"UNLEASHING the UNPOPULAR

Talking About Sexual Orientation and Gender Diversity in Education

Editors

Isabel Killoran , PhD
Associate Professor, Faculty of Education
York University

and

Karleen Pendleton Jiménez, PhD
Assistant Professor, School of Education and Professional Learning
Trent University

Association for Childhood Education International
17904 Georgia Ave., Ste. 215
Olney MD 20832 • www.acei.org

Views expressed do not necessarily agree with positions taken by the
Association for Childhood Education International.

Bruce Herzig, ACEI Editor
Anne Bauer, ACEI Editor
Deborah Jordan Kravitz, Production

Copyright (c) 2007, Association for Childhood Education International
17904 Georgia Ave., Ste. 215, Olney MD 20832

"Unleashing the unpopular" : talking about sexual orientation and gender diversity in education
/ editors, Isabel Killoran and Karleen Pendleton Jiménez.
    p. cm.
 Includes bibliographical references.
 ISBN-13: 978-0-87173-171-5 (pbk.)
 1. Homophobia in schools. 2. Homosexuality and education. 3. Sexual orientation. I. Killoran,
Isabel. II. Jiménez, Karleen Pendleton.
 LC212.8.U557 2007
 371.826'6--dc22

                        2007020508

TABLE OF CONTENTS

ACKNOWLEDGMENTS

We would like to thank Deborah Britzman for allowing us to adopt her phrase "unleashing the unpopular" as our title. Her work inspires educators to wrestle with "difficult knowledge."

We also would to thank the authors for sharing what were often extremely personal and painful experiences. We were amazed by how many people came forward.

A special thanks to Natalia Juarez and Sarah Hawn for their insights and comments.

And finally, a special thanks to ACEI for agreeing to support the educator's need for examples and dialogue on such an important issue.

INTRODUCTION

As educators committed to equity and social justice, we have found a vacuum in support and discourse related to sexual orientation, gender diversity, and education—a paralysis of sorts associated with this topic. While literature, curriculum, and strategies are now readily available in print and on many Internet sites, a gap exists between access to information and the comfort and/or ability of educators to introduce and support LGBTT2IQ* issues in the classroom.

McCaskell and Russell (2000) identify lack of activism, invisibility, hypervisibility, anti-discrimination policy (or the lack thereof), inexperience with other equity issues, and fear of parental reaction as some of the barriers to successfully supporting LGBT students, teachers, and parents in schools. We wanted to hear directly from involved parties the reasons behind their action or inaction, the effects of not having supportive policy around LGBT issues, and possible solutions to the concerns that are raised by the authors. While educators struggle with these issues, children, their families, and their teachers are being hurt repeatedly by lack of progress and insensitivity.

In a meeting at a U.S. conference, Isabel originally suggested this book project because she believed it to be an issue that should be taken up by more educators. A common theme in the discourse around education and sexual orientation is how much "safer" it feels for straight educators to bring up this topic in classrooms. Educators perceived as straight, while still discussing LGBT issues that might provoke homophobic responses, do not have the additional vulnerability of possessing LGBT bodies as targets (Pendleton Jiménez, 2002). Working as teacher educators, we have experienced extreme resistance, including the refusal to engage in the discourse around LGBT equity from some of our teacher candidates. How discouraging, for these are the new teachers entering our schools to guide the next generation. While there is a perception that public sentiment and support for LGBT rights has improved, the readings that follow clearly indicate that the school community has a long way to go.

We wish to acknowledge that given the current North American social hierarchy, which privileges heterosexuals, often through the condemnation or invisibility of LGBT peoples, bringing forward LGBT issues in the classroom is risky work for educators. As human beings constantly exposed to homophobic indoctrination, it is a challenge to grapple with our own fears or prejudices. The stories in this book may evoke feelings of discomfort and disagreement. It is important to realize, however, that these feelings are common and do not mean that the reader cannot develop the compassion and understanding needed to become an even better educator. We hope that these stories will also provide the type of personal perspective needed for genuine connection and understanding. These narratives and essays are offered as an invitation to make room for the questions and discussion that will hopefully lead to more equitable communities. Such dialogue is the basis for critical pedagogy that does not accept the status quo, but rather pushes to eliminate the barriers and boundaries that restrict us (Freire, 1999).

*LGBTT2IQ – Lesbian, Gay, Bisexual, Transgender/Transsexual, Two–spirited, Intersexed, Queer; other authors may use different acronyms.

References

Freire, P. (1999). *Pedagogy of the oppressed* (20th anniversary ed.) [originally published in 1971]. New York: Continuum.

McCaskell, T., & Russell, V. (2000). Anti-homophobia initiatives at the former Toronto Board of Education. In T. Goldstein & D. Selby (Eds.), *Weaving connections: Educating for peace, social and environmental justice* (pp. 27-55). Toronto, ON: Sumach Press.

Pendleton Jiménez, K. (2002). Can of worms: A queer TA in teacher's ed. In R. Kissen (Ed.), *Getting ready for Benjamin: Preparing teachers for sexual diversity in the classroom* (pp. 215-225). Lanham, MD: Rowman and Littlefield.

WHEN SCHOOLS AREN'T SAFE: THE COURTS SET THE STANDARD

Hilary Cook, LLB

*T*his chapter considers the trends in jurisprudence concerning students filing suit against the schools that have failed to protect them. It compares three cases—two in the United States and one in Canada. Judges have increasingly held school boards, schools, and their employees responsible for ensuring the safety of lesbian, gay, bisexual, and transgender students. Initially, judges held schools responsible for dealing with individual incidents. Increasingly, however, courts are asking schools to do more. They want schools to ensure that the environment, the school culture, deals with issues of anti-LGBT discrimination and harassment at a preventive level, so as to stem a never-ending flow of "separate incidents" before they can start.

What is the responsibility of schools to protect all students, regardless of their sexual orientation, from homophobic harassment? Who should bear the burden of making sure that schools are safe for all students? Is a school's culture something that can be guided or influenced by teachers and administrators?

The following account about Jamie Nabozny is adapted from Justice Eschbach's writing for the 7th Circuit Court of Appeals concerning the 1996 ground-breaking decision Nabozny v. Podlesny et al.:

From his birth in 1975, Nabozny lived in Ashland, Wisconsin. Throughout his childhood, adolescence, and teenage years, he attended schools owned and operated by the Ashland Public School District. In elementary school, Nabozny proved to be a good student and enjoyed a positive educational experience.

When Nabozny graduated to the Ashland Middle School in 1988, his life changed. Around the time that Nabozny entered the 7th grade, Nabozny realized that he is gay. Many of Nabozny's fellow classmates soon realized it too. Nabozny decided not to "closet" his sexuality, and considerable harassment from his fellow students ensued. Nabozny's classmates regularly referred to him as "faggot" and subjected him to various forms of physical abuse, including striking and spitting on him. Nabozny spoke to the school's guidance counselor, Ms. Peterson, about the abuse, informing Peterson that he is gay. Peterson took action, ordering the offending students to stop the harassment and placing two of them in detention. However, the students' abusive behavior toward Nabozny stopped only briefly. Meanwhile, Peterson was replaced as guidance counselor by Mr. Nowakowski. Nabozny similarly informed Nowa-

Editors' Note: We have chosen to begin this book with a chapter on legal impact and implications related to LGBT issues. The examples given clearly outline the brutality that many students continue to endure in their schools. Their ability to use the court systems effectively to protect their rights has resulted in case law outlining school districts' responsibility for the safety of all their students.

kowski that he is gay and asked for protection from the student harassment. Nowakowski, in turn, referred the matter to school principal Mary Podlesny; Podlesny was responsible for school discipline.

Just before the 1988 winter holiday, Nabozny met with Nowakowski and Podlesny to discuss the harassment. During the meeting, Nabozny explained the nature of the harassment and again revealed his homosexuality. Podlesny promised to protect Nabozny, but took no action. Following the holiday season, student harassment of Nabozny worsened, especially at the hands of students Jason Welty and Roy Grande. Nabozny complained to Nowakowski, and school administrators spoke to the students. The harassment, however, only intensified. A short time later, in a science classroom, Welty grabbed Nabozny and pushed him to the floor. Welty and Grande held Nabozny down and performed a mock rape on Nabozny, exclaiming that Nabozny should enjoy it. The boys carried out the mock rape as 20 other students looked on and laughed. Nabozny escaped and fled to Podlesny's office. Podlesny's alleged response is somewhat astonishing; she said that "boys will be boys" and told Nabozny that if he was "going to be so openly gay" he should "expect" such behavior from his fellow students. In the wake of Podlesny's comments, Nabozny ran home. The next day, Nabozny was forced to speak to a counselor, not because he was subjected to a mock rape in the classroom, but because he left the school without obtaining proper permission. No action was taken against the students involved. Nabozny was forced to return to his regular schedule. Understandably, Nabozny was "petrified" to attend school; he was subjected to abuse throughout the duration of the school year.

The situation hardly improved when Nabozny entered the 8th grade. Shortly after the school year began, several boys attacked Nabozny in the school bathroom, hitting him and pushing his books from his hands. This time, Nabozny's parents met with Podlesny and the alleged perpetrators. The offending boys denied that the incident occurred, and no action was taken. Podlesny told both Nabozny and his parents that Nabozny should expect such incidents because he is "openly" gay. Several similar meetings between Nabozny's parents and Podlesny followed subsequent incidents involving Nabozny. Each time, the perpetrators were identified to Podlesny. Each time, Podlesny pledged to take action. And, each time, nothing was done. Toward the end of the school year, the harassment against Nabozny intensified to the point that a district attorney purportedly advised Nabozny to take time off from school. Nabozny took one-and-a-half weeks off from school. When he returned, the harassment resumed, driving Nabozny to attempt suicide. After a stint in a hospital, Nabozny finished his 8th-grade year in a Catholic school.

The Catholic school attended by Nabozny did not offer classes beyond the 8th grade. Therefore, to attend the 9th grade, Nabozny enrolled in Ashland High School. Almost immediately Nabozny's fellow students sang an all too familiar tune. Early in the year, Nabozny was assaulted while using a urinal in the restroom. A student, Stephen Huntley, struck Nabozny in the back of the knee, forcing him to fall into the urinal. Roy Grande then urinated on Nabozny. Nabozny immediately reported the incident to the principal's office. Nabozny recounted the incident to the office secretary, who in turn relayed the story to Principal William Davis. Davis ordered Nabozny to go home and change clothes. Nabozny's parents scheduled a meeting with Davis and Assistant Principal Thomas Blauert. At the meeting, the parties discussed numerous instances of harassment against Nabozny, including the restroom incident.

Rather than taking action against the perpetrators, Davis and Blauert referred Nabozny to Mr. Reeder, a school guidance counselor. Reeder was supposed to change Nabozny's schedule so as to minimize Nabozny's exposure to the offending students. Eventually, the school placed Nabozny in a special education class; yet, Stephen Huntley and Roy Grande were special education students. Nabozny's parents continued to insist that the school take action, repeatedly meeting with Davis and Blauert, among others. Nabozny's parent's efforts were futile; no action was taken. In the middle of his 9th-grade year, Nabozny again attempted suicide. Following another hospital stay and a period living with relatives, Nabozny ran away to Minneapolis. His parents convinced him to return to Ashland by promising that Nabozny would not have to attend Ashland High. Because Nabozny's parents were unable to afford private schooling, however, the Department of Social Services ordered Nabozny to return to Ashland High.

In the 10th grade, Nabozny fared no better. Nabozny's parents moved, forcing Nabozny to rely on the school bus to take him to school. Students on the bus regularly used such epithets as "fag" and "queer" to refer to Nabozny. Some students even pelted Nabozny with dangerous objects, such as steel nuts and bolts. When Nabozny's parents complained to the school, school officials changed Nabozny's assigned seat and moved him to the front of the bus. The harassment continued. Ms. Hanson, a school guidance counselor, lobbied the school's administration to take more aggressive action, but to no avail. The worst was yet to come, however. One morning when Nabozny arrived early to the school, he went to the library to study. The library was not yet open, so Nabozny sat down in the hallway. Minutes later he was met by a group of eight boys, led by Stephen Huntley. Huntley began kicking Nabozny in the stomach and continued to do so for five to ten minutes while the other students looked on, laughing. Nabozny reported the incident to Hanson, who referred him to the school's "police liaison," Dan Crawford. Nabozny told Crawford that he wanted to press charges, but Crawford dissuaded him. Crawford promised to speak to the offending boys instead. Meanwhile, at Crawford's behest, Nabozny reported the incident to Blauert. Blauert, the school official supposedly in charge of disciplining, laughed and told Nabozny that Nabozny deserved such treatment because he is gay. Weeks later, Nabozny collapsed from the internal bleeding that resulted from Huntley's beating. Nabozny's parents and counselor Hanson repeatedly urged Davis and Blauert to take action to protect Nabozny. Each time, aggressive action was promised. And each time, nothing was done.

Finally, in his 11th-grade year, Nabozny withdrew from Ashland High School. Hanson told Nabozny and his parents that school administrators were unwilling to help him and that he should seek educational opportunities elsewhere. Nabozny left Ashland and moved to Minneapolis, where he was diagnosed with Post Traumatic Stress Disorder. In addition to seeking medical help, Nabozny sought legal advice.

The decision on July 31, 1996, by the 7th Circuit Court of Appeals in favor of Jamie Nabozny (Nabozny v. Podlesny, 1996) served as a wake-up call to teachers, school administrators, and school boards across the United States to take violent homophobic behavior seriously. In November 1999, the American School Board Journal said that the Nabozny case had opened the floodgates to lawsuits and threats of lawsuits (Jones, 1999, pp. 2-3). Since 1996, many similar suits have been filed. School boards and school staff in jurisdictions across the United States have been told by courts that they will be held accountable for protecting all of their students, including those who are gay, lesbian, bisexual, or transgender (LGBT).

Before the Harassment: Who Is Targeted and Why?

Who are the victims of homophobic harassment in schools? Nabozny was a happy kid and a good student in elementary school. At age 11, Nabozny told his parents that he was gay. While his mother's response was that she already knew, his father was upset and he hoped that Jamie would discover it was only a "phase" ("20 Questions," 1997). Around the same time, an article had appeared in a local paper about a sexual abuse case involving the youth minister at Nabozny's church. Ashland was a small enough town that people were able to figure out that Nabozny was the unnamed victim, and it was this incident that had initially made Nabozny the target of name-calling (Walsh, 1996). The fact that Nabozny didn't deny that he was gay led some at his school to blame him for his troubles.

In another case during the same period, the Morgan Hill, California, Live Oak High School's paper, *The Oak Leaf*, had reported on graffiti at the school that said, "Kill all gays. Keep it in the closet." Three years later, in 1996, Alana Flores entered the school as a sociable sophomore. She asked the students in her math class to stop shouting the word "faggot" at a fellow student, and thus became the target of a three-year long campaign of harassment (Finz, 2004). Flores had had a same-sex relationship the summer before starting at Live Oak. Unlike Nabozny, however, she shared with no one, not even her family, her thoughts about her sexuality (Koymasky & Koymasky, 2004).

Freddy Fuentes became involved in the 1998 Live Oak High School lawsuit started by Alana Flores. Looking back on his school days, Fuentes said, "I wasn't aware that what they were doing, beating me up over and over, was wrong." Fuentes' problems had started well before high school. In one incident in the 7th grade, kids at his school bus stop had begun calling him a faggot and hitting him. When he fell, they continued kicking him on the ground. When the school bus pulled up, the other kids piled on, continuing to yell insults. The bus driver looked at Fuentes bleeding on the sidewalk, looked back at the other kids, and then closed the doors and drove away. Fuentes crawled home and his mother took him to the hospital to be treated for broken and bruised ribs (Dignan, 2004). The school disciplined only one of the attackers (American Civil Liberties Union [ACLU], 2004), and the driver was not reprimanded.

It is not only students who are gay and lesbian, however, who are targeted. In a study of Seattle high school students, 6 percent of all students said they had experienced verbal or physical attacks at school, or on the way to or from school, because someone thought they were gay or lesbian. Two-thirds of those victims described themselves as heterosexual. Forty-nine percent of gay and lesbian students, and 39 percent of bisexual students, said they had faced this kind of bullying (Seattle Public Schools, 1999).

In one Canadian case, Amzi Jubran, a North Vancouver high school student who was not gay, took his school board before the British Columbia Human Rights Tribunal for failing to protect him from physical and verbal anti-gay harassment over a period of five years. Among other defenses, the school board claimed that they couldn't be held responsible under the Human Rights Code for not protecting Jubran because he was not gay. The Tribunal, and eventually the British Columbia Court of Appeal, concluded that the school was accountable nonetheless (*Jubran v. North Vancouver School District #44*, 2002 and *School District No. 44 v. Jubran*, 2005).

It's hard to imagine how school staff could allow such an environment to exist within their schools. Teachers may ignore the taunting because of their own discomfort or lack of knowledge. They may fear that raising the issue will lead them into touchy issues of sex and sexual expression. They may mistakenly conclude that their job is more in danger if they take on the harassers than if they ignore them. In some cases, homophobic teachers may even believe that gay students deserve the treatment they get. In one study conducted in Massachusetts, 53 percent of students reported hearing homophobic comments made by school staff (Report of the Massachusetts Governor's Commission on Gay and Lesbian Youth, 1993).

Kids doing the targeting may be fighting their own same-sex attraction. Studies suggest that men who score high on a measure of homophobic attitudes are also the most likely to respond to gay porn (Adams, Wright, & Lohr, 1996). As Tonya Callaghan later shares in this book, she began hurling homophobic comments after she herself had been the target of them as an adolescent. Are young gay-bashers assaulting other teens in part to draw attention away from their own same-sex attraction? Are they projecting their self-hatred onto their victims? The UCLA Center for Women and Men advises students that:

> Hate crimes and incidents are intended to make LGBT people fearful, keep them closeted, and, in some cases, to punish them for challenging heterosexist norms. They may also result from the perpetrator's fear of being gay and a subsequent desire to lash out at others who remind the perpetrator of that fear (i.e., LGBT people). (UCLA Center for Women and Men, 2007)

This hypothesis seems to be startlingly confirmed by Jamie Nabozny's 2001 statement that 4 of the 10 student perpetrators identified at his trial had identified themselves as gay men (Catholic Pastoral Committee on Sexual Minorities, 2001).

During the Harassment

At School. After speaking up in math class, Alana Flores of Morgan Hill, California, a town about 30 minutes south of San José, began finding threatening notes in her high school locker. At first, she thought it was a mistake, but new notes, which said things like "Die Dyke," were appearing every day. The notes escalated to include pictures torn from pornographic magazines. On one occasion, Alana found a picture taped to her locker of a naked woman, bound and gagged, with her legs spread and her throat slashed. Someone had written on it "Die, die! Dyke bitch, fuck off. We'll kill you" (ACLU, 2004). When the girl who shared Flores's locker found one of the notes, she persuaded Flores, who was terrified, to report the incidents to a teacher, who responded, "Why does that word bother you? Are you a lesbian?" (Koymasky & Koymasky, 2004).

Having taken the issue to Delia Schizzano, the assistant principal, Flores was eventually told, "Don't bring me this trash anymore," and asked again, "If you're not gay, why are you crying?" Flores' meeting with the principal was equally fruitless. Anti-gay obscenities written on, and scratched into, the paint on Flores' locker were left for months before being removed by the school. Flores' request to change lockers was denied. Her tormentors, emboldened by the lack of action from school authorities, began shouting obscenities at her across the crowded school quad. Flores lived with constant harassment throughout her three years at Live Oak High School.

Freddy Fuentes, another of the plaintiffs in the lawsuit started by Flores, estimated he had at least five anti-gay remarks made to him each time he went from class to class (Dignan, 2004). His experience mirrors the 1997 findings of a student group in Des Moines, Iowa, called Concerned Students. They had conducted a study at five high schools in which they recorded their peers' hallway and classroom conversations. Their study concluded that the average high school student hears about 25 anti-gay remarks per day.

In addition to the constant harassment between classes, students at Live Oak High School were able to harass Fuentes with apparent impunity in front of teachers during class time. On one occasion, Fuentes was repeatedly called "faggot" and "queer" by his classmates during a history class. When Fuentes told them to stop, the teacher took him into the hall, "told him he had disrupted class, and shoved him against a wall." During a drafting class, a student told Fuentes, "I want to beat you up after class but I need a baseball bat to hit you because I don't want to get AIDS." The drafting teacher who witnessed Fuentes' daily harassment did nothing to intervene (ACLU, 2004). On one occasion, Flores and Fuentes were approached as they ate lunch together in the cafeteria by a student who handed them an open pornographic magazine with the comment, "It's women, faggot. This is the way you guys should be doing it." When they complained, the nearby campus monitor did nothing to intervene, and the assistant principal told them they were making "too much of a fuss" about the incident. Perpetrators at the school were heard to boast about what they were able to get away with, or about the light punishments they received in the few instances when the school acted at all (ACLU, 2004).

A third case of student targeting was considered by a Canadian human rights tribunal, and subsequently by the British Columbia Court of Appeal. For the five years that he attended Handsworth Secondary School in North Vancouver, B.C., Amzi Jubran "was taunted with homophobic epithets and physically assaulted, including being spit upon, kicked and punched by other students" (*Jubran v. North Vancouver School District*, 2002, p. 1). On one occasion in gym class, Jubran's shirt was set on fire by a classmate. In the spring of his 10th grade, after two years of harassment, Jubran punched and injured a fellow student, who he said had called him gay, an incident that resulted in Jubran's suspension and criminal charges being filed against him.

Schools often react to harassment by placing the burden on the student who is harassed. Many LGBT students are encouraged to undertake independent study programs (which can limit their access to university/college-track curriculum), or to transfer to another school. For example, Fuentes was told by his school that they couldn't guarantee his safety if he stayed at the junior high school where he was assaulted in 7th grade (ACLU, 2004). Not surprisingly, many students who are harassed end up dropping out, or worse. The ongoing harassment against Jubran affected his academic performance and caused him to consider suicide.

The 1995 Seattle Teen Health Survey (Seattle Public Schools, 1995) reflects Jubran's experience. It found that the two-thirds of students who were not gay, but were the targets of anti-gay bullying, experienced the same effects seen among the many gay students who are targeted, such as high drop-out rates, depression, drug and alcohol use, and suicide attempts.

At Home. After Nabozny came out to his parents, they were supportive. Even his father, after seeing what Jamie was going through, came to the conclusion that no one would "choose" to be treated this way. Nabozny's mother repeatedly insisted on meeting with school administrators, some of whom, during the trial, said they could not recall having made such comments as "boys will be boys" and "if you're going to be gay, you have to learn to expect such abuse ("Nearly $1 million," 1996). After Nabozny launched his lawsuit, his two younger brothers, also in the same school, were targeted, and anonymous callers threatened to burn down the Nabozny house.

Flores went it alone until she came out to her family in the aftermath of a suicide attempt. Her family rallied around her. After Flores filed her suit, her younger sister was put in the position of having to defend her at her former school. At one point, the false story went around that because of Flores' lawsuit, the school would be unable to afford desks for the students. In fact, as in other schools, the case was funded by the school's insurance company.

Interestingly, these three cases were all launched by youth whose parents accepted them and supported them. Was this the base from which these young people found the strength to come out; to find a lawyer who would take their cases; to go through depositions, where they must testify about what happened to them and face aggressive cross-examination by lawyers for the school district; and to face the attendant publicity?

After

Nabozny had sued not only the Ashland Public School District, but also the individual school officials who had refused to act: Mary Podlesny, William Davis, and Thomas Blauert. The school board's argument, that the school board or its employees could not be held responsible for the harm caused by individual students, proved to be unsuccessful. In a subsequent trial, a federal jury found the three administrators personally liable, and the parties settled for $962,000 U.S. in damages. Lawyers representing school boards across the country began to advise their clients that here was a financial risk to be taken seriously. By the fall of 1999, the National School Boards Association was holding a session on sexual orientation legal issues at a meeting of their Council of School Attorneys.

Flores filed her suit, Flores v. Morgan Hill Unified School District, nine months after she graduated from Live Oak High School. After three years of constant harassment in her school, and a suicide attempt while in her senior year, Flores' fear turned to anger (Koymasky & Koymasky, 2004). Her suit must have touched a nerve, because she was soon joined by five other plaintiffs—four girls and one boy—from the same school district, all alleging that school district employees had repeatedly ignored or minimized reports by the students that they were the victims of anti-gay abuse.

In the Flores case, once the federal court of appeals cleared the case to proceed, the school district settled for more than $1.1 million and agreed to implement a program to combat anti-gay harassment for administrators, staff, and, particularly important, students.

In the Jubran case, as well, the British Columbia Human Rights Tribunal (in a decision upheld by the B.C. Court of Appeal) made it clear that it was not enough that the North Vancouver School District had punished each of the individual offenders. Unlike Nabozny's school, Jubran's school had responded to his complaints, investigating, then warning, disciplining, and, in some cases, suspending the students who took part. The harassment had continued nonetheless, with an ever-widening pool of participants. In some cases, the friends of those disciplined by the school had even taken revenge on Jubran.

The North Vancouver school board argued that it had done all that could be expected, but that it could not be held responsible for eradicating discrimination among the school population. The tribunal, however, found that the school could and should have done more: addressing the issue of homophobia or homophobic harassment with the students generally, for example, or implementing a program to address the issue. The tribunal pointed out that the administration had insufficient training and education to deal with harassment, and didn't seek assistance until after Jubran filed his human rights complaint (Jubran v. North Vancouver School District, 2002, p. 39). In other words, the school had begun by dealing with each incident of harassment as though it were an individual event. The tribunal decided that the school, once its initial efforts proved unsuccessful, should have accessed the expertise that they lacked, and trained their staff and gone into the classrooms to deal with the problem systemically.

Several themes emerge through an analysis of both the victimization and resistance of these youth as they navigate systems of education. There is a catch-22 for many students; on the one hand, they are required by law to attend school, but on the other hand, their attendance may threaten their physical and psychological health, with possibly fatal consequences. Ultimately, the violence inflicted upon them is not taken seriously. Their safety is not a concern. Compassion does not seem to be enough motivation. In cases in which parental pressure and student complaints have been insufficient in invoking basic caring responses, let alone systemic change, perhaps the risk of financial liability will push schools to do the right thing. These cases, courageously brought forward by students, clearly indicate that the bar has now been raised for schools and that courts are holding schools accountable when they fail to rise to the challenge.

References

"20 Questions: Jamie Nabozny." (1997). *Philadelphia City Paper* (May 1-8, 1997). Retrieved April 1, 2006, from http://citypaper.net/articles/050197/articleop.shtml

Adams, H. E., Wright, L. W., Jr., & Lohr, B. A. (1996). Is homophobia associated with homosexual arousal? *Journal of Abnormal Psychology, 105*(3), 440-445.

American Civil Liberties Union. (2004). *Case background: Flores v. Morgan Hill Unified School District.* Retrieved April 1, 2006, from www.aclu.org//LGBT/youth/11947res20040106.html

Catholic Pastoral Committee on Sexual Minorities. (2001). *Jamie Nabozny kicks off 2001-2002 speakers' series by sharing his shocking and inspiring story with his first Catholic audience.* Retrieved August 27, 2006, from www.mtn.org/cpcsm/Nabozny_11-14-10.htm

Dignan, J. (2004, January 8-14). Important victory for gay students: Six gay, lesbian former high school students win $1.1 million. *Gay City News, 7* (New York, NY).

Finz, S. (2004, January 7). Settlement in gay suit. Ex-students claimed harassment. *San Francisco Chronicle,* A-15.

Jones, R. (1999, November). I don't feel safe here any more. *American School Board Journal,* 2-3. Retrieved April 1, 2006, from www.asbj.com/199911/1199coverstory.html

Jubran v. North Vancouver School District #44, British Columbia Human Rights Tribunal, Member Carol Roberts, April 8, 2002.

Koymasky, M., & Koymasky, A. (2004). *Alana Flores. Biographies* (June 14, 2004). Retrieved April 1, 2006, from http://andrejkoymasky.com/liv/fam/biofl/flor1.html

Nabozny v. Podlesny et al. (7th Circuit Court of Appeals) 92F. 3d 446; 1996 U.S. App. LEXIS 18866. pp. 8 to 14.

Nearly $1 Million Settlement Reached in Anti-Gay Student Violence Case. (1996). *The Electronic Gay Community Magazine, Land of Awes Computer Information System.* Retrieved August 27, 2006, from www.debtaylor.com/deb/stuff/eauclaire.html

Report of the Massachusetts Governor's Commission on Gay and Lesbian Youth. (1993). *Making schools safe for gay and lesbian youth: Breaking the silence in schools and families.* (Feb 25, 1993)

School District No. 44 (North Vancouver) v. Jubran, 2005 BCCA 201

Seattle Public Schools and the U.S. Centers for Disease Control and Prevention, in subsequent analysis by Public Health – Seattle and King County. (1999). *1999 Seattle teen health survey.* Retrieved August 27, 2006, from www.safeschoolscoalition.org/quickfacts.pdf

Seattle Public Schools and the U.S. Centers for Disease Control and Prevention. (1995). *Seattle Public Health 1995 teen health survey.* Retrieved June 23, 2007, from www.safeschoolscoalition-wa.org/83,000youth.pdf

The UCLA Center for Women and Men. (2007). *What's your concern?: Sexual orientation.* Retrieved January 30, 2007, from www.thecenter.ucla.edu/sexorien.html

Walsh, J. (1996). *Jamie Nabozny, 20, of Minneapolis, Minnesota. Profiles in courage* (February 1996). Retrieved April 1, 2006, from www.youthorg/loco.PERSONProject/Alerts/states/minnesota/jamie.html

THE STUDENT EXPERIENCE

Sky—Age 10*
This is Sky with his two moms.
They are playing on the swings in the park under a rainbow.

* Drawing originally appeared in Foster, D. (2005). *Growing a family? The experiences of planned two-mother families.* Unpublished doctoral dissertation, University of Alberta, Edmonton, Alberta.

Introduction to "The Student Experience"

While it is impossible to ensure a school setting where boys and girls are free from insults, steps may be taken to provide a more comfortable environment. Homophobia is already a problem in elementary school, so it is not too early to discuss, in age-appropriate ways, related topics. Themes around gender and family provide natural entry points to discuss sexual orientation, gender diversity, and the definition of family (Bickmore, 1999). A common fear is that these discussions will lead to conversations about "sex." However, it is possible to offer age-appropriate answers to any questions the children may pose; thus, this fear should not be a deterrent to providing the opportunity for all children's experiences to be reflected and validated in the curriculum.

Educators need to raise awareness around issues confronting students with nonconforming gender expression; teachers might not know that these students are sometimes targets of ridicule. They also might not know what form the ridicule will take, and what moments in schooling are exceptionally prone to such behavior. Schooling situations that require separation based on the biological sex of the child often place children with nonconforming gender expression in awkward positions (e.g., physical education classes, health classes, classroom play areas, bathroom line-ups). By making assumed distinctions more visible, those who do not clearly fit into such categories are more easily spotted and criticized (e.g., "That's not girl hair," "Boys don't cook," "You don't belong in the girls' line-up.").

Children of LGBT parents also encounter both homophobia and heterosexism in schools, but the issues often emerge in areas specific to assumptions of "normal" parenting. For example, celebrations of mother's and father's day, projects that require students to articulate family membership and genealogy, discussion related to marriage, parental permission forms, school performances or socials to which parents are invited, and even the daily dropping off and picking up of students are all moments of potential exposure of LGBT family configurations. They could be moments of pride and validation of LGBT family, or they could lead to feelings of invisibility and possibly make these children targets of taunts from their peers. Educators who provide inclusive policies, structures, assignments, and discussions that recognize the diversity of families can better support these students as they negotiate the position of their LGBT families within the school system.

The collection of children's responses in this book documents the frequency and vehemence of homophobic insults in schools. They pose a critique of school policies and teacher practices that lack the consequences needed to effectively confront homophobia. They also present some strategies developed by children within same-sex families to cope with negative reactions: the love of family, the screening of the values of potential friends, and the message to other children in same-sex families that they are both OK and not alone.

As you read the stories, think about the following: How would you validate same-sex parents and diverse family make-ups? What are some common school practices around celebrations that need to be rethought? What occurs in schools that forces gender separation? What complications may arise around parental consent? How would you proactively introduce LGBT issues in the classroom rather than waiting for an incident to occur? What policies does your school have in place to confront homophobic insults on school grounds? How do teachers in your school respond to homophobic insults?

References
Bickmore, K. (1999). Why discuss sexuality in elementary school? In W. J. Letts & J. T. Sears (Eds.), *Queering elementary education: Advancing the dialogue about sexualities and schooling* (pp. 15-25). Lanham, MD: Rowman & Littlefield.

My One-armed Barbie in a Window Box

Niki Dame

Buried from the ones that tease
Staying late and watching girl guides after school

Classroom with a Berlin Wall
My kin on one side far from me
And seeing something false
Not seeing I'm their sister

But, one-armed Barbie buried between classes
Was my friend-in-waiting
Forbidden by those who should have known better

And I taught myself to tie knots
On my own
And sewed on badges
Of my own
And still sew badges none can see

A merit badge of compassion
Another of understanding
And always, always forgiveness

By watching sisters
Learned as best I could
A solitary path? Perhaps

But, one-armed Barbie buried deep
And naked though she was
As anatomically perfect
As a seven-year-old needs

Covered with the leaves and dirt
Of classroom breaks
I dressed my dolly with my dreams

And dreamed
The change
The change that hits all boys and girl

The change
Spoken of with pursed lips and hidden meaning
Held hidden promise
That god would fix what he had broken
As simply as a one-armed Barbie

Now History and Herstory
And Heritage and Hisitage
Are memories that sculpt me now
Past sadness, past tears
Past violence done to me
Past the violence that I did to others

Those memories must be cause for peace, compassion
and forgiveness
Or else, I taint the memory of a one-armed Barbie

So I remember her stringy hair
And the dirt on her cheek
No clothes or house or Malibu car
Just a dirt filled window box
That I could conceive of as a grave
If I so chose
But that's not my choice

She came into my life unexpectedly
The cast-off toy of another
Luckier
Girl
And she left the same way too

Discovered by a zealous gardener
Who only saw a discarded thing
I cried when I found her gone

A crappy piece of broken plastic
A treasured childhood toy
A friend
A moment from the gods that offered hope
She is beautiful in my memories
And so am I
And so am I

I've earned my tears
I've lived my scars
I've journeyed hard my years
And I have learned
The gods love buried one-armed Barbies . . . Like me

Copyright Nichola Ward - reprinted with permission

Liam—Age 7*

I am the smaller one; the guy with the acne is my 14-year-old brother Louis. The women in the middle are my moms.

Brittany N. Guiney Yallop—Age 7

* Drawing originally appeared in Foster, D. (2005). *Growing a family? The experiences of planned two-mother families.* Unpublished doctoral dissertation, University of Alberta, Edmonton, Alberta.

"Shut Up!" Or Why I Ended Up in the Hall

Katerina Cook, age 9
as dictated to Karleen Pendleton Jiménez

*K*aterina's story shows the painful consequences of removing the child with the concern for LGBT issues, rather than the child who is making homophobic comments. Educators might explore what fears guide a decision to remove the victim rather than the perpetrator. Literature can serve as an excellent part of the curriculum for students and teachers to explore LGBT issues together, before classroom homophobia surfaces. How might LGBT issues be included as part of a literature unit on Shakespeare (and other authors who explore similar themes of gender and desire)? While it is difficult to know the strongest or most apt response at the moment of a homophobic comment, what are possible strategies for addressing issues of homophobia in the days that follow?

Go away to when you were a kid and imagine that your mother or father was in love with another boy or girl. And all of your friends knew about it and they laughed and laughed and laughed and laughed at you.

So one day you were in class and the teacher was reading *Twelfth Night* and they were just at the part when Olivia figured out that Violet was a girl. And then some girl or boy in your class said, "Ewwwww, they're so lez," and made a face, the same face that they would have if they were picking their nose, except they were smiling at the same time.

I yelled, "Shut up!" but the teacher didn't do anything about it. The teacher was surprised and was just looking down at us with big eyes. Silence. I was even surprised that I didn't get in trouble for shouting "Shut up!"

I felt like I wanted to kill Fleur. I was looking at her. She was smirking at me. She was thinking, "You're gonna get in trouble because you just yelled 'shut up' at me." My face was probably turning red because that's what my friend Zoe told me after.

Pause.

And then I was told to go outside to calm down, but the other kid wasn't told to go outside. And then I was crying in the hall and this grade 5 boy came along and asked me if I was crying because I was getting punished. "I'm not getting punished."

"Then why are you here?"

I didn't really answer. My head was against the wall.

He ran to join his friend.

I thought about how evil Fleur was. I thought of her being tortured by me. Because I am a violent child and I'm not afraid to say that. I didn't really like being outside in the hallway. I didn't like older people looking at me and being puzzled why I was crying, so I just went back in.

The reason Zoe is my best friend is because she is the only person that doesn't care that lesbians are different from straight people. She is actually the only person who understands and tries to tell Fleur. It would've been helpful if she could've said something to Fleur. It would've also been better if the teacher just didn't ignore it.

All the other kids, but mostly Fleur, say that lesbians are totally different from straight people and they're disgusting and all about sex, which is totally not true. I feel like saying that Fleur is such a bitch. Except that the teachers, the people who are reading this right now, might be freaked out that I said the word "bitch." Because I am only 9 years old, 9, 9, 9, 9, 9, 9, 9!

Fleur's favourite colors are pink and yellow, the main flower colors. And whenever we're told to do a drawing of something, she always draws a picture of her name. And ever since that day, she never hesitates to say bad things about lesbians and gays when she is near me.

Epilogue: This teacher was approached by one of Katerina's lesbian parents subsequent to the incident described. The teacher was very concerned about what had occurred and decided to lead a lesson to explore LGBT issues and to educate against homophobia.

THE GAY DISASTER THING

Carter Cook, age 10
as dictated to Karleen Pendleton Jiménez

*I*n his telling of the perils of the playground, Carter articulates the emotions he experiences when homophobic insults are hurled outside of teacher supervision. His story provides one model of pedagogical action, offering students the opportunity to discuss the feelings and understand the reasoning of all parties involved. Are there forums in your schools available to open conversation about same-sex families? How would you frame questions for students who have either inflicted or received homophobic insults?

One time my friend Dylan and I had gotten into a fistfight in bad places: the waist, the side of the head, and the stomach. Usually I find I'm in a difficult situation and a teacher can't hear me. Unfortunately, there is also a rule in my school: If the teacher doesn't see it, it doesn't count. How, exactly, is a teacher going to see a kid being beat up on the other side of the playground?

We were near the sandpit where bunches of boys hang out together and usually start fights. It was afternoon recess—I guess you could say the time I dread. That's the time I get most beat up or name-called. I believe this is because the kids find they can get away with stuff easier. Well, it's the time and place you're most likely to get into a fight, a bloodthirsty type of fight.

Right before we had the gay disaster thing, you know, the fistfight, someone was teasing someone else, etc., etc. Adriana, a girl who is usually picked on by bunches of boys, was once again getting picked on. They call her things like a pig or an octopus or a rude name that describes how she looks. But that day they used a word that really didn't work well, especially with two people standing nearby who had lesbian parents—to be precise, me and Sami.

We heard this comment and obviously that is how the bloodthirsty fight began. They didn't even use an anti-gay word, it was something like, "You were created by five men." She wasn't even really human because she was made by five men, not the best thing to say around people with lesbian parents. Or, maybe they just called her a fag, I don't know which.

So I slapped him.

Do you want me to describe how that comment felt? Like me and my friend Sami were created by a bunch of freaks (which is not true). Actually, it felt worse than that. Basically, they were saying that we were sons of bitches.

And after that we came in and everyone was shouting about it and telling the teachers everything that happened. The teachers were trying to settle down a huge raging fistfight instead of a riot. I found what they did was the best solution. They tried to calm everyone down first. You can never get anything out of a kid who is not calmed down first.

And so the teachers called a meeting. And everyone sat down in a circle and they discussed things. At the beginning, they said they're having a meeting for the predicament, argument, fight, etc. that happened outside. Then they would pass the heart pillow to someone else to speak about what they thought. They would pass around a heart cushion to each other every time they wanted to have a turn to talk, so no one would interrupt. Let's say they said how they felt about it and how they might have been scared that this person is beating them up. Or someone else says, "I was mad because they were making rude comments about my mom." We really didn't appreciate our moms being talked about in a rude or racist way, and the other people said that they couldn't understand why we would beat them up just for them teasing us.

And then the teachers would take the heart back and talk about something like, maybe ask us a question like, "Well, why were they teasing you? Did you insult them first? Did you say a rude comment about their moms first?"

The meeting was very effective because they don't let anyone talk except the person who uses the talking heart. And then they would pass it back and forth, with everyone explaining what they thought, felt, what happened, or why they did something. It was a good way, because everyone could express how they felt and others could find out why they were so upset about something. Kids get mad because something in their mind seems easy, but really it's quite hard. And so everyone gets to say how they feel and as you probably know, expressing your feelings helps you calm down.

Louis—age 14*
That's me on the left.
Monica [social mom] and my mom are in the middle and that is my little brother Liam upside down next to our dog.
We are out front of our house.

* Drawing originally appeared in Foster, D. (2005). *Growing a family? The experiences of planned two-mother families.* Unpublished doctoral dissertation, University of Alberta, Edmonton, Alberta.

Hi. My name is Madison Bouley-Picard, age 9. I think having two women around the house is cool but I try not to mention it at school because people make jokes about it. Like "You're gay" or "You are lesbian." I get offended by that, because my mom is lesbian, so why should people joke about it if it happens in real life. People use it like a fighting word and they think it means "you're dumb," but it doesn't mean that. People have it out there so it could be insulting. To you, it's a fighting word, but to people who are gay or lesbian it hurts. Next time, when you are about to say a mean word like those, stop and think about how it feels. I just wish people would not use gay or lesbian as a joke.

—Madison Bouley-Picard, age 9

I am Jordan, age 11, and I think it is a bad thing at my school because kids go like, "Oh, that kid's gay," "That's a gay thing," or they say, "You fag," or things that could hurt kids. Usually I ask, "Do you make fun of gays and lesbians?" before I make friends. I still have problems on my bus—"Ha, ha, your mom is a lesbian." I hate it and I get mad. I don't care and you shouldn't either. "It's not a bad thing," that's what I say to him.

At my school, when a kid says that word in front of a teacher, the teacher says, "Don't say that word" or something, like it's a bad thing. I wouldn't like it even if my mom wasn't a lesbian. I think we should talk about it more in school because it shouldn't be something not to talk about. If I was a teacher, I would talk to small [kids, in 1st-, 2nd-, 3rd-, and 4th-grade], and [say] it's okay to be it.

I have a dad who is married and I have a step-mom and step-brother. So I am fine with it and fine with going to my dad's, then to my moms'.

I am fine with it almost all the time. I think it's okay to be gay. It's okay to be a lesbian. Don't let kids bully you because your mom or your dad is gay. I think it is okay for everyone out there. If they want to be gay or a lesbian, they can!
P.S. It's alright!

—Jordan Bouley-Picard, age 11

"You're gay!" "You fag!"

These are the most-used mean names in my high school. You can be walking down the hallway and be guaranteed to hear at least one of them on your way. "You fag" is now the new "You're a loser," sadly. In my high school, you can find teachers who will either dismiss these words or speak up. In our school, for the most part not too much will happen to you if someone hears you. If the teacher hears you and decides to take action, I believe the most you would get is a detention, but I am not even sure. In our school we do have a Gay/Straight Alliance, but unfortunately, I don't think most people in our school know that we do. In our school, I really wish that people would stop using these words as bad things to call people.

—Jacky Bouley-Picard, age 17

Kory—age 14*

**Mom is pushing Chris [younger adopted brother]
on a swing in the park.
We go to that park lots to hang out and have picnics.
That's me off to the side with Barb [social mom].
I'm the one with the Donald Trump hair.**

* Drawing originally appeared in Foster, D. (2005). *Growing a family? The experiences of planned two-mother families.* Unpublished doctoral dissertation, University of Alberta, Edmonton, Alberta.

PRETTY

Karleen Pendleton Jiménez

*I*n *this narrative, Pendleton Jiménez retrieves her 13-year-old voice and memories from junior high. Teachers and teacher educators receive an insider's perspective on the stressful results of systemic gender enforcement for those students with nonconforming gender expression. "Pretty" provides a look into the specificity of living as a boyish girl at an age when most children face changing hormones and accompanying social insecurities. In addition, the perils of language and labeling are addressed through the term "pretty," illuminating layered meanings and implications for pedagogy. The account prompts further questions for educators: What type of language and activities that draw upon student appearances might support and develop positive body image, and How can the social rituals of schooling be planned carefully to include and value a diversity of gender expression?*

When you hit the 8th grade, you think you're the coolest person that ever breathed. The top of elementary status. You've worked your whole life to get there. It's the year before high school when the world crumbles—when you have to start again from the bottom and don't come anywhere near the top 'til you're 50, if ever.

And the 8th-grade teachers threaten you to enjoy your happiness before it's too late. They devise little dances and sports tournaments and contests to show you how wonderful life is. The most popular by far is the beauty contest in the spring. And if I had ever believed that I was happy, it ended that afternoon on stage.

K-a-r-l-e-e-n—P-e-n-d-l-e-t-o-n. Karleen Pendleton. In between Amalia Lopez and Lisa Ashley. Karleen Pendleton—beauty contest nominee? The teacher said it the same way she called out my name every day for attendance. Like it didn't mean nuthin' different between my two most hated enemies. Well, maybe she didn't know they were my enemies; *they* probably didn't. I mean, I never talked to them or nuthin'. I just heard about them way too much from Sal. It made me sick. Here he was spending all this time with me, talking about them. How pretty they were, how he'd heard that Amalia would kiss you after school if she liked you. I thought they were whiny and weak. That's all there was to it. Who cared if they could bleach their hair and put makeup on?

OK, I gotta confess it. I would have worn makeup if I had thought he would have liked me more. I even snuck into my mom's makeup case once. I sat down at this little table she had with a light-up mirror and everything. I only got as far as opening the one I think she used for her cheeks. It was this orange-red, greasy looking stuff worn down to the bottom with a little cotton pad. I thought of my mom rubbing her face with it. I thought of all the girls at the school doing it too. That's something they did. Something they just did. Automatic. They didn't think about it like me, sittin' there lookin' at my face all round and puffy in a magnifying glass mirror. I got more interested in the magnifying glass part of it than the makeup. I imagined creating a big fire with it in the backyard.

That must be the difference. The automatic part. I've just never had it. I mean, my brother told me at the time that I needed to start dressing more like a girl because it would "look bad" for my mom.

But I honestly had no idea how to do it. I had never really looked at girls before. Never even thought about it 'til that second. Girls just looked like girls, all put together in pretty outfits. Never thought about separating out each part to see how they did it. I spent too much time looking at boys' clothes. Boys dressed easier. Or it was easier for me to dress like a boy. One of the two. The only thing hard about it was lookin' exactly how I wanted. I didn't understand how I could put the same exact clothes on as Sal and look completely different. I'd even stolen his pants before, thinkin' that they would be what was needed all along to make me look right. It didn't work. My stomach pushed up under the zipper. But they were too big on my waist and way too long on my legs. Not to mention that no matter what shirt I was wearing, I couldn't hide *them* anymore. Those painful circles rubbed against my t-shirts. It got me so sad. I kept getting bigger clothes so at least sometimes I could pull off lookin' like a boy. But I never really looked liked one of them. Because even though people thought I was a boy half the time, they thought I was a dorky one, never one of the cool ones.

I didn't know my nomination was a joke. I didn't. I swear it. I thought maybe it was a break for me. Maybe Sal'd like me after. I'd always wanted to be popular. I'd always thought I was. Not popular like Lisa or Amalia, but cool popular. I hung out with the boys that got in trouble. That got sent away, but still called me. And most kids wanted to hear about what was happening to them, but when I think about it, maybe it was only so that they could make sure it wouldn't happen to them. Nothin' really to do with popularity at all.

I was smart popular, too. I was even voted smartest girl of the 8th grade by everyone. I had all kinds of awards to show for it, and enjoyed beating some pretty pissed-off boys. But smart people are never respected. Not by kids. At least it gave adults something to say about me. I heard it all the time. They told my parents how smart I was, and my parents smiled and thanked them or told them other ways I was smart and everybody was happy.

I wasn't stupid. I knew they said it 'cuz they couldn't say how "pretty" I was like they did all the other girls. Not that I wanted them to. I mean that would have been embarrassing. I felt sorry for girls having to hear it all the time. I just wanted to hear it once, that's all. That's why I walked on stage. I thought it could be true. How stupid. How ridiculously stupid of me. I should have refused to get on stage. Called the whole thing stupid. Said I was better than some stupid beauty contest. Then it never would've gotten so bad. He never would've said that to me. "Joke." It was a joke that I'd been nominated. And I never would've ignored him and acted like I didn't know what he was talking about. I never would've thought about all those kids eating their lunches lookin' up at me and laughin'. Me in my bright girl's shirt, stepping up, smiling like an idiot.

I haven't ever made that mistake again. I can live without being "pretty." I've done it for years.

Helen Soliz saved me, or at least found a man to. He was only 14, but he was a man with broad shoulders, brown rippling muscles, and a so-so face. Every nominee had to bring a date to the dance. Helen volunteered him to be mine. He shook my hand hard, like we were both guys, and smiled. I looked at Helen and felt my cheeks and eyes squeeze up. I wasn't sure this was such a good idea. I could pretend I was sick or somethin' or just not show up, or walk to the library instead when my mom dropped me off. Only the library wasn't open that late, and I knew my mom was going out on Friday and expecting my dad to pick me up at the dance. And I knew she'd be mad if I was home alone that late or if she had to talk to my dad about it. I started picturing her yelling at me or him, when Helen picked up my hand and played with it in her fingers. "Come on," she said, "you gotta go. It'll be fun. I promise."

Helen wasn't a best friend or a good friend or anything close to that. She was just someone else in my class, but someone who would do me favors. Favors that I didn't ask for. Once I forgot a pencil and she saw me searching and gave me an extra one. I'm not even sure how she knew what I needed. Sometimes she'd talk to me during PE when I didn't know any other girls to talk to. And I'd tell the other kids to shut up when they sang, "Helen Soliz has hairy moles," which wasn't even true. She only had that one black mole on her cheek but it wasn't hairy. I'd even heard the lunch ladies tell her it made her pretty. Mostly, we just knew to trust each other in little moments when other people started acting stupid.

So I looked back at her big dark eyes sitting in a freshly made-up face and decided to believe her, like she said.

I went to every single dance at my school. But I hardly ever danced. The Rosemead Community Center filled with balloons and cookies on a Friday night only meant one thing to me. Ping-Pong. I was the Ping-Pong champion of Muscatel Junior High School. I even beat the boys who owned their own rackets. Boy after boy would line up to challenge, and I'd love creaming them all.

Stepping five feet back, I balanced the featherlight ball between my thumb and index finger and smacked it 1/4 inch above the net. Half the time, they couldn't even return my serve. It was serious business for me. I even dressed appropriate to the game, in a T-shirt and sweatpants—to the disapproval of my classmates. To tell you the truth, I never even thought about it until John Osa, a boy I beat in math competitions, sneered at the sight of me in my favorite gray sweatpants. "Don't you think you should dress nicer? It *is* a dance."

"Naww." That's all I had to say back. Why? I was just going to play Ping-Pong. It never occurred to me to wear anything else. And I brushed him off, but worried about it from that day on. I decided it would be OK dressing up for Ping-Pong, since that's the only place anyone would see me. Not dancing. Or, maybe only for 10 minutes the whole night, if at all. And after that, one boy at the beginning of 8th grade wanted to slow dance with me. I never went back. Besides, I wasn't very good at it. And I only like doing things I'm good at.

The beauty contest extravaganza put all my worst skills together—dressing, dancing, and acting like a girl. I figured I'd just hide out in the game room. If Ping-Pong was too visible, pool would have to do. I could hold my own there, too, and people wouldn't be looking at me. And that man that Helen picked out would just have to find someone else to dance with. After all, I wasn't going to win the contest. The joke would never go that far. They wouldn't risk Lisa's and Amalia's reps over me. They'd already had their laugh at lunch. So who cared where I was when they announced the winners?

Unfortunately, my game room competitors thought it was a good reason to get me off the tables. They might have respected my game, but they were also sick of me. Hyun Song laughed and said I had to go compete for my beauty instead. My "shut up" came out weak, and so I decided I had to go to the bathroom.

The Aqua Net burned my nose before the door was half open. And there they were. I should have known. All the beauty nominees lined up in front of the mirrors. Tight black miniskirts, long white dresses. Bra straps, dress straps, purse straps of every color inched carefully over each other, make-up cases cluttered along the sinks, eyelash contraptions, eye pencils, lipsticks, hair picks, and me standing there in my maroon corduroys with a plaid shirt and tennis shoes that I thought had looked nice two hours earlier. I was standing in the wrong bathroom and I knew it. I didn't need to be told. I couldn't even breathe. I left before they noticed me. I went through the dance floor, gave Helen's man a nervous smile, and walked out into the gated night.

Big, black, pointed bars surrounded me. They said they were for keeping unwanteds out of our dance. "Those evil high school kids." Like any of them would ever have been caught dead there. I knew it was a way to trap us. But at least I could breathe. The air was cool in my mouth and my lungs took it all over my body. There were no stars or moon, only clouds glowing from the city lights. I liked standin' out there. It was my favorite place after the game room. I liked bein' alone. Most kids wanted other kids around, but I liked getting to be by myself sometimes. Gave me a second to think about how weird everything was and to wonder why I was in the middle of it. I mean, all I was doing was sitting there when she called my name. How could I get to be a beauty nominee without ever having done anything for it? I never wanted it. OK, maybe just for a second, just before I thought about it. When I thought it could be true. That it was exactly what I needed to get the other kids to shut up about me lookin' like a boy and all. But I never tried for it. It just hit me when I was doing nothin' at all but talkin' to Perla about a history test or somethin'.

That's what got me. I kept doin' nothin' at all and things would happen. Like that old lady in her big orange flower dress who told me I was in the wrong bathroom at the library. Didn't even let me say anything. Just pointed and sent me out. I held it for three hours 'til my mom came and picked me up and it hurt bad. I guess it did feel good when I finally got to go at home. Actually, nothin' ever felt so good in my life. But god, I didn't need all that goin' on. I just needed to study, that's all. . . .

Helen snuck up behind me.

"Karleen?"

"Yeah," I answered, surprised.

"Whatta ya doin'?" she asked and slid her fingers around the bars next to me.

"Nuthin'," I said, pushin' my hand into my pocket. I was hopin' if I didn't say much, she would leave.

"Why aren't you in there for the contest?"

"Don't believe in it," I answered, so I'd sound like I had a real reason and then I remembered the man. "Oh, sorry about the guy. I mean I really appreciate you gettin' him for me and all, but I. . . ."

"That's ok," she broke in. I was glad 'cuz I didn't know how to end the sentence. She looked down, scratchin' her shoes on the cement. "I get it. . . . You don't look right all dressed up with makeup and all that anyway."

I turned and grabbed the bars. I was thinkin' that was just what I was thinkin'. All I was doin' was standing there by myself enjoyin' the night and then Helen had to come right in front of me and bug me. Talkin' about dresses and whatever. The things I hated most. I was so sick of it. I hated that place. I hated my brothers and the woman with the orange dress and the teacher for sayin' my name as a nominee and David Twirp for callin' me a joke and even Helen. I hated Helen standing in front of me tellin' me that I didn't look right. I hated them all. I didn't care how I looked. I just wanted them to leave me alone.

My hands were sweaty in my corduroys. Helen looked at me all sad like I could be a kitten she found out there or somethin'. I was starting to think the fence wasn't so tall and I could get out of there after all. I didn't want to walk home in the dark or nothin', but I could have done it. It had to be safer than in there.

"Karleen. I didn't mean it bad. I think you're pretty without all that stuff. That's all."

Oh god. Not that word. "Pretty." She was callin' me pretty. Shit, when was this shit gonna end. I was sick of it. I hated that place. Shit. Damn. Shit. She was still lookin' up at me. I had to get outta there. Stop. She was gettin' closer. Stop. Shit. Stop. Stop lookin' at me so much. Her eyes were so big. I didn't want her to see me. Stop. Shit. Helen, leave me alone. Pretty. Pretty. I hate pretty. Shit. Shit.

Her lips hit mine soft they were wet they tasted like Kool-aid and cream cookies her eyes were closed mine were open hers were covered in colors her lipstick stuck to me she pushed again I pushed back I didn't know how to stop it if I should have told her to stop it or not I didn't know I only knew how the lips tasted her hand touched my stomach and my stomach got hot on the inside, hot so fast like a doctor's needle that hurts in the middle of your body after 3 seconds when the medicine hits you only this didn't hurt I liked it I liked her it felt good my back fell on the fence her hand pushed me pushed on me the bars were hard on my shoulders I didn't say it I didn't want the pushing to stop stopping it stopped I didn't say anything but it stopped. Stopped all of a sudden. Her hand stopped. Her lips stopped. Her eyes were open. Our eyes looked at each other. Hers were big. The black parts were big. I didn't know what mine looked like. Her lips smiled. They were dark and crooked. I didn't smile. I didn't breathe. I watched her walk away. She said she'd see me Monday. Soft. Friendly. Her breathing was the same.

There were pins in my stomach. My skin was shaky. The bars were pushing in against my back. They were hard and cold. My skin was too warm for them. My skin was hot. I couldn't be so hot. My mom would think I was sick. She would touch my skin and think I had a fever and then she'd be sad. I didn't like her eyes big and sad when they get wet and look like marbles. She'd ask what happened and be sad that I stood there outside when I could have been inside without a fever. I wouldn't tell her. I wouldn't be so hot. I would breathe big. Big cool air. Cool air in my mouth and my lungs took it all over my body. I would breathe it for a while and not look inside for Helen. I wouldn't try to find her. I would only look outside at the night. I would only look up at the sky. There were no stars or moon, only clouds glowing from the city lights.

THE LETTER

Barbara Brush

M y only regret about being gay is that I repressed it for so long. I surrendered my youth to the people I feared when I could have been out there loving someone. Don't make that mistake yourself. Life's too damn short. —Armistead Maupin

In this love letter, Brush recounts a history of unrequited desire originating in her admiration for a 7th-grade science teacher. Her words attest to the beauty and value of the love she offers, in contrast to the world that misunderstands and seeks to stifle a young child's passion. What mentoring is available for teachers who are learning how to navigate student crushes? What representations of LGBT desire exist in the classroom for LGBT students to learn about themselves, and to imagine what futures are available to them?

Dear Squirrel,

By now, you know, and most of the people in my life know. My friends, my family, my colleagues. I do all the stuff. I have HRC [Human Rights Campaign] checks and HRC shirts and rainbow beach towels and bumper stickers on my car. The only time I ever missed a Pride parade was when I was in Norway. A couple weeks ago, for National Coming Out Day, I took HRC's online "How Out Are You?" quiz, and my results said, "You're so out you could be the 5th Golden Girl." And it's fun, and it feels good to be a part of something; but it's more than that. It's fighting back, and not just against the world outside.

I wear my rainbow pendant every single day. It's a ritual. In the morning when I wake up, I put it on before I put on my glasses, before I put my feet on the floor. At night I take it off after I am in bed, after the lights are out, after I cannot see anymore. It is there to make me remember. It's the only piece of jewelry I've ever bought for myself and I spent a chunk of money on it, because I needed it to be something really beautiful that touches me every day and reminds me every day and is beautiful every day. Because I am a warrior, and I need a shield, and the demons are always out there, and the demons are always in here.

It was Texas, you understand, small-town Texas in 1981. Texas, which gave us Dubya. Texas, where in 2005, a state constitutional amendment banning same-sex marriages, civil unions, and domestic partnerships passed with 76 percent of the vote.

As a 7th-grader, I had no sense of myself as a sexual being, no awareness of any such drive or desire. I failed to understand the fuss about boys; I didn't dislike them, I just found them fundamentally uninteresting. But I didn't find myself attracted to girls, either. I knew that I preferred their company, and felt more comfortable with them; but I didn't connect that to anything physical. Mostly what I cared about was horses. It was Texas, after all. And I cared about science. My favorite T-shirt had a detailed image of a strand of DNA in white on a navy blue background. When I wasn't riding, I was in my room with my watercolors, rendering molecular structures, mitochondria, double helices.

And that was where *she* came in.

She was the Life Science teacher. An imposing woman: sharp, trim, very butch (though I didn't know that word then), with a couple of fierce silver streaks in her short black hair. A tough grader (the challenge excited me, though few of my peers shared the sentiment). She told me I was "hyper-analytical," which was true and I was happy to accept it as high praise. And she awarded me first place in the class science project competition.

I walked past rows of black lab tables and up to her desk to claim the prize. When she gave it to me, she also gave me a really nice hug. I felt completely blissed out in that moment: warm and special and honored and close to her. I felt a sense of connection. I wanted to preserve that feeling, to give it a form, and to share it with her. So I wrote the letter. I told her how much it meant to me, that connection, how good it made me feel. I hoped it would please her. She took it, as I believed then, all wrong. She took it, as I understand now, pretty nearly right.

After school the next afternoon, I was sitting in the living room with my brother, watching *The Partridge Family*, when my parents came in looking grim. They'd been called in to talk with the principal. Did I know why? I didn't, I said. I hadn't done anything wrong. They asked very seriously whether I'd written a certain letter to my science teacher. Yes, I had. What did that have to do with anything? And how did they know? *She* never said a word to me about it, then or later; but she'd given away my letter to the principal and the school counselor, who showed it to my parents at their meeting the following day. The counselor felt it was beyond her. The recommendation was regular sessions with a shrink.

I met with the first guy, a psychiatrist, only once, and I remember about our meeting only that he was angular and cold and shriveled and grey, with black square-rimmed glasses. He scowled and jabbed little notes onto his pad, and focused what I considered an absurd amount of attention on my wardrobe. While as a young girl I'd favored lace and frills, as a junior high student and an equestrian, I was more comfortable in jeans and t-shirts. He seemed inordinately displeased by this revelation. I was displeased by the fact that he was a moron.

The second guy, the psychologist, I had to see once a week for several months. He was younger and rounder than the first guy, but just as pompous and self-satisfied and annoying. He was fairly interested in my habit of carrying my spiral notebook with me everywhere and writing everything down; he never asked me for it, but I started keeping it locked in a box under my bed, nonetheless. The only thing I considered to be a real issue in my life was the one that he casually dismissed: the fact that rumors had quickly spread throughout the school that I was toxic, and no one would have anything to do with me. My two best friends, Vicki and Crystal, had stopped speaking to me. I don't know what they had heard or where they heard it, but a few days after my parents' meeting with the principal, I was waiting after school in front of the building for my friends to come outside so we could head to Vicki's house, as we often did, to go riding. When they finally did appear, they ignored me and walked in the opposite direction.

I followed stupidly. "Aren't we riding today?"

"No," was all Vicki said. Crystal didn't say anything.

"Why not?" I didn't get it. The buses had left, and I'd told my mother I was going to be at Vicki's, so I didn't have a ride home from school. What was up with the sudden change in plans?

"Because if we keep hanging around with you, people are going to start thinking we're gay, too," Vicki shot over her shoulder. I was so shocked by this, and by the loathing and disgust in her voice, that I had no idea how to respond. Where did she even get such an idea about me? I wasn't like that.

I'd never even thought about it. In my mind, it was supremely ironic that they were rejecting me for something that wasn't even true—though I doubt it would have been easier if I'd known that I was what they said.

Soon everybody "knew," and everybody kept their distance. The brilliant psychologist told me that everyone feels like an outcast in junior high. I don't think it ever even occurred to him that occasionally people feel that way because it's actually the case. He told me a stupid story about how when he was 13, he had a friend called J.T. He'd thought this was very cool, to go by one's initials, so he tried it, but his initials were D.L., and somehow that just wasn't the same. He was right about this much: It wasn't the same thing at all. I never understood the point of these sessions and felt they were an absolute waste of time. Fortunately, my parents eventually concluded that they were also a waste of money.

Things finally started to turn around my sophomore year in high school, when I found friends among the musicians, the bookworms, and the drama queens; my closest friend wore a rebel disguise, with multiple piercings and purple hair one week, a black mohawk the next. In reality, he was a quiet, introspective, wonderfully talented visual artist. He was also gay, though this was never discussed while we were in school; he didn't share it with me until a year after we had graduated. He kissed me once, having asked my permission, while we were in the neighbor's pool; this was exciting for both of us in that it meant we could both then say we'd kissed a member of the opposite sex. The act itself was one of friendship, and in all other respects it was wholly unremarkable.

I was 24, a graduate student, when I found myself drawn to a woman in a way that was not only romantic but powerfully and unmistakably physical, and I finally began to ask myself the questions for real. The very first thing I did upon recognizing what I felt for her was to go to the library. I was looking for confirmation. I wanted stories, descriptions, definitions, language in which I could recognize myself, say *Yes, that's what I am.* I didn't find any. They did exist, as I later discovered, but they were not on the library's shelves.

When I first saw *Fried Green Tomatoes*, like most straight people, I failed to recognize it as a lesbian film, because there was no overt sex scene. I hadn't yet heard of butch/femme, so I didn't see how clearly Idgie and Ruth represented those identities. Still, I knew I wanted what they had: their loving, intimate relationship, their life together.

It wasn't until I took a women's studies class called "Lesbian Lives and Cultures" that I learned what should have been obvious all along (though, in my own defense, I've found that most straight people don't get it any more than I did): A lesbian identity isn't just about sex. According to many, it wasn't even *primarily* about sex. It wasn't simply a matter of wanting to sleep with women; it was about wanting to *be* with them, forming attachments to them. Falling in love with them. That was a definition I could own without any doubt or reservation; and if I'd known about it, if there had been anyone who could have explained it to me, I could've owned it 10 years earlier. Even now, though I'm conscious of physical attraction as an undeniable part of what I feel for you, it's that sense of closeness with you that I want most of all—so much it eclipses nearly everything else. Times when I want to touch your hair with my fingers; when I want to kiss you, softly, perfectly, though I'm sure you will never let me. Times when, sitting next to you on the sofa, I feel such a warmth of affection and tenderness that I want only to lean against you, to rest my head on your shoulder, to feel your presence there with me and know that you're not on the verge of running away.

The woman in grad school—the woman for whom my feelings were intense enough to lead me to a new identity—could not accept it. She surely must have suspected—you know I'm ridiculously unskilled at hiding such things—but both knowing and fearing the power of the words, we never spoke them. I've still never said it out loud—not to you, nor to anyone else: *I love you.* In part, it's protective of you: Knowing you don't share my feelings, I'm hesitant to put you in the awkward position of having it said to your face. I know you wouldn't lie, and I don't want you to lie, and it's not fair to force you to cast about for some magical response that would allow us both to feel okay. But this particular silence is also the final layer of self-protection. You already know, and you've accepted it, and still that surge of panic burns all the way through me any time I even think of actually speaking those words in your presence.

After the last time, I promised myself I was never again going to be in any relationship where I had to feel guilty or ashamed or like I needed to apologize for loving the person. I have, and I have not, kept my promise. I've kept it in the sense that you have never asked me to break it. You have never guilted me or shamed me or asked me to apologize. But I have. I'm trained to feel those things and I don't know how long it may take me to unlearn them altogether. I am well trained to fear the consequences, and however much I want to trust you, however much I *do* trust you, some of that fear won't go away. But I believe this love is a good thing, and I need to believe that. I believe it should be celebrated, and I need to celebrate it. It feels good and it makes me happy and it is *so* important to be able to genuinely, honestly, love somebody and not have that be a bad thing, not have it be an ugly or a shameful thing, not have it be a problem, not have it be something I'm supposed to be trying to fix or undo. To love someone and have that be welcome and safe.

Love always, Moose

At One Time, Fontana Was the Working-Class Eden

Cindy Cruz

School offered Cruz "a safe space" away from the danger her young, queer, brown body faced on the streets. Her queerness was located as much in her butch presentation as in her assertive approach to the education that would move her away from the poverty faced by her hometown. How does one's (student's/teacher's/parent's) race, class, gender, and body shape desire and aspiration influence others' hateful exchanges and loving relations? How might education be offered to LGBT students as a tool for survival?

Education, like it is for so many families of color, was our ticket out of the gritty neighborhoods where we lived. At one time, Fontana, California, was the working-class Eden—a company town that recruited union workers, where their labor was paid what it was worth, where a ranch-style home with a pool was within reach. Fontana was an energized place where we played ball in organized leagues and had huge company picnics at which my parents played games in the park with the other Kaiser Steel parents. We believed in the American dream—some of us in the family still do—and thought that if we worked hard in school and at the job, we would be rewarded. I already had a taste of those rewards, little teasers from my teachers, who recognized I didn't talk with an accent (our family didn't teach us Spanish), I could read, and I enjoyed the attention I got when I raised my hand in the classroom. I didn't "play" like a good Chicanita was supposed to—I was not quiet, I was not humble, nor was I in any way going to submit to any boy. I was loud and boisterous and a show-off. My mother taught us to be assertive and, most importantly, we were allowed to question our teachers. I took this seriously, as I knew I could ask questions other students didn't dare (or didn't think to) and I knew my parents would always side with me. Consequently, my report cards showed high marks in my academic work but poor marks on "respect for authority."

When I was in the 4th grade, a new girl in my school thought I was a boy and said she liked me. We all laughed, my friends and I, when we heard that. She even tried to talk with me during recess, but I was too busy playing soccer to listen to this girl who was so dumb that she couldn't tell if I was a boy or a girl. I went home later and looked at myself in the mirror. I looked good and hard at this androgynous body that enjoyed running, playing any kind of sport, and was as good as, if not better than, any boy my age, even kung-fu mock-fighting with them, in these clothes my mother picked out. Simple clothes—a sweatshirt over blue jeans. Maybe it was my hair cut short by my *tia* who just graduated from beauty school that confused this girl? Was it my boots I wore every day? Or the silver cowboy belt buckle my father got for me at the Date Festival rodeo last year?

I knew very early on I was different. But I thought it was because I could read. My mother made sure of that. I had a house full of books that my parents never touched, but I did. I read them all, two or three or more times. New books would come every month in the mail and my father built huge shelves to house them all. I lost myself in these new worlds, in *1001 Arabian Nights*, Twain, Hardy, Melville, Steinbeck, Poe, and Hawthorne. My father and my uncles collected comic books and swapped them with each other, and I found myself awash in hundreds of issues about Wonder Woman, Spider-Man,

Tarzan, Batman, and John Carter of Mars. I read Emily Dickinson's poetry, Sue Kauffman's nascent feminism, the entire Encyclopedia Britannica, and the medical books my father brought home from the thrift stores. I read through these books, looking up terms such as "tomboy," "homosexuality," and "lesbianism." Since the medical books I had were old, everything I read talked about "deviance" and "disorder"; I had no idea homosexuality had since been removed from the psychiatric manual. I didn't think I was deviant or disordered. I was an "A" student, I won awards for my academics and athleticism, I played in the band and was All-State, and my parents were proud of me. So what if I read these stories and switched the genders, or that I identified with the male characters?

When I got older, it did matter to people that I looked or played or walked like a boy. People felt free to police my gender—my clothes, or the way that I talked, or my haircut. Sometimes adults said things about my androgyny even while I was standing in the grocery line with my mother! My mother would tell them to mind their own business and a few other things. Other boys and girls didn't like it that I was faster, stronger, and smarter. By the 5th grade, I downplayed some of my abilities to fit in, but it didn't matter to some of my classmates. They knew I was different, but they didn't know why. And some of them thought they knew what to do with my difference.

I walked home from school every day with my next-door neighbors. One day, however, I was late as music rehearsals kept me later than I usually was. Noticing the time, I grabbed my instrument case and made my way home. The streets were so quiet. My boots echoed through the empty streets and I heard whisperings on my left near a row of vacated houses: "Wetback, go home." I bit my lip nervously, as I was a little scared of older boys. They seemed to be the ones most outraged at my gender transgressions and they were probably bigger than me. I walked a little faster and noticed who lived nearby, just in case I had to make a run for it. I heard those words again, "Wetback, go home." This time, it was a little louder. I stopped in the middle of the street and shouted back to them, "Don't call me a wetback, you assholes!" Three white teenagers walked out of the house on my left, blocking my way home. I froze. "Calling us assholes, you little spic?" said the tallest boy, SWP (supreme white power) tattooed on his left arm. "Are you a boy or a girl?" the second one sneered. "Maybe we should find out," said the third and he started toward me. I tried to shout for help, but my vocal cords wouldn't work. As the third boy grabbed me and started to drag me into the empty row of houses, the adrenaline rushed through me and I slammed my instrument case into his groin. He fell to his knees in pain and I sprinted away from the other two boys, who now had to help their fallen Aryan companion get out of the street.

When I got home, I thought that this must be the beginning of how people would react to me and my boots and short hair and cowboy belt buckles. I felt sick and insecure about my "looks"—I allowed my hair to grow out and wore more clothing made for girls. I hated how men and boys would look at me. By junior high, other students made obscure comments about my sexuality, or lack of one. Other classmates were more blatant, scrawling "jota" or "dyke" on my locker in *placas* (signatures) that I recognized. Didn't the medical encyclopedia state that I would grow out of this developmental phase of "tomboy"? But the words did not stick to me and I was fortunate to have been placed in a pre-college track at my school. It kept the overt heterosexuality at bay. But the storm of drugs, sex, and alcohol swirled around me nonetheless as I buried myself in my books.

If outside the classroom was about the brutality of adolescent boys, then inside the classroom I found an environment in which I excelled, where literature took me far away from my dusty hometown. Then the steel mill closed. My father and all the fathers around us lost their jobs, and I didn't dare ask for money for books. So, I shoplifted what I wanted and searched the thrift stores for literature.

I could get Michael Herr's *Dispatches* or James Baldwin's *The Fire Next Time* for a quarter, or five books for a dollar at the local secondhand store. I was fortunate in high school to have teachers, some of whom were lesbian or gay, who loaned me books or allowed me to search through the department libraries for literature and poetry. After the steel plant closed, Fontana turned into a city of thrift stores, pawn shops, and fast food malls. There were no more company picnics, the union was shattered, and my father was working for minimum wage at a poultry farm. The recreation leagues were eliminated for lack of players. The city replaced the union jobs with fast food. There was still work at Kaiser Steel, but it was to help dismantle the mill for shipping to China. We went to a lot of funerals at that time, and the violence escalated all around us—fathers who didn't see any way out other than suicide, drive-by shootings, my best friend who turned to prostitution to pay for her drug habit. I knew there was nothing left for me in this post-industrial town. It was as if someone had ripped the heart out of the city, its streets left limp and lifeless.

During my first year of college, someone gave me a copy of *This Bridge Called My Back: Writings by Radical Women of Color*. I was profoundly affected as I read these testimonials from working-class writers of color; *Bridge* was a space where women of color, particularly lesbians of color, were at the center of a radical politic. Their critique of U.S. imperialism, of racism, and of homophobia, and the image in the foreword of a world on fire reverberated through my own histories and those of my family. *Bridge* gave me a language to use to begin making sense of my world, as I read the narratives of these writers who have made the political decision to be the connections between communities. But I was most affected by the stories of Gloria Anzaldúa, Nellie Wong, Cherríe Moraga, and Audre Lorde. I felt an intensely personal connection to their brutal honesty about their mothers, their families, and how the shit comes down on women of color and their families in this country. I recognized my histories in their words, my history of rewards for my family's assimilation into the language of this country, my own queerness. I recognized my own resiliency. Despite all they've experienced, these writers still choose to use their own bodies for political work—the human bridge, the back that gets walked on over and over.

Teaching is also about making connections. Working with youth in Los Angeles is about recognizing strength and resiliency. The writers in *Bridge* are using their own bodies to build coalitions. It made sense to me that this was the role of lesbians and gay men of color—a role I have made my own. It is what I teach to the young people I work with in Los Angeles—these queer youth of color who are now in my own classrooms. It is about empowering a new generation of young scholar-activists to build community and coalition in their own lives. And it is also about empowering myself.

I believe that my experience growing up queer didn't necessarily mean "homosexual." In Fontana, it was a "queer" thing to want to go to college. I sincerely believe that my socialization as an assertive and righteous girl cut me out of the crowd. Maybe it was the fact that I didn't speak with an accent or maybe it was my refusal to play by the rules ascribed to my race and gender. It made sense to call myself a lesbian early on, as it was a term that might describe what I was experiencing, but maybe the term "dyke" would be a better fit for me—one that announces my hard-scrabble, working-class history. Sometimes when I hear other people tell stories about growing up and going to school, so normal and unassuming, I hesitate to tell my own stories. School, at least in my classrooms, was a safe space for me. I didn't really have to "come out" of any closet, but maybe my closet is one where race and capitalism and gender are hopelessly entangled. Whenever I claim my own queer body, my life moves away from those I went to school with. I am convinced that had I not been a lesbian, I would not have survived this. I would not have survived.

WHEN MATT BECAME JADE: WORKING WITH A YOUTH WHO MADE A GENDER TRANSITION CHANGE IN HIGH SCHOOL

Dale R. Callender

This chapter was written with full permission and authorization by Jade.

*J*ade's story demonstrates the courage and strength of Jade and her family. It was an experience that shifted and touched many for their commitment to ensuring equality and compassion. It is important to note that being transsexual for Jade is a reality—not a choice or decision. She finds it quite difficult to be referred to by, hear, and/or read about her previous gender. She was always Jade. "Matt" was just another name she went by to survive in the world until her transition. She finds it very uncomfortable to be constantly reminded of the transition by the use of "that" name and the male pronoun. It is with this in mind that I only use the name of "Matt" for the sake of helping to educate and clarify.

With thanks to all those who have assisted in the formation of the manuscript with their input, guidance, thoughts, and opinions. In particular:

Jade
Jade's parents, Anne and Michael
Delisle Youth Services staff, management, and board members
Northern Secondary School support staff members
Bob Milne, Northern Secondary School Principal
Tony Kerins, Northern Secondary School Acting Principal
Steve Solomon, TDSB (Toronto District School Board) Human Sexuality Social Worker
Jake Pyne, The 519 Community Centre Social worker
Scott Pope, Director Atkinson Counselling and Supervision Centre
Jane Steelemoore, Northern Secondary School Parents Council Chair
Leslie Scrivener, Toronto Star reporter
Paul Zalewski, Teacher/Editor of initial drafts
Nancy Matthews, Edits

Looking in the mirror these days, Jade says she "feels right." "I just feel more comfortable viewed as a woman. I think what might be useful is that no one knows why exactly someone becomes transgender and feels the way they do. The cause is unknown. I do know I need to express myself and have the world view me as who I really am."

Working with transitioning youth appears to be an emerging focus within educational settings. As you journey through this chapter, question and challenge the following to help guide your path:

Is your educational system/structure supportive of all gender diversities? Do you have a basic understanding of transgender issues? Are you familiar with basic sensitivity protocols for engaging transgendered youth? Are you aware of the current laws and rights of transitioning youth with respect to accommodations and prevention of harassment and discrimination? What would you do if a student approached you about transitioning in his or her school setting?

Background

Delisle Youth Services is a multi-service social service community agency based in Toronto, Ontario, committed to supporting the developmental, emotional, and social needs of youth and their families. One component of community partnership is their school-based prevention and intervention model, the Delisle in the Schools program. The Delisle in the Schools model serves young people who are at risk of dropping out of school or experiencing lack of success in the schools due to a variety of complex personal and social problems in their daily lives. The agency works with the community to bring supportive services into North Toronto schools. Its model goes beyond simply placing a worker in the school, making its full range of services available to the school in an effective and efficient manner. Working with the school team, the Delisle staff develops an individualized plan that helps each student cope with his/her particular areas of need. The youth workers provide support to students experiencing issues beyond academic problems and needing the opportunity to discuss and explore their issues in a confidential and supportive atmosphere.

About Matt, Who Was Jade

Matt was a 17-year-old male attending a high school in North Toronto, Ontario. Even with 2,000 students in the school, he was hard to miss because of his imposing stature, standing 6 foot, 4 inches tall. He had just been elected incoming Student Council President for the 2004-05 school year. His performance during the campaign seemed to enlighten the assembly; after that, there was a buzz around the school about this young man. He seemed to be someone who would now be noticed. He had a wit and bite to his humor, which helped him relate to his peers, and attract those who didn't know him. He was, by nature, an introverted person—he did have a small group of close friends, but seemed to shy away from public gatherings and activities.

As the Delisle worker, but also sharing my time with involvement in school activities, I was the student council staff adviser. I met Matt for the first time during a meet and greet session for the new Student Council. Matt seemed focused, driven, and excited about the upcoming school year and about what the Student Council could do for the student body.

Matt came to see me to get support and advice on stressors in his life. When asked to explain further, he found it difficult to express—he was not one to usually speak to someone about personal things. One major anxiety in his day-to-day functioning was his ability to conclude an ongoing fantasy that he had been working on for years. The struggle for Matt was not *how* to end the story, but feeling like he *needed* to end the story.

Matt wanted to talk more about his longing for an intimate connection with a female he knew of at the school. He just didn't know how to begin trying to break down the barriers of approaching and getting to know her. We talked about developing the skills and opportunities to get to know others . . . the basic social skill to meet and greet and instigate conversations.

"I have this overriding sense of confusion at times. I just can't explain it. I feel at a loss, not knowing what to do—it just hits me," he said, and then began to cry—sob, really. He appeared to lose his

ability to engage in a dialogue, waving me off to give him some time, crying, drooling, breathing hard. He needed several minutes in silence just to regain composure. *"This happens periodically,"* he told me. *"Happens at home or when I'm walking down the hall in school. I have this sense of crashing, needing to be away from others."* It appeared Matt was struggling with some degree of a social- or anxiety-related condition.

I brought up his potential struggle with sexual orientation. It was a thought that came to me as I was beginning to develop an assessment of some of the reasons behind Matt's anxiety and confusion about wanting the relationship with the young woman. I shared with him that throughout adolescent development, sexual awareness emerges, the capacity for close friendships develops, older role models become mentors and idols, and awareness of a variety of attractions grows. Some people will be confused by their feelings or experiences. Equally important is the fact that emerging homosexual feelings are both unexpected and unwelcome to most adolescents. And most will go through a period of not wanting to be gay or lesbian. The fear of rejection and stigmatization can be, at times, the basis for denying, rejecting, and fighting against those feelings. The conflict between the feelings and the fears results in confusion.

Matt seemed to have a hard time verbalizing the exact nature of his feelings and his challenges. His behaviour indicated that these feelings of confusion, perhaps concerning his sexuality, were contributing to his anxiety and his substantial need to develop an intimate relationship with the young female at the school. Matt appeared to be acting out anxieties, conflicts, and confusion through his daily life. He willingly shared his distress. Was Matt struggling with confusion about his sexual orientation, or was Matt struggling with a specific or generalized anxiety condition? Or both?

Just as we were wrapping up our second appointment and scheduling another session, Matt calmly stated, *"Oh, something else; I also like to dress up in women's clothes."* I was caught off-guard for a moment . . . it was not something that had come up as part of the counselling I had done. This was a new revelation that increased my understanding about Matt's sexual identity and stressors. "Tell me about that," I asked. He explained that the most difficult thing about it was finding clothing to fit him because he was so tall.

"Who else knows about this?" I inquired. Matt replied, *"Not a lot of people. I'm not really comfortable yet telling my mom. And my Dad is out of the question."* I told him I thought we should explore the issue more as it may provide some insight as to his current stressors, and provide exploration opportunities concerning some of his anxieties and feelings of confusion.

I had a lot of questions to ask Matt about what it meant for him to dress as a woman. How important was this part of his life in his overall daily functioning? We agreed that our next meeting would focus more on how this part of who he is affected his life. Just before school started again in September 2004, we had our next meeting. Matt had spent some time relaxing at his family's cottage with his mother during the last part of the summer. He had progressed in his evolution towards identity clarity. Matt told me he had talked with his mother about his need to dress like a woman. He said it was one of the most uncomfortable things he had ever done. *"Even though my mother had come out as a lesbian, to talk to her about something as personal and different as this, was so difficult,"* he said. *"Trying to identify as a female in a male's body is not something that is easy to talk about with your mother. I really didn't know how to first describe it. Just more or less as the need and desire to dress in women's clothing was the start."*

Since coming out as a lesbian, Matt's mother had always been hopeful that her children would see the importance of being true to oneself. As she tried to understand exactly what Matt was saying, and needing, she realized that Matt was telling her something about who he was at this point in his life. Transgender to Matt in that early stage meant *"being born in the wrong body."* Not feeling like, or identifying with, the gender that corresponded with his sex and genetics. He had felt this way from his earliest memory: *"I knew for the longest time . . . but . . . wasn't ready to deal with it."*

His fixation on the young female at the school continued. He felt an overriding need to connect and develop a relationship with her, despite his need and desire to dress as a woman. My idea in this initial stage was to try and refocus away from relationship development, and move toward coping strategies and skills to help ameliorate his confusions and anxieties. Massive feelings of depression and helplessness overwhelmed him. These feelings would arise very quickly, with no real gradual transition. He experienced rapid thoughts, not being able to concentrate, feeling like he was afraid of something, and finding everything either positive or negative—nothing in between. Could it be that aspects of his identity and personality were repressed for so long that now these feelings were flooding out into all different aspects of his life? It seemed, at times, to be practically unbearable for him.

Matt decided not to come out at school that September. Instead, he would dress as a woman at home. His mother and he went shopping for clothes. He would slowly begin the transition to being who he really was and letting others know when he was ready. But this still wasn't enough for him. He was not happy to have to hide, to "be in the closet," away from others. He would come to school and walk the halls, be in the community, hang with friends, do his student council activities, and all the while he felt a longing to be who he really was. It just wasn't good enough to be at home dressed as woman. I really felt that Matt was on a course of self-discovery, where the evolution of becoming what had been repressed for so long was just a matter of time.

The Centre for Addiction and Mental Health in Toronto has a gender identity clinic and Sunnybrook and Women's College Health Science Centre has an anxiety disorder clinic. I recommended to Matt and his mother that they consider using these facilities.

Matt and his mother gave me permission to speak with Matt's individual guidance and support counselor. The counselor and I had come to similar formulations as to what would be the most beneficial in better understanding Matt and his struggles. This individual had been focusing on helping Matt explore his sexuality and would now begin to assist with his sexual identity supports. My work could focus on continuing to provide a more immediate on-site school support to Matt and his daily struggles with anxiety and identity.

Schoolwork seemed fine for Matt. However, Matt's internal struggles continued to surface, and did so more frequently. In intense moments, his emotional feelings apparently would come to the surface all at the same time—episodes possibly relating to internal conflicts between male vs. female, building an intimate relationship vs. the need for social isolation, and safeguarding his true identity vs. the fear of being found out.

For the first few months, Matt wore women's clothes only at home. While isolated, he did experience a sense of freedom. An opportunity came up at Halloween with a student council dress-up day. Matt decided to dress as a woman at school. Dressed in a pink dress and wearing a wig—there was no mistake, Matt was dressed as a woman. He had brought the outfit to the school and changed in the student council office. People thought it was funny and he did get a few "odd looks"—but it was Halloween, after all. This proved to be a testing ground for Matt. Could he stand the comments and the looks, and would he have the confidence to dress the way he felt and live his life the way he wanted? Soon afterwards, we talked about how this day went for him. Matt said he felt very positive, carefree, relaxed, and engaged with everyone: "I really didn't care what people thought."

Near the middle of November 2004, Matt began to discuss for the first time the possibility of regularly dressing as a woman at school. He had begun to wear women's clothing in the community, on walks around the block and shopping with his mother. He also had begun to consider attending a Transgender Teen support group run through the 519 Church Street community centre in Toronto. He had a desire to connect with others who had the same interests. It was clear that Matt appeared to be taking that invisible step-by-step process to test out his comfort/safety and seek out support resources to help him move along in his transition.

In our November 19, 2004, counselling meeting, Matt let me know that he wanted to come to school dressed as a woman. How could he do this? We had an open discussion about the most immediate concerns and considerations: Would the school allow this? How could we ensure his safety? How did his parents feel about this? When could he begin? Was he ready emotionally? Who needed to be consulted? While a lot of questions needed to be addressed, Matt seemed ready and he needed my help to move forward.

The Starting Point . . . Educating About the Differences Between Gender Identity, Sexual Orientation, and Transgender

Making a clear distinction between "sexual orientation" and "gender identity" was paramount to understanding the shift within Matt. Being transgender for Matt was seeing himself as a female in a male body. Although Matt had an emotional and perhaps sexual attraction to both genders, his desires concerning his gender presentation reflected a need to begin a lifestyle—be who he really was. Questions could and did arise—"Is he gay?," "Is he a "cross-dresser?," "Does he just want to dress in women's clothes?"

The biggest misunderstanding to overcome was assuming that because Matt dressed up in women's clothes, he must be gay—thereby tying his sexual orientation to how he wanted to present himself as a member of the opposite sex. It was interesting that if the transition was as simple as Matt being "gay," it would be more easily understood and perhaps accepted. Matt's need to express and present himself as a woman was not understood, and was disturbing and confusing to many at school.

Matt was transgender. He saw himself as a female in a male body. He wanted to live his life as a woman. He may or may not be gay. A sex reassignment/change may be something he would explore in the future.

Preparation for the Change

Matt was clear that this change was something he needed to do. He had already begun to dress as a woman at home and in the community. School, where he spent almost 8 hours a day, was the last place left where he needed to make the transition. For Matt, it wasn't just about the need, it was also about the right to be able to do what he thought was just a natural extension and representation of who he was.

The challenges were many. How would we start? Who would we need to get "permission" from? Who do we need to involve? How would Matt's role on the student council be affected? What were the safety precautions that would need to be considered?

Under the Toronto Board of Education policies and equity foundation statement guidelines, Matt had the right to make the transition and the school had the responsibility to grant him that right and to ensure his safety and comfort. It was clear, with regard to their statements, that students have the right to learn and work in an environment free of restricting biases.

So the policies and practices were clear—Matt had the right to dress as a woman within the school system. But, how would the school interpret those policies and practices to ensure the principles and values of the policies were followed?

How To Begin

The school first needed to examine the potential barriers/considerations to the school's "position" of support and how to concretely make the transition begin. It was decided that in order to have some direction and feedback regarding the considerations, a social worker from the Toronto District School Board Sexuality Program would be invited to attend a meeting with the administration members of the school to discuss the transition.

After meeting with the local school team and Matt's core subject teachers, the vice-principal sent out a memo asking specific staff to attend a meeting. I remember this meeting well. I announced that Matt had decided to make a "gender presentation" change at school and that he would begin living his life at school as a woman. There was silence in the room. Everyone needed time to digest the situation. Then, a few questions came up. Isn't there a special program he can go to? Doesn't it make more sense for him to wait until the end of the school year when he has left Northern? The school administrators who were present reiterated the equity policy and stated that Matt indeed had the right to do this. They added that conversations and consultations with Matt's parents and community resources would obviously take place, and that plans were being discussed to make this as smooth a transition as possible. What support would they require in their individual classes? I would be traveling with Matt on that first transition day from class to class. Would the teachers need to address this change in the class? Were they comfortable doing this themselves? How would they be comfortable dealing with any class discipline problems? The meeting did not go on for too long; the purpose was to involve them in the planning and knowledge stage, and have them approach the people working directly with Matt to hear their questions and share concerns.

Involving Community and School Support Resources

Contact was made with two key sources: the 519 Church Street community centre in Toronto (www. the519.org) and a social worker from the Toronto District School Board Sexuality Program. My most pressing question in working with a youth going through this transition concerned whether any written documentation or information existed detailing how to bring about such a transition into a regular high school environment. The answer was "NO!" Thus began the process of piecing together direction about how to work with a youth who is beginning the transition of acknowledging he is transgender and applying those principles, values, and rights/responsibilities to this particular situation and environment.

When the social worker from the sexuality program came to speak with the administration at the school, it was more of an informal discussion and question/answer time than a step-by-step process of what to do and not to do. Collectively, we arrived at a consensus for which directives we would follow. There were basically no right or wrong answers—paramount were the rights of the individual, how the school could best accommodate and support him, and how best to involve and balance the desires of Matt's parents in dealing with this transition.

We believed that having his parents at this initial planning meeting would not be helpful, as the school needed time to plan, consult, and be given possible direction as to what could or couldn't be done. They needed to get their thoughts and ideas together before involving the parents. Matt and his mother were supportive of this need on the school's behalf.

Issues and questions/answers that eventually arose from meetings with staff, other parents, and students were:

1. What name would Matt like to be addressed as? "Jade."
2. How would he dress? He would go by appropriate dress expectations, as per regular student population rules.
3. What are the school's plans to address the teachers? Engage his core subject teachers first; then address departmental curriculum leaders, who can filter the information to their staffing groups. Local school team meeting was addressed.
4. The staff would need education about the equity policy. Provide written information about the policy to staff group.
5. Early in the new school year (January), provide professional development information about gender identity and forum for questions or concerns to be raised. This would be facilitated by this author and the Toronto District School Board Sexuality Program social worker.
6. What washroom would Matt use? He will use the first floor unisex staff/special needs washroom. Matt could get the key from the principal's office.
7. Safety concerns. Consider having Matt take a less-traveled route to school through more residential areas. Need to report any harassment, taunts, and incidents. Follow-up meeting with School's Youth Services School Liaison police officer should occur regarding safety planning.
8. As soon as possible, hold a face-to-face meeting with Matt's mother (preferably, with both parents) and Matt to discuss his desire to make the transition at school.
9. The principal then would have a face-to-face meeting for follow-up and discussion with Matt.

We had a rich conversation about the need to inform Matt's father, who, at the time of the meeting, had not been informed about the transition. Matt and his mother had contact with his father; up until that point, however, neither had informed Matt's father about what was in the planning stages. The school staff questioned if they were required to do so. It would be best if Matt's father knew about the transition, in order to avoid Matt's father finding out about it without prior knowledge or involvement. It was legally evident, however, that while, as a secondary caregiver, Matt's father could ask and inquire about academic matters within the school, the school would need written permission from Matt himself to inform Matt's father about nonacademic matters, such as what was currently being discussed. Informing Matt's father was the responsibility of Matt and/or his mother.

The meeting involving Matt's family and himself took place the day after we met with the school administration and the Toronto District School Board Sexuality Program social worker. We were just expecting Matt and his mother, and were still uncomfortable about Matt's father's apparent non-involvement. However, we were quite surprised and relieved when we entered the meeting in the principal's office and saw that Matt's father was present. When Matt's father had learned that Matt was cross-dressing and he wanted to begin a transition at the school, he came over to the house that evening. He didn't want Matt to think that he had hesitated for a moment. "In theory, I had a choice. In reality, it was a no-brainer," Matt's father said. "There was nothing to do but be completely supportive. It was a turning point." Matt's father became emotional as the news settled in: "My first reaction was sadness and fear for the future—that he was exposing himself to a lifetime of hardship. Life is hard enough. My second reaction was sadness for the past. There were many periods of Matt's childhood when I wondered why Matt wasn't happier. I was now able to understand that Matt, for his whole life, felt uncomfortable wearing clothes we'd bought for him. My third was admiration. You tell your kids to respect others despite differences . . . to be themselves and not what other people want them to be. I was proud to have a child who had the courage to do that." But what lay ahead? "I wanted to make sure my child was doing this with his eyes open, so he understood from an adult perspective what this meant. Was this something you need to do at school; could you pick your times—after school, weekends, social occasions? Beyond school, there's university, and beyond university. . . ."

Matt's father wanted his son to consider all of this. But he never wanted to talk him out of the change. "Here was a child who had wondered, does my father really support me? I realized how important my role was."

Matt's parents were very appreciative about how much time the school had taken to try and cover everything and how much sensitivity they had shown. Matters were left such that Matt would need to finalize a decision with his parents and then the principal would have a final meeting with Matt to confirm that he would indeed go forward with the transition at school. We had looked at a potential start date in about two weeks from the meeting with Matt's parents—just before the holiday break. We would now wait to see if we moved forward.

The next day, I received an E-mail message from Matt:

"I still want to go through with it, but my parents wish me to wait probably until 2005 because they want to work things through with my sister. The point was made that her life, although in [another local school just down the street], may be affected by this and [they] just want to ensure she doesn't suffer any serious backlash.

"Personally, I'm really annoyed. I know the risks, but it's been 15 years coming and I know this is what I want and need to do. If you have any suggestions on this, don't hesitate to contact me. I've also sent an E-mail out to the other members of the student council informing them of the situation. But since my parents insisted, I guess I can hold off."

Matt's E-mail conveys his feeling of frustration. I think he struggled with the belief that his parents, while understanding and supportive, also wrestled with what they faced ahead. They would require the same courage, effort, commitment, and love that is needed when anyone is forced by circumstances to face facts that one would prefer to deny or to ignore. Matt didn't ask to be transsexual. He faced the terrible risk of rejection that such a disclosure could entail, and found himself in a situation in which the pain was undeniable. Matt reached out to his parents and others, and it appeared he was close to being able to realize that he could begin living his life as he needed to. His parents were concerned for their son, but also needed to be concerned about the potential impact on Matt's sister. Matt's sister was already aware that Matt was cross-dressing at home and in the community. The worry was that, due to Matt's prominence as the student council president, talk could filter over to his sister's school and have an emotional toll on her. Matt's parents were not sure that his sister would be ready to handle such a toll. Adults could possibly understand the complexities of the transition, and deflect negative responses, but a 15-year-old with friends who might label her the "sister of the transsexual" may not be able to.

Matt sent the E-mail to the other student council members. There was also a discussion about how to broach the transition with the student body and parents. Should the school send out a general memo to be read in class; should there be a general announcement over the P.A.? Should a letter be sent to families? It was decided that none of the above should be pursued, since doing any of those things would present the "exhibit" of the transition, which was counter to getting on with the business of being a student. As mentioned previously, Matt needed a smooth transition to becoming Jade. Therefore, the parents council was duly informed about Matt's transition to Jade.

Safety Considerations

We decided it would be best to meet with the school's community police officer. This way, we could provide some direction to Jade and her family in regards to providing some safety considerations while the transition was happening, and gain information about available supports if Jade was feeling uncomfortable or victimized. While the school could provide a more contained and controlled environment, it was acknowledged that the community at large presented more challenging safety issues. We considered the most appropriate travel routes to and from school—Jade usually walked to and from school each day, so traveling on public transit was not too much of a concern. (Jade had already acknowledged that taking public transit was still anxiety-provoking for her—she had taken it, but usually felt more unsafe with more people around.)

It was important to catalog the support available along Jade's typical travel route from school—pay phones, stores she could go into, the community centre and as a last resort, knocking on doors along the street for help, if needed. We also strongly recommended that Jade have a cell phone with her. Jade also was advised to never go into a secluded area, and to be always aware of her surroundings and observant of individuals seen in her travels.

Jade decided on two separate travel routes to and from school. This way, she could change the routes if feeling vulnerable. She did get a cell phone for the initial purpose of calling home prior to leaving school so someone would know she was on her way. If she didn't arrive in the 25 minutes of typical travel time, someone would be alerted that Jade might need help. Jade would communicate any changes in her plans or timing.

Jade's best defense was not to become a creature of habit. She should create a commotion if she was feeling targeted or in danger while in the community. The unusual is always an easy target, and Jade needed to be aware that sometimes people decide to act on feelings of discomfort.

A letter, a joint effort by the Toronto District School Board sexuality counselor, Matt, his parents, the administration, and me, was sent out in a sealed envelope to all staff. The letter was sent out after it was firmly decided that Matt indeed would begin dressing as a female at school by a particular date.

Letter Sent Out to Entire School Staff

DATE: 1 week prior to transition start date
TO: All staff
FROM: The Principal
One of our students, Matt, has made a "gender presentation" decision (which is defined as the way we show ourselves to the world—by way of sex, gender or sexual orientation). In the near future, Matt will be dressing as a female at school and in the community. During that time, he would like to be known as "Jade." You will appreciate that this has been a highly personal and difficult decision for him and his family.

TDSB equity policy supports Matt's right to make this decision and states that the Board shall respond effectively to the needs of students who identify themselves on the basis of sexual orientation or gender identity . . . and assure all students experience personal growth and reach their full potential in academic and life paths.

Matt is a wonderful and courageous student. It is his right to live his life in the manner he chooses, both at school and in the community. Matt will be as smart and funny and nice as before, except he will be dressing differently in order to feel more comfortable. It is our professional duty, as Board employees, to support Matt to the best of his abilities. As well, it is our responsibility to help each other and our students to respect Matt's decision and not tolerate harassment or bullying in the school and ultimately to get on with the main task of educating students.

There are two important messages that Matt would like to communicate to staff:

i) He anticipates that this change may make others uncomfortable and they may need some time to adjust and

ii) He is not an "exhibit," but a student who would like to pursue his education, like all the other students in his classes.

Matt has asked that this decision be shared with you and anyone else you feel is appropriate.

In the near future, the TDSB Sexuality Program Social Worker, who has been guiding us in our deliberations, will present a workshop to the entire staff on "Sexuality and Gender Identity." This should assist us to meet the diverse needs of students in our school.

Please be assured that we have engaged in numerous meetings with Matt, his family, Board personnel, our own counselors and Matt's teachers to make this as seamless a transition, as possible, for all involved. On the occasion of Matt's "gender transition," a counselor will be in each of his classes to assist as needed. As well, our other counselors will be available to discuss any concerns with students.

Attached, please find a list of resources to assist you in learning more about "Transgender Youth and Their Families" (i.e., a person who wishes and seriously acts upon the sense of having the wrong body), should you want to explore this area in more detail.

I realize this is a complex transition which will require great sensitivity on everyone's part and should you wish to discuss this further, please drop by.

Thank you.

Start Day. Support and Challenges. What We Did. The Questions Asked.

"Is this for real? Why is he doing this? Is he gay?"

On her first day at school as Jade, she changed in the student council office. She had decided she just wasn't ready yet to walk to school dressed as a woman. She met me in my 3rd-floor office, a half hour before school start time. Jade has since admitted she was frightened that first day as she walked through the school. Yet her fear was also balanced by a new feeling of being comfortable for the first time. She was very tuned in to what was going on around her; there was some laughter, but no one came up to her directly. She found the day "kind of surreal." *"I never expected anything to happen after years of longing."*

We had discussed how Jade would get through her classes that day. Would she need and want support? Should I go to the individual classes prior to the start date and have a discussion with the class? It was decided that Jade and I would go to her classes that first day together. As I was a well-known figure in the school, it would send a visual message that Jade had support and that incidents wouldn't be tolerated. Having already heard back from Jade's teachers that they didn't feel they had to specifically address Jade's start date in class, this author and Jade went to the home form class and she sat in her regular seat, while I sat in close proximity. I needed to balance providing Jade visual and emotional support, but also respecting a certain degree of privacy and providing space for her to deal with questions/comments or participate in the class on her own. That's what she wanted.

The most interesting response was not necessarily comments, but looks and stares. I observed many occasions in which students in the class were just looking at Jade in her presentation and you could literally see them processing the situation. Transitioning from class to class during the breaks was also noteworthy. It appeared that some students were caught off guard as Jade rounded a corner of the hall and met them face-to-face. Some students would approach other students to whisper or bring them closer to see Jade. There were some giggles, laughter, and snide remarks. However, all were within the expected "not sure what I'm seeing/uncomfortable" category.

Jade and I had lunch together in the cafeteria. We carried on a conversation as if we were oblivious to all those around us. Jade then decided that she needed some time alone to sit and reflect, so she went to the student council office. We met up again after lunch. Her afternoon classes were with teachers who fully supported her and were more than comfortable providing advocacy or placing limits on anything that would occur in the class as a result of Jade's presentation. Therefore, these teachers let me know that I did not have to accompany Jade to those classes; she went to her afternoon classes by herself, and she handled the transition periods between classes as well.

At the end of the day, Jade and I spoke in my office. Jade said she had thought the day had gone very well, and she was ready for tomorrow.

Jade also decided to do an interview with the school newspaper, the *Epigram*. In it, Jade answered the questions students may have been too polite to ask: questions concerning what transgender meant, which washroom was Jade using, what Jade's sexual orientation was, would she be having a sex change, and what advice she would give to other questioning youth.

Jade said, "The world around us, it seems, is becoming more and more accepting of differences. However, very many people will never be comfortable with individual living choices or differences among peers, which they were taught to be wrong. Exposure to different cultures and lifestyles will make us more accepting. Nevertheless, high school can be a very intimidating community in which to reveal oneself when maturity can be scarce and experience lacking."

It was important to Jade that the transition be transparent. She didn't try and hide it. She said, "This is what I'm going to do—I'm not embarrassed and I won't allow myself to be a target." Jade did not remove herself from her group of friends, or stop doing what she typically did on a regular school day. She walked down the same halls in the school, and went to the same meetings. It appeared most thought of her as the same person—she had just changed her look.

Added Challenges

The fact that Matt was now identified as "Jade" did bring up some discussions concerning the role of student council president. Some believed that the student council president should more closely reflect the majority of the students. "As a student, he has the right to express himself in his own way, but as a representative of the school—maybe some things should have been brought forward in the campaign. I voted for Matt, not Jade," said one student. Some students began talking about impeaching or removing Jade from the role of the student council president, but this movement did not gain sufficient support.

Dealing with diversity straight on, the administration made it clear that such a "movement" would not be allowed to even be brought up. The school could not say they respected Jade's rights and then stand by and allow a movement to grow towards denying Jade's right to hold office. It was felt that Jade and Matt were one and that she represented the school as before, except that the way she presented herself had changed. Therefore, Jade could continue as student council president. The difference now was that we had to consistently plan how to deal with potential problems or disruptions. The rest of the members of the executive student council, of which Jade was a part, didn't hesitate to involve Jade, nor did they ask if there should be a difference in how Matt was involved in council affairs, or how "Jade" should be involved. It was simply expected that there would be no difference.

Jade's first public appearance at an entire school event was at the "holiday assemblies"—two gatherings of all grades within the auditorium. There was a set agenda, and Jade was assigned to one aspect of the assembly. It was really the first forum where Jade would be seen in front of a large crowd. Jade was situated on the stage as part of the "platform party." We had already discussed with the student council and Jade what to expect from the crowd—to be prepared for snickering and for more movement and activity within the crowd than usual. We agreed it was important to keep focused on the topics being introduced, to stop if the noise level became too loud, and if need be, to have a staff member address the crowd to settle them down.

At one point, Jade got up and addressed the crowd about a specific holiday celebration. It seemed to go off without a problem. In the crowd were also the various teachers and staff members who had brought their classes down to the auditorium. They subtly addressed any chatter/shout-outs or unusual large-group disruptions.

Jade's position in the school did raise some questions. What part, for instance, should she play in public events in the community, such as the Grade 8 orientation assembly and meet and greet? In response to an administration member, who suggested considering having someone else introduce and welcome the students from feeder schools, someone asked, "If this is a role typically performed by the student council president, then why would we be considering having someone else talk to the students?"

The initial position was that perhaps the school didn't want "Jade" to be the focus of the assembly. Following the practice of rights and roles, it was concluded that the school could not have it both ways. They couldn't talk about and practice supporting and respecting Matt's rights to identify as Jade, but then, when it came to certain events, not allow Jade to represent who she truly was. Then they started talking about a compromise in terms of allowing Jade to be in the auditorium but not directly addressing the students from the stage. This suggestion was discounted for similar reasons. Eventually, we resolved that Jade and the vice president of the student council would address the audience together, thereby acknowledging Jade's status as student council president but also diluting the focus on Jade.

It was even considered whether or not to inform the feeder schools about Jade. The conclusion was that Jade was not the reason students were coming to the school, it was the school itself. Actively informing the schools would simply draw attention to the situation and have people formulate their judgments before entering the school. While there was a bit of laughter when Jade did speak at the opening part of the assembly, it seemed the older students provided modeling for the younger students through stern looks or comments. The laughs faded. The older students set the tone and maintained respect for whoever was addressing the crowd. The student body's incredible progression in support of Jade was evident in June at Jade's last presidential speech at the closing school assembly. She received overwhelming applause.

One of the next "big hurdles" was the pre-booked exchange trip to France in March. Obvious concerns about Jade attending were on the minds of everyone. Initially, no one was sure whether

Jade even wanted to go to France after the transition. The France trip had been planned and paid for prior to Matt's final decision to make a transition. In December, as the transition was initially being planned, the priority was to get through those first days and then worry about what the plan would be for the trip in March.

After the transition, Matt decided that he wanted to travel to France as "Jade." The travel agent raised several concerns regarding the distraction of Matt traveling as Jade and that the "homestay" part of the trip (where Matt would stay with a billeted family) would be out of the question as it would not be fair to the family because it had not been the original plan. There was also a concern about who would be Jade's roommate in the hotel stay, as each student did need to have a roommate. The travel agent was prepared to provide a full refund.

After investigation, it was deemed that Matt's rights to participate in the trip were protected under the sexual orientation clause under the Ontario Human Rights Code. The travel agency could not restrict who Matt self-identified as. Instead of filing a human rights complaint, Matt and his family decided that they wanted to try and make something work for the trip. As the consultations continued, the travel agency was reasonably accommodating in trying to work out the situation.

In consultation with Jade's family and the travel agency, a plan was formulated in which Jade would go on the trip. For the first part of the planned trip, she would share a room with a friend of hers. The peer had been consulted and was very comfortable with the arrangement. In dealing with the billet family issue, all were in agreement that a shortened trip would be best (with full refund granted to Jade for that portion); Jade would return home early to avoid any need for separate room accommodations (which would have cost an additional sum of money for Jade).

Planning for safety on the trip was the next issue to be discussed. Jade, the teachers accompanying the trip, the school administration, and Jade's family were part of the discussion. The following was decided:

- Jade would travel as "Matt" to and from the airport and while traveling aboard planes.
- Jade would need to get "some distance" away from the airport prior to changing into women's clothes, the concern being that Jade would present a security concern if seeming to be in disguise.
- Jade would need to be addressed as "Matt" in the airport, due to her name being "Matt" in official documents.
- Jade should anticipate the need to be more aware of safety issues in another country.
- If needing support around any safety/security problems, Jade would seek out one of the staff immediately. (As per regular student trip expectations, no student is allowed to travel alone; students always must travel with two or three other students.)
- Jade would need to let school staff know where she is going during her free time.
- At all times while in France, Jade would carry an official letter of recognition. This letter could be used if security personnel or others questioned her about her presentation.

Jade went on the trip in March with no apparent disruptions and/or problems as a result of being transgender. School staff reported that individuals who came into contact with Jade were respectful and appropriate. While we planned for the worst case scenarios, most people were respectful within appropriate social norms.

With June came the regular high school "formal," consisting of an end-of-year celebration dinner and dance event at an off-campus locale. Jade, as the current student council president, and as a graduating student, was certainly leaning towards attending the formal and was encouraged to do so. She was worried, however. Large events seemed to create more feelings of being overwhelmed and she just didn't appear comfortable at these type of events. Ultimately, she decided to attend, viewing it as a "right of passage." We briefly talked about the usual safety concerns and her comfort level attending such an event. However, Jade was clear that safety precautions were unnecessary, as these were her peers and they already knew who she was and how she presented. Afterward, she said, "Overall, it was a good night, and I'm glad that I came."

Jade had decided to leave home in the fall to go to university in another province. She had obvious anxieties about this big shift. Jade and her parents researched how open and welcoming the university would be. It was important for them to let the university know of the special considerations and circumstances that Jade potentially presented. She looked forward to university and her ability to live her life more independently.

Counselling Matt Who Was Jade—What Did He/She Want and Need?

Jade is content cross-dressing for now, although she hasn't ruled out the possibility of a sex change operation. By law, she would need to live as a woman for two years before beginning the process. *"A lot of people think because you're transgender, you have to be very femmy. . . . In the transgender community there's a wide spectrum, many different people and some get into looking like Barbie dolls, very, very feminine. Some don't feel the need to express femininity. It's more or less how your brain is—it's not dependent on interests."*

Jade wanted people to know there is nothing wrong with her, and that she didn't go rushing into this. Coming out as transgender changed her life and it was frightening, but it is completely natural for her.

Views and Perspectives of Working With Matt/Jade

Working with a transgender youth was a new experience for me. Although I am aware that any special issue or concern could be brought up in my professional work, I was initially taken aback and unsure how to proceed. However, the internal connection with youth clicked on once again. Matt was asking for help, support, and direction. It was not something that had to be rushed into, and I was clear from the beginning that this was a new experience for me. (It was for Matt, too.) Being open, honest, and straightforward with him throughout the process was what was needed. His agenda, his pace, and his goal were the foundations to the work. Matt was the driving force with respect to his wishes, confidentiality, and the complexities of needing other people's involvement.

It was critical that other professionals who needed to be involved in the transition were allowed to participate and help in a multi-disciplinary approach. Being aware of rights, policies, and procedures as they related to sexual identity and orientation provided a legal foundation to Matt's transition.

In dealing with this transition, many things seemed to align in a positive manner. The involvement from parents and school officials was positive, and students showed respect. Despite a sometimes uncomfortable and unknown topic, most things worked out in Jade's favour. Surprising! And perhaps a rarity? We anticipated many risk areas, but we did not need to deal with them. It was, however, beneficial that we had anticipated and planned for some occurrences.

I had looked for a "handbook" on how to work with a student transitioning in high school. I couldn't find one. A lot of what we had to do was "new"—even though trans youth have been with us for years.

Through the experience, I did unearth some information concerning guiding principles in working with trans youth:

Don't panic:
- A counselor has a very important role in reassuring parents, families, and other service providers that trans people are healthy, happy, and whole people
- Preventing a youth from being transgender is not possible and should not be considered as an option—supporting the youth and his/her family is the best option.

Build trust:
- Listen; professionals who are not listening may be seen as the ones standing in the way of the transition
- Transitioning is necessary; for many trans people, living as their birth gender is not possible
- Trans youth may be in a hurry to make decisions because their bodies are changing in the opposite direction from how they feel
- If not supported, many youth will find other means of transitioning that are less safe
- Be aware of the extreme discrimination that trans youth may be facing and the frustration that this elicits
- Be aware of your own feelings about this issue (seek outside support for your concerns); trans youth should not be expected to educate the adults around them.
  Provide training for staff:
- Advocate for all professionals involved to get the training they need to work effectively with this community.

Inform youth of options:
- Involve youth in the process every step of the way
- Youth will need all the information they can get to make a good decision
- Support youth to research safe resources themselves.

Connect trans youth and their families with community resources:
- Trans youth often exist in isolation from each other, which is a major factor in low self-esteem, self-harm, and suicide risks
- This is a challenging process for any family, but resources for parents and families exist to help them learn to accept and appreciate a trans youth.

I was honoured to work through this transition with Jade. She allowed me, as a professional, to experience and support her through one of the most sensitive, intrusive, and revealing periods of her life. Adolescent sexuality is usually a topic that most adults discuss with some discomfort. It raises many perplexing moral, emotional, and practical issues for adults and caregivers. But the experience, while universal, is highly personal and unique to all and should be treated with patience and compassion.

Although it is obvious that attitudes towards this specific population may have begun to change, young people like Jade are still vulnerable to all of the perils inherent in having to live their daily lives as they need to. Open, accessible, and supportive services and professionals need not be shaken or hesitate in working with and interacting with new populations. There are exciting opportunities of growth and more exciting developments in helping those in need.

The opportunity to document this experience provides a foundation and resource to the many individuals, services, and organizations that work with vulnerable populations. Hopefully, readers will find this chapter to be a framework for guidance and resource.

LOCATING OURSELVES: TO BE OUT OR NOT TO BE OUT

Introduction to
"Locating Ourselves: To Be Out or Not To Be Out"

When we initiated the plans for this book, we imagined the powerful stories we would collect. We knew LGBT students and educators to be beautiful, resistant, subversive activists who disrupt "business as usual" with their very bodies and actions. We knew we would be presenting painful stories as well. What we did not anticipate was how intense the fear is and how long the hurt lingers when a decision must be made: Will I, as a student or educator, at this moment, be "out" or not? Such tension emphasizes the gap between increasingly tolerant human rights legislation in North America and the lived realities of confronting systemic homophobia in education.

Coming out is not a one-time only event. One comes out over and over again. One comes out in different ways and for different reasons. And, as several of the pieces in this section indicate, it is not entirely clear what one should come out as. We embody multiple identities at any given time, some visible and some invisible, to those with whom we share our classrooms and school campuses. Consequences result when those parts of our lives deemed unacceptable by those around us are willingly or unwillingly exposed. We face consequences when we neither match nor fulfill social expectations concerning out gender, class, race, or sexuality.

Many reasons are offered as to why one might come out, or why one might not come out. The educators in this section draw upon theory and stories to both construct their strategies and reflect upon their past decisions. We put other coming out stories in the next section, because they are connected to strategies in schools. Questions about the nature of effective pedagogy are considered alongside issues concerning the quality of one's life. Coming out is understood not as an individual experience, but as one that can impact partners, family, friends, colleagues, teachers, and students.

What these narratives and essays share is the predicament of being perceived as the problem. If those considering coming out speak out, they become the problem for those unable or unwilling to accept this level of honesty. If they remain silent, they become the problem for those who wish they spoke and publicly allied themselves. It is a classic blame-the-victim scenario, homophobia trumping the range of possible responses. There is no unproblematic way to conduct oneself as an LGBT educator or student.

What these educators and students share is an unwillingness to be controlled by social expectations, to have one's humanity reduced to a single possible identity—a stereotype. They follow neither mainstream heterosexist ideology, nor any standard LGBT activist response (if such a thing exists). These stories express a refusal to abide by norms—these authors embody a sense of power and freedom. The stories also show the human cost of this refusal, however: the doubts, the reactions, the isolation. Their resilience lies in their education, migration, politics, passion, families, ritual, and even appearance—how to wear one's hair and clothing, how to walk into a room, how to arm oneself and present oneself to the world.

surviving the elephant

janet romero-leiva

"do you have a boyfriend?"
cautious to answer
i avoid
they
crazed by hormones devouring familiarity
curiosity-filled bodies heavy with questions and feelings
unheard
unspoken
undoing a previously comfortable existence
watching each other watch each other
(she likes him) (he likes her)
me
running
their hunger for understanding and belonging falls heavy on my tongue
cannot answer a simple question
"do you have a boyfriend?"
cautious avoidance
"i have a partner"
they
sitting/pondering in silence
my response not satisfactory
creating confusion and excitement
partner?
me
walking
satisfied smile on my lips
anxiously awaiting the next inquiry
"do you have a boyfriend?"
"no, i have a girlfriend!"
they
wide-eyed
attempting to swallow the elephant sitting among us
me
sadly aware of this rejection
a discomfort eleven year olds were previously incapable of in my mind
we
sink into queerness
drowning
fighting
surviving the elephant

THE MISUNDERSTANDING?

Lisa Ortiz

In "The Misunderstanding?," Ortiz describes the painful direction she received from an administrator to hide her lesbian identity, her partner, and her true relationship as parent to her own child. She chronicles how her confident position as an out-and-proud lesbian teacher becomes increasingly conflicted and diminished by the principal's insistence on her invisibility. How do we confront homophobia when it is spoken by colleagues we genuinely like and respect? What do principals have the right to ask of teachers regarding their family; what type of advice constitutes care and what constitutes a threat? What is the role of a teachers union in providing an inclusive environment and protecting and advocating for its LGBT members?

I sat on a cushy, floral-print sofa in front of an antique table, laden with an eclectic array of cups, a plate of homemade cookies, and a pot of ginger tea, waiting for the inquiring masses to arrive. The intimate space was made smaller by hundreds of cards papering every wall; mobiles, fairies, and streamers enlivening the air; Celtic music whispering in the background. This was the scene for a most unorthodox interview. Though it was odd, I felt comfortable. I knew the school needed me . . . my credentials that is, and the interview was just a formality. I sat for three hours while teachers came and went during their lunch breaks in groups of two or three. The most professional question I was asked was, "What's your favorite children's book?" To which I responded, "A Mouse and His Child," even though it had been a decade since I'd read it and then only once, but it had been a profound experience at the time. Mostly, they asked questions that are pretty much illegal . . . about my family, what I do in my spare time, why I moved, etc. Given such real-life questions, I felt at ease to give real-life answers . . . and provide photos. I was, after all, a very new and very proud mom. "This is my partner, Georgia. And this is our daughter, Malena." That response led to further, even more personal, and definitely illegal questions, which I blithely answered. I have always been out and proud. Some say overly so. Stare at me and I would hold my girlfriend closer or maybe even kiss. Whisper to your friend, point or laugh, and I might approach you . . . dare you to say it to my face. I was a coordinator for Pride in a large metropolitan city. I worked with queer youth. I was a leader in my university LGBT group and hosted dozens of events. I've sat on panels—from an advisory group for the superintendent of city schools to educational panels for teachers. I have facilitated anti-homophobia (Challenging, Learning about, and Understanding Heterosexism, CLUH) workshops for businesses, youth groups, and universities. I'd never been in the closet in my life and wasn't about to start. They would know what they were getting.

In the end, they hired me and I was confident that I had found a safe haven. Heading up this haven was an Earth-Mama named Cathy. Cathy had long brown hair with just a touch of grey. She wore long skirts, no makeup, and resembled a pixie elf. She even danced a spontaneous jig on occasion. She had very precise diction, an unidentifiable accent, and the voice of a poet. Her eyes sparkled and she was passionate about learning. From the moment I met her, I was awestruck. She was brilliant and creative, and the school was an artistic wonderland. Murals, sculpture, gardens, textiles, children's art—not crafts or cookie-cutter—were everywhere. I worshipped her. Not in any sexual way, but rather as a mentor—a blend of parent and teacher. She inspired me. I wanted to *be* like her. After meeting Cathy, I figured if I couldn't make it there, I couldn't make it anywhere in the state and we might as well pack up our stuff and head back to the rat race we had come from.

New places and new people are tricky. What you see at first are the spotlighted showcases. It can take a while to get around to looking in the dimly lit corners, shadowy halls, and darkened rooms. I knew this to be true from past experience and expected that this place was no different. Nevertheless, I was surprised to see how quickly I began my acquaintance with the shadows. My position wouldn't begin for three months, so I subbed—mostly at my new school. My first assignment was a one-month stint for a class of 3rd- and 4th-graders. Their highly organized teacher had a rotating list of parent volunteers for each day of her absence. The class had been studying the human body and one of the areas yet to be addressed was "disability." The students had just finished a unit on "the senses," so I decided to invite Georgia to speak about being deaf. So began the dots. Malena came with Georgia . . . DOT. Georgia, Malena, and I have the same last name . . . DOT. This was a smart group of kids. They started asking questions . . . and didn't stop. They knew Malena was my daughter and Georgia had introduced her as her daughter . . . DOT. "Do you live together?" "When Georgia goes on vacation, do you go with her?" "How can a kid have two moms?" I answered as I always have: Georgia and I are partners, some kids have a mom and a dad—Malena has two moms. I adopted Malena before she was born. DOT . . . DOT . . . DOT. I knew I was in over my head but didn't want to appear shameful—not to the students, nor to Molly's mom who was this day's volunteer. I had been teaching and out for the exact same amount of time. I always had pictures of my family on my desk and when questions arose, I gave these same answers. But never had students questioned beyond my answer, "She's my partner."

Two days later, Cathy called me into her office and told me to close the door. "I need to talk to you . . . Molly's mom called . . . wah wah wah wah wah." Her poetic, perfect diction trailed off inside my head. Fairies and rainbow-colored cards swirled in my field of vision. Smell of fresh flowers . . . moss . . . tea. I sank into the soft sofa and, for the first of many times to come, hugged the sofa-guardian—a stuffed dragon with amber eyes. I re-entered the conversation to hear Cathy say, couched in tones of concern for me and my family, "You can be Malena's mom or Georgia can, but not both of you." Had she really said that? And did anyone else hear it? Surrounded by whimsy, I was introduced to Fear.

Some characters we meet and then never see again. Fear and I, however, would develop an intimate relationship over the next year. In a closed-door session, Cathy relayed a complaint about Georgia's presence at school, saying it was putting my sexuality "in people's faces." Could we be more "discreet"? Georgia was a volunteer, teaching her third session of Advanced American Sign Language—an enrichment class. Each session, we had dealt with odd, homophobic incidents. First, Georgia's name was omitted from the advertisement of the class. Instead they had listed me twice—at the same time, in two different locations. The second session, Georgia's first name was listed, but not her last name—my last name. The other 17 classes were listed with teachers' full names. Prior to the third session, I checked the list. Again, Georgia was listed by first name only. I told Cathy's secretary to change it or cancel the class. She changed it, none of the students quit, and the class began and ran smoothly until our "in people's faces" conversation. Georgia's class was cancelled mid-session. Four students were left without a teacher or the class they loved.

Several other closed-door sessions were held regarding my teaching style, my communication style, and the fact that change takes time. Cathy always seemed sympathetic. She seemed to take my side—telling me the words to use to placate the offended/irritated party. Closing the door became a bit of a joke between Cathy and me. We also joked about the "suits" that would come for her someday to move her to a different site. Districts often don't like to leave principals in place for more than four or five years, lest they incur too much loyalty. Cathy was on her fifth year. I vowed my loyalty and we laughed about seceding from the union. She genuinely seemed to like me. She commiserated, telling me about her experiences trying to "win over" her husband's family—they were Jewish, while she was Pagan. She had us over to dinner, had me privately assess her daughter for learning disabilities. She confided in me . . . but maybe she "confided" in everyone.

Fear returned in another closed-door session, when Cathy told me about a fight on the playground. Evidently, one boy had called another boy a "fag" and a fight ensued. Parents were called in and the offending boy's father said, "What do you expect? You even have a gay teacher. We've seen the bumper stickers." OK, I know what you're thinking. This is ridiculous. Yeah, I started out laughing, too. By the end of the discussion, though, Cathy was warning me that she feared "a tidal wave of protest . . . media . . . wah, wah, wah, wah, wah . . . wouldn't want anything to happen to your family." Fear. As I drove home, anxiety kicked in full throttle. I was looking behind me to see if I was being followed, and took a rambling route home via the police station. Visions of the terrible possibilities—the many ways my family could be taken from me—flashed through my mind. I was crying, near hysterical, when I got home. Georgia "honey, honeyed" me and forbade me from removing my stickers. But she didn't understand. She couldn't. Everything depended on me.

The next morning, armed with a knife hidden in my bag, I drove halfway to work and pulled over on the side of the road. I couldn't do such a thing in front of my own home. Not in front of my baby. I looked at the proud rainbow strip under my rear window . . . teacher-perfect, "Celebrate Diversity" on a rainbow. If I was going to remove one, I would remove them all . . . "Attitudes Are the Real Disability." I sliced and pulled and scraped . . . and bawled. My stickers, like badly mutilated bodies, were unidentifiable, but I punished my own weakness by leaving the carcasses for me to see each day. I was so ashamed . . . but that was nothing compared to what I would feel when Georgia saw what I had done.

Each time events such as these occurred, I would cry and wail at home and consider moving. I was terrified. My wife and baby depended on me for everything. We had moved here to give our daughter a quality of life that we thought impossible to attain elsewhere. We'd given up three-quarters of our pay to live this life. I could not lose my job. And I could not deal with the fear that who I was could cause my child harm.

Near the end of my second year, the situation had me so stressed that a simple, "How are things going, Lisa?" would lead to me crying hysterically. Matt, a 5th-grade teacher who was a favorite of mine, asked this innocuous question. He believed in and practiced inclusion of students with special needs and sometimes team-taught with me. Matt also happened to be our school's union representative and, as I then learned, had lesbian moms. We were kindred. Matt offered to attend a meeting between Cathy and me to inform her that her behavior was cause for grievance and must stop.

I would like to say that this story ended with a grievance filed with the union, a million dollar settlement, and/or new legislation, but I can't. Cathy claimed every event was a misunderstanding . . . every quote mistaken and/or taken out of context. She said that she was hurt that I felt the need to bring in Matt instead of just speaking with her. Whether or not it was true, having someone I worshipped say she was "hurt," and that I was the cause, crushed me. Matt said he would support me in a grievance, but I was too confused and scared. Maybe I *had* misunderstood. Maybe I *was* too sensitive. I couldn't be blacklisted. I needed my job. My family was depending on me. The closet door creaked open and slammed shut firmly behind me.

"That's So Gay": A Narrative Vignette of One Lesbian's Experience in Alberta Catholic Schools

Tonya Callaghan

In this narrative, Callaghan recounts a lifetime of navigating through the homophobic environment she encountered within Catholic schools in Alberta, Canada. As both a student and teacher, she was immersed in homophobic comments and conversations, even as she hid her sexual identity. As a teacher, she faced intense isolation and was concerned about keeping her job and not becoming the personal target of prejudice. How can staffroom homophobia be addressed with or without known LGBT colleagues present? How do sexist conceptions of a woman's role both limit her options as well as contribute to homophobic behaviour? How does religion shape cultural expression and sexual identity?

I was born into an Irish Catholic family in a rural community on Prince Edward Island, the smallest maritime province in Canada. Both my mother and my father come from large Irish Catholic families that count nuns and priests among the siblings, uncles, and aunts. The promise of a better economic future convinced my parents to move our young family to western Canada. In Calgary, Alberta, my sister and I both attended Catholic school from kindergarten to Grade 12. We attended church regularly, assisted with minor tasks during Mass, and happily sang along with the church hymns.

As an upper-elementary student, I can remember paying close attention to the priest's homilies every Sunday. They made me uneasy. I didn't like the stories that portrayed women as temptresses of men, as weak and punishable, or the idea that women should obey their husbands. As a young girl, I learned very early what it meant to be an ideal Catholic woman. Catholic doctrine's patriarchy and sexism were reinforced in the day-to-day operations of the Catholic schools I attended as a child.

In the classroom, boys were expected to be leaders and girls their followers. When it came to electing a classroom representative, the person selected was almost always a boy. Boys were regularly asked to assist with supposedly "heavy" tasks, such as moving books from one shelf to another—a task that girls clearly could also easily do. When administration asked for assistance in setting up the gymnasium for events such as assemblies, masses, or final exams, boys were sent to help, even though the job only entailed arranging chairs in rows and setting up tables. Girls were regularly viewed as the weaker of the two sexes, in need of male protection and assistance.

In Grades 5 and 6, I remember developing crushes on the few other girls who, like me, did not fit the Catholic ideal of female behaviour. We were the ones playing "cars" in the sandbox or hanging by our knees on the monkey bars. It was on the elementary playground that I first heard the word "lezzie," and the scrapes on my knees from being pushed to the ground taught me its meaning. I was running to secure the four-square court for the lunch hour game and a boy called out: "Don't let her have it, she's a lezzie!" Then, I felt a quick shove in the small of my back and my hands, knees, and shins came in contact with the gravelly pavement. Whatever "lezzie" meant, it wasn't a good thing.

Later, I asked my mom what that word meant, and she told me it was short for the word "lesbian," which she said is a woman who prefers to have relationships with other women rather than with men. When she asked why I wanted to know, I just told her that was what some people were calling girls at school. I never told her the name-calling was directed at me.

In junior high, I learned I could be safe from such assaults by being tough myself and by tossing around homophobic phrases like the best of them. I regularly uttered statements like: "That's so gay," "He's such a fag," and "Don't be a dyke." No adults ever reprimanded me for saying such things and my peers either feared me or thought I was cool. My strategy was to get a tough reputation so I wouldn't get picked on.

In the 10th grade, I made the mistake of acting on one of my crushes when I was out with three of my best girlfriends at a drive-in movie. I made the suggestion that we could kiss each other as practice for when we'd go on dates with boys, and I was the first to volunteer. After my friends in the front seat saw the kiss I gave my friend who was with me in the back seat, they said they didn't want to do practice kisses on one another and abruptly left the car to get more junk food. The next Monday at school was a tough one; none of my friends would talk to me. I couldn't figure it out until a girl I sometimes went skiing with told me that word had spread that I was a lesbian. I denied it, of course, saying that I had just made a stupid suggestion that we try some practice kisses. But no matter what I did to explain it all away, I still had to get a new set of friends after that. Throughout the rest of high school, I kept my lesbian feelings underground and it wasn't until I was in university that I was finally able to come out as a lesbian.

Later, when I became a teacher and taught for some years in international schools in Europe, I came back to Canada and found myself teaching in Catholic schools. This was primarily due to the fact that public schools were not hiring at the time and my Catholic background qualified me for teaching in a Catholic school. The longer I taught, however, the more I recognized versions of my own experience among the students I was teaching: the closeted students, the tentative students who still weren't sure, and the students who teased and punished each other with the phrase "That's so gay."

Well, as a Catholic teacher, I was "so gay." I was a healthy, somewhat athletic, young woman in my late 20s. I liked to wear pants a lot, I sported a short haircut, I had thick, dark eyebrows, and there was no boyfriend in sight. So, what's a good Catholic girl to do in a Catholic school where being "so gay" was an insult? I made a conscious decision to stay. I wanted to be there for the queer students because I knew how important it would have been for me to have had a positive role model. Of course, I couldn't be "out" to my students in a Catholic school but, as an English teacher, I could inform my students about the backgrounds of some of the writers anthologized in the government-approved texts. I told my students, for example, that Audre Lorde was a lesbian and that Tennessee Williams was "so gay."

Working with the students in the classroom was the least of my worries as a lesbian teaching in a Catholic school system. The heterosexist culture of the entire organizational structure and the regular, homophobic comments of my colleagues were constant sources of anxiety and stress. I was frequently asked about my marital status and why I did not have a boyfriend. On the topic of one of the greatest joys of my life—my life with my partner—I had to remain silent. I even pretended that my partner was just some writer I knew when her image started appearing on posters around the school promoting a writer-in-residence program. Colleagues would say: "Hey, don't you know her?" And I would have to mumble something like: "Yeah, we went to school together." I was fiercely proud of my partner, but I had to suppress that pride.

While I was "out" to some select colleagues, for the majority of the staff the truth of my life was so distorted and censored that I came across as a boring straight person who did nothing of any interest on the weekend. I couldn't say, "We went hiking," because that "we" would signal a whole new arsenal of rat-a-tat-tat questions aimed at finding out who that "we" was made up of and if I was seeing someone. If I said I went to a play or a movie, the usual follow-up question that I could predict with astonishing regularity would be: "Oh? Who did you go with?" When I said, "Oh, some friends of mine," that signaled that I was a single woman who frequently went out with her girlfriends and needed to meet a man. The matchmaking efforts would begin and I would have to find polite ways to refuse to meet my colleague's brother or good buddy from university. The matchmaking game started to peter out, though, when I entered my 30s and switched schools—the people at the new school either did not have enough time to get to know me and my marital status, or thought I was too old for matchmaking and didn't bother.

No matter what school I went to, however, I regularly witnessed homophobic jokes or comments on current events, such as same-sex marriage, during staff room conversations at lunch or during meetings. I started to grasp the full, institutionalized nature of the homophobia when I made an anonymous call to my union representative to inquire as to what would happen if it became known that I was co-habiting with my same-sex partner. I was told to keep quiet as I could be fired if anyone found out—having a same-sex partner is contrary to Catholic teachings. I didn't bother asking my second question about getting my partner signed up on my benefits package.

I found out that other gay teachers had troubles with the benefits package too. I came across a 30-something gay math teacher one day in the staff room who had just come into a type of long-term temporary contract that entitled him to benefits. He told me that when he called the district office to see about getting his partner on the benefits package, the administrators told him to bring his "wife" down in person along with the marriage certificate and they would be happy to set "her" up on the benefits package. The fact that he was co-habiting with a same-sex partner is almost irrelevant, since co-habitation outside of wedlock is contrary to Catholic teachings and the benefits package is only available to legally married, Church-sanctioned couples.

Years of practice meant that I had developed sophisticated coping mechanisms for functioning in such a repressive environment. Unhappily, this was not the case for the lesbian, gay, bisexual, trans-identified, and queer (LGBTQ) students I was encountering in Catholic schools. Sensing that I would be sympathetic, some of these students came to me with their stories of bullying and more subtle forms of mistreatment. A tall, slender gay boy with dyed jet-black hair and nail polish to match suddenly started joining my teacher advisory (TA). After a few days, I asked him what was up and he told me his assigned TA was a big homophobe, and he asked if he could please join my TA. Without making a big deal about it, I made the switch with the administrators in the office and he was clear to stay.

Earlier that same year, a lesbian in Grade 12 came up to me to ask what I was teaching and requested to be in my class. She wore oversized boys' clothes, had an asymmetrical and spiky haircut, and kept her wallet in her back pocket attached to a chain on her belt loop. Though she didn't say so, I knew she approached me because she recognized some kind of affinity, something sympathetic about me. Sadly, I wasn't teaching Grade 12 English that semester, so I never had the opportunity to teach her, but we always acknowledged one another in the halls after that.

She knew she could trust me and later came to me to ask for advice about how to handle the homophobic bullying she was experiencing at the school. The bullies were calling her names, whispering about the sexual things they would like to do to her, following her around after school, taunting her, and even occasionally throwing rocks at her. We both went to speak to the principal about the problem on separate occasions; each time, the principal said she could do nothing about the incidents since they occurred off of school property. Because this student was living with her girlfriend and not her parents, I knew her case would be hopeless; administrators would try to please parents so they won't take their child out of the school (along with the funding that is attached to that child). I advised her to transfer out of the school, and she came to visit me later to tell me that she was much better off in her new, non-Catholic school.

I knew I wasn't going to be able to deal with this homophobic environment much longer when a promising drama student in the Catholic high school where I was teaching committed suicide after suffering several months of bullying due to his sexual orientation (as was confided to me by his friends after his death). Our school failed this boy, who did try to seek counselling at the school but clearly did not receive satisfactory results. The only way the school responded to his death was to bring in grief counsellors for a few days afterwards. Dissatisfied with this response, I felt compelled to take action regarding the Catholic school system's sanctioned and institutionalized homophobia by engaging in research about it.

Religious institutions have been among the most invasive cultural forces in making certain that there are negative consequences for living queer. Contrary to a commonly cited Catholic value to treat all individuals with dignity and respect, officials in Catholic schools are doing a disservice to vulnerable queer youth and staff whom they regularly dismiss and fail to keep safe. The pervasive heteronormativity of the Catholic environment encourages homophobic attitudes in staff and students, and alienates some LGBTQ students to such a degree that they drop out of school or, like the gay drama student, commit suicide. The tragic death of this student compelled me to write about the ways that many publicly funded Catholic school districts in Canada ignore their legal, professional, and ethical responsibilities to protect *all* students and to maintain a safe, caring, and inclusive learning environment. I was ultimately "so gay" that I could not bear teaching for the Catholic school system anymore. Consequently, I decided to pursue graduate studies as a way to express my experiences instead of always having to suppress myself in the homophobic environment of the Catholic school system.

ON LATE NIGHTS: LIVING IN MY QUEER TEACHER BODY

Karleen Pendleton Jiménez

In this personal essay, I document the complex consequences that an educator faces after coming out to students. In a society where LGBT people are targets of attack by both outsiders and internal demons, such exposure brings forth questions and fears. What kinds of resources, interactions, and/or practices may help to protect and replenish us so that we can continue to provide social justice education and feel strong in our own bodies?

"I'm scared all the time and when I am not scared, there is no chance for change. In me." That's how I teach writing. "Go toward the fear," I tell my students. "Feel its pulse. Let it speak to you." . . . writing can sometimes force action in yourself and others. Sometimes. Sometimes you read or write words you got to live up to. (Moraga, 2000, p. 185)

4:45, almost evening. The last day of the term. In the long classroom, in this concrete slab of a building, the sunset and city lights shining into the lesson. But it's too long, it's too hard to project, and the round tables make it easy for turned backs and gossip. You stop taking the time to hassle with opening the heavy beige curtains. You find yourself in a large, bland vacuum in front of 40 students.

There is something wrong in this room. I have sensed it from the first day. It has something to do with the woman with the baby blue Roots T-shirt and the dark eyes. Her pupils are too small or too solid. I cannot see her. I've no idea what she's thinking. I find myself worrying that it has something to do with me being a dyke.

See, in an appropriate hermeneutic moment, two-thirds of the way through the term, Shakespeare and I come out to the class. Hope it's OK with him. I don't normally support involuntary outings. But he's such a popular guy in English classes, and I see nothing wrong with a little queer exploitation of colonialism.[1]

Once, during a debate over whether to be out or not while teaching, an instructor told me, "But look at you, Karleen, you don't have a choice. You're out as soon as you walk into a room." Which I've got to admit I found flattering. But even if everyone in the class thought I was a dyke, it would not be a topic of classroom conversation unless I spoke it first. At least not conversation that could be heard by everyone. I come out so that we can talk about it, so that it becomes personal to the bodies in the room. I come out because too many pictures of hurt queer bodies roll through my head.

I used to teach a Saturday writing group for queer youth—dedicated teenagers who showed up voluntarily with pens and notebooks to write their poetry, who sometimes showed up with freshly taped-up gauze around their wrists. I remember long-sleeved shirts on hot summer days. I didn't get it. Another student nudges me, "Carla's had a bad week."

"What?" I shoot a look at a young woman lying on the floor. She rests on one elbow and writes away in her notebook. A navy blue oxford shirt covers her.

"She's hiding her wrists," he tells me.

"Oh."

It wasn't clear to me that coming out, writing stories, graduating from school, any particular accomplishment meant that these students were safe from their own knives. It was a continual struggle for the imagination to live. Forget role models; I come out to be basic evidence of queer life. Other teachers do this for me whether they know it or not.

Twice a year at conferences I meet up with a woman in her 50s named Dr. Rusty Barceló. She is the vice president of the University of Minnesota. She is another fair-skinned, Chicana, soft butch walking in university hallways, only she wears three-piece suits to work now. We might have a drink together, tell of our latest relationships, describe books we've read. Mostly, I just want to look at her, hug her body when we greet, know her to be alive, and know that it's possible for me to grow older. That's it. That's all I need. I consider her presence a precious gift.

I also have the luxury of a queer supervisor who is out to me, who brings me unconscious calm at school. Amidst theory and methodology talk, I have the pleasure of normal everyday conversation: who's "cute" or "sexy" down the hallway, what movie we've seen, what ideas we're thinking about. Our girlfriends weave in and out of the conversation unselfconsciously. My learning with her happens on that quality of ground.

I want to bring that quality to my own classrooms. I come out to my students every term. As what, exactly, changes. Mostly I come out with the word "gay." "Thought it might be important for you all to know that I'm gay." "Lesbian. Lesbian. Lesbian." I am that word, I am proud of that word, but I still find it hard to say in front of an audience of students. It sounds dirtier, and I worry about what expressions it might provoke from their faces. And "transgender"? It has the effect of wrinkling the brow of the most liberal of students. Like the night of the last class.

The frizzy-haired, formerly goth student outs me by saying, "Did you write that transgender children's book that's at the bookstore?"

Forty eyes shoot up at me. I laugh, "Ha . . . ha . . . ha, yes well, that is, um, in fact, me, ah and really, it's just a sweet book, you know, about a kind of tomboy-girl who's being picked on for looking like a boy and acting like a boy and yeah, right, it is, I would call, a transgender book."

And the questions flow. . . . "What's that mean? Are you transgendered?"

"Yeah," and then I'm there and I'm not sure how I've gotten there. The lines between the desks and walls and faces become more extreme. They leave lingering patterns in my vision. A smile forms across my face. I answer, "Well, it can mean a few things. What it means to me is that I'm a masculine woman and also that sometimes I feel like a man and sometimes like a woman."

"But that's not really how you feel, it's that we lack the language to describe it," one of the women offers at the front of the room. I am proud of her for thinking on her feet, and using her learning from the discourse analysis lecture of a month ago to save me. Save me from the frowns and open mouths.

"No," I tell her, "it may be a limitation of language, but then also the way I feel has formed itself around this limitation of language. I do feel like both a man and woman."

The closeted gay man in the course told me afterwards that he panicked at first when the questions began. He wanted to tell them to stop. He wanted to protect me from the personal intrusion. But then he watched and felt awed by my willingness to talk freely. He said that the scary charge of such topics as transgender, queer, his own gay life, became less powerful.

I run into my supervisor later, sit in her office and rehash the transgender classroom conversation. She studies me and asks with what I think is partly disbelief and partly admiration, "It doesn't bother you to talk about that stuff, does it?"

"Naww," I say, my chin up, my bravado given away by my leg bouncing.

Three hours later, I realize that a smile is on my face. The house is quiet; my girlfriend and children are in bed. I am sitting on my couch in the dark, watching Open Mike: Mike Bullard asks a male hockey player for love over the telephone. I shake my head and take another sip of pastis. Over the past year or so, I have watched Mike make passes at nearly every male guest on his show as well as his musicians and audience members. Then he laughs a full head-shaking laugh and looks back at the camera for recognition of a gay joke well-delivered, I think. Only, is he gay or what? It's so confusing, and yet entertaining. Homo love sells.

I swallow more of my warm licorice drink. Was I entertaining? They couldn't stop asking questions. Here you go, one butch dyke before you, ready for consumption. And I don't care if we say that the consumption model is a product of capitalism and marketing and talk shows. And that our classrooms should be student-centered, not teacher-centered; it is a thrill to be consumed, to be the object of fancy. I get a buzz from it. And I don't think I'm the only one.

It's a buzz that's good at the time, but smacks you later. Liz Newbery, a friend, described it as "alluring but disturbing. There's something not quite right about it." I feel it as a burning that runs for hours. I find what's wrong about it in my frozen smile. It's my father's smile. His nervous smile. He never got over being a disappointing son, or a girly boy. He is plagued by panic attacks. He has never found a way to raise his chin and speak up. He finishes any given statement with a smile and mumbled laugh. He is embarrassed by his own voice. I hate when I feel the creases of my own mouth shaped into his. How long has it been this way? Am I nervous or embarrassed? Is it my body or my words that take me here tonight? Do I look like the weakness I see in him? What is it I'm afraid of?

The TV turns to kitchen infomercials at some point and I begin to walk around the house, answer E-mails, write, listen to the radio.

I'm afraid of student evaluations. Students hold a funny place in my life. They are familiar strangers. Strangers on the street sometimes yell obscenities at me; a couple of times, they've thrown stuff. It has not hurt me yet. People I have known who can't deal with me have gone away. The only people who address hate to me with any continuity is a minute portion of the students in my teacher education courses. And, of course, I remember their words the most clearly, rather than those of the supportive majority.

Right, so, I have to confess that I wrote this part and then I went through all my evaluations to find the real juicy horrible lines from students to deliver to you as proof of homophobia, only the worst ones, and I found only two that directly named anything queer: 1) "I learned about multiculturalism and homosexuality. That's pretty much it." And 2) "All the readings are centered on only sexual orientation issues. Teach us how to teach English!" I think this only winds up proving that I've kept imaginary harsh evaluations with me. These remarks are condescending; they misrepresent my work, but they are not so heavy with hatred.

I used to be afraid of Chicana/o communities, the places and people I consider to be my home. But in the four years and 15 classes of teaching in Chicano studies, I only once received any negative evaluations. I have to wonder if our shared culture and struggle against California-style racism kept us closer, or at least more protective.

I'm somewhat afraid of E-mails, small electric packets delivered daily, and the most popular medium for the news of bashings and suicides of everyday queers. Often, photos are attached, earlier portraits with smiles. I print them out and carry them around with me, like tiny altars in my backpack. I peek at them. I study the clothing, their eyes, their lips, and then return them again to my bag:

July 2001. An E-mail [telling me] that Mandy, a buddy of mine, drove off the road into a canyon for no apparent reason. Her body was found months later. She was a butch dyke, the former executive director of San Diego Pride, who was going through a rough time socially, struggling with the rise and fall of life in the queer community. She was in her mid-thirties; I've heard people say that she might have meant to do it.

September 2002. E-mail of a black trans man who committed suicide; political activist, community worker, Alexander John "Bear" Goodrum. He was in his 40s, he was out, he supported younger queer folks. Aren't these the tasks achieved by the survivors?

October 2002: E-mail about the murder of Gwen Araujo, a 17-year-old Latina trans woman from the San Francisco Bay Area. It was the first time she wore a dress in public.

May 2003. E-mail of the bashing of friends of mine, another trans man of color, his femme girlfriend and a sister—Prado, Mariah, and Yvette—outside a San Francisco gay bar. They have charged the perp with assault and fight him back in court. They are asking for as many of us as possible to come to the courtroom dressed in red, as a symbol of the blood spilled.

I don't know what exposure to hate does to a body. Don't know if the damage we endure will heal like lungs when offered clean air, or build to excess and die as a liver would. Don't know how you can live 41 years, work as a highly visible queer activist, and then need to end your life. Don't know what that means about the stability of my own. I know I'm being dramatic, but I'm not exaggerating. And really, if you can't be dramatic when you're afraid, when can you be?

On such fearful nights, I eventually force myself back to bed, back to my girlfriend. I hold her close to me. I use that very love that makes me vulnerable as the source of my protection.

References

Moraga, C. (2000). *Loving in the war years: Lo que nunca pasó por sus labios* (2nd ed.). Cambridge, MA: South End Press.

Note:

[1] English literature, and particularly the writing of Shakespeare, has been used as a tool to colonize many parts of the world, to simultaneously impart the value of English culture and devalue native cultures. Because he has been held in such high regard, both for his literary merits and through the disturbing connection to the British empire, I imply here that it might be useful to note that he wrote about his desire for men as well as women. I want to appropriate his worldwide reputation to showcase bisexuality.

DON'T FENCE ME IN

Celia Haig-Brown

Paper prepared for the EGALE conference, Montreal, QC. May 19, 2003

*T*o come out in class or not. This perennial question has been, with good reason, at the forefront for many of those involved with schooling—particularly with children—for years. (See Didi Khayatt especially—a number of articles over the years.) In your reflections as you read this piece, you may wish to answer the following questions: What are the differences between sex and gender? Although categorizing people is a convenience in some ways, these categories are also subject to change. What might it mean for our teaching and learning if we were to take that seriously? Does this possibility of change extend beyond sex and gender categories? How might the ways we categorize people or even ourselves be dangerous to our students or even serve as a form of violence? Can you think of a time when you were hesitant "to come out" about some aspect of who you are? What did that feel like? How did you resolve it? Did you resolve it?

(un)Categorically Sexual

Some time ago, in an effort to be true to my own inclinations and in response to the postmodern turn to suspicion of categories, I found myself coming out in a graduate class as "(un)categorically sexual." It worked for me. (I sometimes wonder how that is received, and take time to offer a bit of explanation.) First of all, "(un)categorically" allows play with words—play, as you will see, is part of what sexual and sexuality should be about in my books. In the central word—"categorically"—we have the meanings of "absolutely, without qualification, unconditionally"; then, with a sleight of tongue trick, we bring the "un" to bear to slip in the notion of "not pertaining to a category." With one and the same word, there is the possibility of an absolute claim to being sexual (i.e., belonging to a (broad) category), juxtaposed with an immediate refusal of being shoved into one specific category. As for the explanation of sexual, I leave that to you.

For me, those two words—partly a joke and partly very serious—catch the notion of embracing being sexual, and simultaneously refusing to name one sexual category as an identity. The words also serve me well in that they have refused and continue to refuse an answer to the question, Coming out as what?

A number of years ago, when I asked the man I was living with to leave because I was falling in love with another person, a woman, he wrote me a letter that included a statement of claim. He wanted money. Among the list of amounts that I owed him and the reasons I owed were these words (honest: I am quoting), "I also think I contributed domestically and collaboratively to your attainment of tenure and a clearer idea of your sexual orientation to the tune of (tab, tab, tab) $15,000."

I thought to myself then and I think to myself now, "Hmm, what exactly is that clearer idea?"

His very statement is for me an effort to categorize and control—an effort that had frustrated him and me throughout our relationship. I refuse the categories. It also gestures toward larger questions of power and control that gender our relations, sexual and otherwise.

Coming Out As What. . . .

Okay, imagine this: Fifty head of wild horses running hard: eyes on any path to freedom, brush cracking in their ears, jumping fallen tress, branches whipping across muscled chests as they crash through the bush, nostrils flared, ears pricked, running, running, to what they can't really know. What they do know is that there are four well-placed cowboys hard on them and then one breaks out in front of the lead mare, a splashy paint, and dives through the gateway to the open grasslands, praying that the mare will follow, bringing the herd behind.

Today, I come out as a cowboy. That category I embrace. It's one I love to use on people who see only a greying professor in front of them. I am the "cowboy" diving through the gate.

When I was 5 growing up on Vancouver Island, I had a Golden Book called *The Littlest Cowboy's Christmas.* All I ever wanted were the guns and the horse and I knew then my life would be perfect. Never got the guns—not the toy ones from the well-fingered Sears catalogue—but I did wrangle the horses (so to speak) into my life. I went on to read *My Friend Flicka* and *Thunderhead* and found myself clearly identifying with Ken. At some point, I remember realising that when I had an image of myself doing something, it was really an image of my older, hero brother. (Of course, that's not all that was going on in my head but it plays a major role in how I explain myself to myself these days. I also have been known to say I want to live all the lives—then and now, the categories can still feel confining.)

I did become a cowboy and I married one, too, just to ensure the legitimacy of my position. I married the toughest cowboy I could find. We had a rodeo outfit—that means bucking horses and bulls and Mexican steers—and eventually we had—well, I did most of the work—three children. I also became a teacher, because someone had to bring in regular money and, anyway, I needed my independence.

Imagine this: High school rodeo. 1975 Kamloops, British Columbia—semi-desert, sagebrush, and rattlesnakes, cowboy country. It's hot and dry and the kid cowboys are strutting their stuff in tight-fitting jeans, black cowboy hats, and dusty boots. Horses, goats, steers, concession stands, smells of hay and manure, animal sweat and human sweat, country music whining on the PA system: the usual fare at a rodeo. Cut to the arena: The cowboy is on a powerfully built mare with a big white spot on her belly. The rest of her is a rich brown and she is a beautiful creature. The music fades and the announcer grins as he introduces the "cowperson" who is working the calves out of the arena. In the next instant, a difficult calf turns back and runs under the horse's belly. The horse, as they say, explodes. In a frenzy. The cowperson grips hard and weathers the first few leaps, but this is the horse they told her to "get on or she would go to the can." (In cowboy parlance, that refers to being made into dog food.) And the mare really can buck when she wants. The rider hits the ground hard. Her students are astounded to see what their English and biology teacher does on the weekends.

Resistance to Categories: Living All the Lives

What is all this resistance to categories about? What is this desire to live all the lives?

In retrospect, I would say that there is a clear, although tacit, recognition on the part of some children about where the power and the freedom lie—what little freedom there is. The power to make choices and to experiment with life can be partially a dimension of privilege and an accompanying sense of entitlement, although the possibility of squandering privilege is real. When a person decides to cross boundaries and challenge assumptions, the costs and the benefits mount up and they don't necessarily lead to a balanced budget. Why the attraction to cowboys? It's related to romantic notions of power, control, and freedom. And if we gender those notions, challenging sexism comes in.

We continue to talk about and try to address sexism in many contexts. Some days, it seems that things are improving, and sometimes it doesn't. (Check out the top 10 CEOs in Canada in an article published in Toronto's *Globe and Mail* daily newspaper. Surprise, surprise: They are all white men.) One thing is for sure: When we talk about sexism, we are talking primarily, if not exclusively, about one-way discrimination (i.e., against women). Building on a recent talk given by Didi Khayatt at the Hearts and Minds Conference sponsored by the Centre for Gender Diversity at the University of Toronto in 2003, I want to say that what we are really talking about is misogyny. Khayatt argues convincingly in her paper that we need to take gender seriously if we are to begin to address homophobia. Without going into the intricacies of what she says, it comes down to homophobia being based in misogyny: the palpable fear is that somehow men might become like women—and that is the despicable thought, not the sex acts that they perform.

Misogyny is not the sole purview of men, of course. We women can internalise it well; some of us reinscribe it in our heterosexual relations with men, and decide to spend a good portion of our personal lives negotiating the contradictions and tensions of being feminized women, albeit in a relatively liberal North American context. While it may put a negative spin on a little girl who saw herself as a cowboy and worked to get there, one way to think about a trajectory that leads to wanting only to be with "the boys" and to be one of them is to understand it as a desire not to be controlled by them, not to be lesser than. The desire also may be manifested in wanting to be both man and woman, one and then the other, or both in the same moment—messing with the categories. Avoiding sexism/misogyny is one explanation for the conflicts that we find ourselves in as we try to make sense of gender identities—masculine and feminine, butch and femme, tops and bottoms, flaming faggots and bull dykes. In this day and age, these tensions can lead to resistance to a singular gender definition and/or the embracing of a perverse one. We can play with gender—we can cross-dress because we are driven to it or because we like to play. We listen to Micky Gilbert, who is sometimes Michael; we read Leslie Fienburg and think of the moment when she stole into her father's closet and put on his suit—seeing her future, feeling "right" for the first time. And in the next instant, feeling oh so wrong when caught in the act by her frantic and punishing parents: their horror palpable as they try to force her back into her assigned position of "girl."

If we could ever, as a society, move beyond this hatred of women, this fear, manifested in the desire to control them, would there be some ideal world where people would perform their gender in whatever ways moved them without repercussions? Would it be any fun? Would the notion of coming out in class fade as wide-ranging gender play became an accepted and acceptable part of life? My ex-sister-in-law talks about life in her First Nations community in British Columbia. There is a man there who is very effeminate and who spends his time with women. The people there say about him, "He is the man who makes baskets"—no judgment.

The Misogyny

At this point in my life, I am forced to look at what it means/meant to reject being with women and to choose to spend time with men. How does one assume that stance and then find oneself not only in love with a woman, but planning to spend a lifetime, a lovetime, with that woman? I conjure up

Monique Wittig's provocative claim, "I am not a woman." Women exist in relation to men. Even the word exists in relation to men. I don't live in relation to men and, therefore, I am not a woman. Well, I am not really prepared to give up that category. What I am prepared to give up is living an intimate and daily life in relation to a man. I choose woman. And in so doing, I sidestep existing problematic gender relations. I sidestep sexism, I sidestep misogyny and embrace woman—myself and my lover.

What is there to fear? To worry about? In coming out? I had to conjure up the moments to get at the fears. I stand in front of my undergraduate class of preservice teachers. We are talking sexuality and schools. "I've never met a lesbian," says one student and goes on with her statement. I don't miss a beat and respond to her without any acknowledgment that she is talking to one now. What is that about? I tell myself, and you, that it is about fearing the loss and wanting the best of that specific pedagogical moment—a moment when the discussion can either flow in productive ways or come to a grinding halt—when a student is being open. A moment not to be dismissed lightly. Strategically one chooses. Will the students be well-served with the disruption that the teacher could bring at that moment: "Yes, you have met a lesbian. You are talking to her now and she is going to grade you." Or is the pedagogy of the discussion that ensues from not claiming the turf at that moment worth the moment of self and group denial that one faces in not coming out? This question is one with which teachers struggle regularly, and not just in relation to sexuality. And, of course, the loss of a pedagogical moment is never an absolute. One situation calls for a coming out; another calls for a staying in. The choices to be made are part of what it means to be a teacher and to be a lesbian in the classroom where many students continue to assume that there aren't any of those there and if there were, it wouldn't be the teacher.

And the other reason I fear is the effect that coming out might have on those I love. In my case, I am careful around my kids, their friends, and those they work with. Of course, the best-laid plans of mums go oft awry. I didn't know that my then-teenage daughter had been reading my E-mails to my lover and had reported to her classmates that her mother was a lesbian. She told me later in the day that her boyfriend had been losing an argument in class and had shouted at her, "At least my mum isn't a lesbian." So much for protecting the children. I watch my children, who have grown to wonderful, thoughtful, and sexual adults, negotiate the coming out process—whether in relation to their own sexuality or to their mother's or their friends'. But there I was the other day, with my daughter's work colleagues, saying, "Yes, I am going to Corfu in June with my sisters and my, uh, friend." You can see the sentence coming out of your mouth as if it is in slow motion. Your brain is watching and deciding—to come out or not—and like a train picking up speed, the moment of decision roars toward you, reaches you, and then, in a split second, the decision is made and the rest of the sentence clacks on by. A moment of denial with reason or with perceived need. Later that day, my daughter says to me, "And mum, that business about 'friend' going to Corfu: Just say 'partner.' Nobody cares."

Back in the Saddle Again

Final story. As chair of a university senate committee, I am working with the secretary of the committee and he tells me that one of his colleagues has asked him if I used to be a nun. He laughs and says that he told her I used to be a rodeo person. I can't stop thinking about it. The next day, I wear my cowboy boots and jeans to work. The next time I am in a meeting with the person, I make sure that I mention my three children. I come out as not a nun.

Nothing wrong with nuns—unless, of course, you are (un)categorically sexual. Nuns are not sexual and if I am going to claim anything, it is that I am sexual. But there is a deeper worry—nuns are not in control, they vow obedience, and ultimately they obey men: the priests, the bishops, the Pope. Is this misogyny at work—in the sets of relations and in my response?

Imagine: You look in the closet—clothes closet, I mean. Your eyes move past the business suits and you reach for the Wranglers. You slide each leg, first one and then the other, into the stiff denim, feeling the tightness grasp your body, a bit rough against your skin. Push the shirt tails flat inside. The satisfying zip of the fly, slip the metal button into the hole and reach for the tooled belt. Slide the end through the loops, reaching around behind and then through the clasp of the silver buckle. Push your feet hard into the leather boots. Pull your pant legs down around the boot tops. Check once in the mirror and head out to work at the university.

COMING OUT AS WHAT. . . .

Didi Khayatt

In this personal essay, Khayatt explores the way she has come to be recognized as possessing certain identities, specifically as lesbian, feminist, and "old." At times, the labels are thrust upon her; at other moments, she hungers for the meanings they offer and embraces them. They are only partial descriptions of who she is: they are never completely solid, they are named in relation to those around her, and they can change over time. When an educator becomes known as being lesbian, gay, bisexual, or transgender, how is that person veiwed by his or her students and colleagues? Do other aspects of his/her identity become less visible or valid? How do issues of race, class, age, geography, and politics influence the way sexual identity is expressed?

Several years ago at a sexualities conference in Toronto, Elizabeth Kennedy and Madeline D. Davis, authors of *Boots of Leather, Slippers of Gold: The History of a Lesbian Community* (1993), were in town giving a talk about their groundbreaking book. One evening, after the conference ended for the day, a whole group of women went to a local lesbian bar for drinks and dancing. I was in my early 50s then, grey-haired and fit. The place was packed with women, all dancing and talking. I was dancing, sort of moving to some very loud music with one of the two authors, getting to know her despite the thumping beat and pressing bodies. As we talked and swayed, a young woman turned toward us and said: "It is so nice to see old women still dancing." Well, I never had thought of myself as an "old woman" and the remark took me by surprise. This chapter, "Coming out as what . . .," will locate my position as a lesbian whose years of life have overtaken her rather more quickly than her ideas about herself growing old.

When I was approached to write this chapter, I quipped: Who said I'm out! But later, it occurred to me that I have spent a lifetime coming out as a lesbian, a process that is never-ending for the simple reason that, because of my age (almost 60), I have witnessed and participated in a long history of lesbian politics, beginning with my coming out to myself as a teenager in Egypt, to browsing through my mother's French books as I looked for inspiration regarding my identity, to anguishing over whether I could be a lesbian or not after reading the psychology books of the era that provided characteristics to recognize lesbians. One way to identify a lesbian, the books said, was to note whether she could whistle or not, and since I could not, I wondered maybe if. . . . My first sexual encounter with a woman, at the age of 19 (in Egypt), still did not convince me that I was a lesbian. Maybe I was going through "a stage," as per the thinking of the era. Maybe I was bisexual (somehow that sounded better to my very young ears, more of a sexual adventurer than a sexual deviant). It took graduate school in Egypt and several prompts from my family that I should get married to make me realize that marriage did not have a place in my plans. Instead, I left for Canada. Here in Canada in 1967, far away from my family, I had no trouble knowing who I was and am (sexually), but I had trouble with others knowing my sexual identity. The late 1960s and early 1970s in Northern Ontario, where I lived and taught high school, was not a place nor an age open to calling oneself a lesbian. To come out publicly as "lesbian" is to make a political statement. I had the fundamental understanding of what it would mean to be recognized as a lesbian, and a lesbian of colour at that, and I knew that I would have to forfeit my job, at worst, and would be ostracized, at best. The real problem, of course, was that I was just terrified of being recognized for the lesbian I was. I was just as afraid of being seen a woman of colour. I passed. I had shoulder-length hair, was young and pretty; I mostly looked white and straight. My difference became my charm, my secrets my own.

I have written often about my life, my coming-out process, the genesis of my political awakening, and today I want to write about coming out as an "old lesbian." I want to be clear that it is not an identity I embrace so much as it is one that is thrust upon me. I am old because I am perceived to be so. I am old because younger women have ceased to see me. I am old because I am settled with a lover and I have ceased to look at younger women. Of course, coming out as anything is more complicated than that.

Coming out is a process. It is not a one-time moment in one's life. It is a political move because, whether one is aware of it or not, it forces one into a community that shares a history, if nothing else. Coming out is a process that privileges one part of an identity and compels the individual into being reduced (even just momentarily) to this one facet at the expense of the whole person. In other words, when I come out as a lesbian, you do not see as clearly that part of me that is a woman of colour, my history of privilege, or my able-bodied, if aging, being. Coming out highlights one aspect of a whole person, and in emphasizing it, makes it the person, which is perhaps why we say: "I am a lesbian" rather than I perform "lesbianly." Simply put, coming out forgets the individual who is behind the category. Yes, of course I am a lesbian, but I am also so many other things. One reason why the title of the 1982 book *All the Women Are White, All the Blacks Are Men, But Some of Us Are Brave* (Gloria Hull, Patricia Bell Scott, and Barbara Smith, editors) is brilliant is because it calls attention to how categories work: when you say "women" many think of "white women," when you utter the word "black," black men often come to mind. And, of course, when you say "lesbian," white lesbians are implied unless otherwise specified. As I wrote in another paper, it is not that "lesbian" as an identity is necessarily white, so much as it originates in the white history of 19th century Western Europe.

I speak of myself as a lesbian when I want to claim a sexual identity. I do not say I am "queer" because I came out in the era when such a word did not exist except as a pejorative, a term used as a mainstream shortcut to denote "homosexual." I do recognize, however, that "queer" is more inclusive than "lesbian" when it implies a fluidity within the sexual. It is restrictive, however, for someone like myself whose politics are implicitly denied as an older lesbian, and whose history it forgets when the term "lesbian" is subsumed under "queer."

In 1980, I left my teaching job in northern Ontario and came to finish my Ph.D. in Toronto. It was then that I was introduced to feminism. For me, it was like coming home for the first time in my life, and that includes coming out and living in a settled lesbian relationship with another teacher for over a decade. For the first time, all the ideas I had been anguishing about, all the questions that I could not answer, all the contradictions that made up my life, all came together and began, through a process that would take years, to make sense to me. It was through feminism that I finally understood the consequences and responsibilities of coming out. Coming out ceased to be a moment of courage and became an instantiation of a conscious political act. Feminism allowed me to recognize my rage against an unjust and misogynist social system, and to understand that this injustice was personal and also therefore political. Feminism informed my analysis, framed my research, and challenged my thinking. Feminism is not an identity so much as a political perspective, a process that has acted as the foundation of my thinking and theorizing. To me, this is the identity that I claim with pride and with fear—pride in the political stance I undertake in naming my beliefs and in my insistence for social justice, and fear in that I can never live up to the term in its implications and demands for a just world.

Finally, if "coming out" means everyone knowing about my sexual "identity," then I am out to different degrees, depending on the context. In my daily experiences of going about my business in the world, I am almost always out with friends and my immediate family, and I am out at work with respect to the administration of the university (I am, after all, the president's adviser on sexual and gender diversity issues). I am out with my colleagues and with graduate students, and I am out differently with my preservice students. Although I almost never use the declarative statement of "Hi, my name is Didi Khayatt and I am a lesbian," I have written extensively about how I "come out in class" and any one of my students who is interested in my work will know that I am a lesbian. At work, most people know that Celia is my partner; some recognize our relationship, and others prefer to play at being discreet. So, am I out? Out as what?

Reference

Kennedy, E., & Davis, M. D. (1993). *Boots of leather, slippers of gold: The history of a lesbian community.* Florence, KY: Routledge.

IN THE SCHOOL, CLASSROOM, AND CURRICULUM

INTRODUCTION TO "IN THE SCHOOL, CLASSROOM, AND CURRICULUM"

Drawing upon critical theory and pedagogies of social justice, educators share their successes and failures in their attempts to implement LGBT issues in the classroom and/or school community. They provide us with strategies for introducing, supporting, and engaging students in dialogue, advocacy, and arts-based activities. They frequently confront teasing and insults between students, unsupportive comments from colleagues, reprimands from administrators, resistance from established school culture, and unchallenged protocols. LGBT educators experience the awkward and potentially dangerous position of having their personal identity collide with their pedagogy. One of the most important findings is the need for educators to be willing to risk discomfort in order to tackle sensitive issues within the school community (see April Whatley Bedford's chapter).

We begin with a piece on the Toronto District School Board and their equity policy. This is followed by two pieces based on extensive interviews with preservice and practicing teachers about their experiences as LGBT educators. Then we include specific approaches to working with anti-homophobic curriculum, such as arts-based initiatives, theatre of the oppressed techniques, and the use of children's literature. To further support educators in their quest for social justice and anti-bias curriculum for their students, we have included a final chapter of resources for embracing LGBT families in the classroom.

Homophobic Graffiti on the Portable Wall

John J. Guiney Yallop

In late May
one of my grade five students ran
back into our classroom at the end of the day
out of breath
and shaking.
She told me there was something written
on the outside of our portable about me,
something bad;
it had a swear word in it.

Outside I read the message
delivered the length of our classroom.

Fuck you, Mr. Guiney. Suck your gay dick. Remember me.

My students were gathered
beside and behind me
like worshippers shocked at a violation
of their sacred place
and their holy leader.

This one
more visible than any of the others
named me
named my identity
and was signed by

Remember Me.

Previously published: Brock Education, 14(2), 139.

Fighting Homophobia in Toronto Schools

Tim McCaskell

*T*he last chapter in the first section spoke of Dale's and Jade's experiences within the Toronto District School Board. Many people who hear of this experience wonder how and why the Board became so supportive. Below is a description of the history of the Toronto District School Board's equity policy. What is it that made the most difference in shifting the attitudes of Board members? Do you think this type of support is possible in all boards? What do you think should happen if a parent disagrees with a board's equity policy?

As part of its equity policy, the Toronto District School Board (TDSB) recognizes the impact of individual and systemic homophobia on students, parents, and employees and commits itself to ensuring that "fairness, equity and inclusion are essential principles of our school system and are integrated into all our policies, programs operations and practices."[1]

Experience on the ground in schools demonstrates that the Board still has a great deal of work to do before achieving its lofty policy goals on homophobia, not to mention the other areas highlighted in the equity policy: racism, sexism, class bias, and equity for people with disabilities. But compared with most public school boards across Canada, the TDSB's anti-homophobia practice may indeed seem remarkable.

The Board runs the Triangle Program, Canada's only full-time secondary school classroom for lesbian, gay, bisexual, transgender, and queer students facing difficulty in mainstream schools. The Human Sexuality Program in the Board's Social Work Department has a full-time queer social worker providing counselling to LGBTQ students and their families. Its Equity Department produces documents and resources on anti-homophobia education and support for classroom teachers. Anti-homophobia workshops led by community speakers are commonly delivered in both elementary and secondary schools. The Human Rights Department has the responsibility for investigating incidents of homophobic harassment. There is recognition for lesbian and gay domestic partnerships in employee benefit packages. The Board regularly sponsors a school-bus float in Toronto's annual Pride Parade. Representatives from a community-based Anti-Homophobia Equity Coalition sit on the Board's ongoing Equity Policy Advisory Committee, and openly gay and lesbian individuals are trustees.

Why Should Toronto Be So Progressive?

The answer to that question lies in demographics, history, political context, and activism. The Toronto Board's policies and programs didn't fall from the sky, nor were they born of some administrative epiphany. They were the result of years of struggle; the context of municipal, provincial, and national politics; and, to paraphrase Oscar Wilde, too many evening meetings.[2]

Up until the 1960s, Toronto was still a typical English Canadian city, dominated by a patriarchal Anglo Protestant elite. With the loosening of racist immigration laws by the end of that decade, however, Toronto's complexion began to change. The city experienced a demographic shift. Growing immigrant communities from Catholic Europe, Asia, and the Caribbean made up an increasingly significant percentage of families with school-going children, and these families often found the public school system oblivious to their needs, if not culturally insensitive and racist.

The 1960s and 1970s were a time of social ferment and transformation. Previously silenced voices from these new communities began demanding changes in the school system to better meet the needs of their children. Reform trustees were elected and began to challenge the old order. By the end of the 1970s, the Toronto Board of Education was addressing multiculturalism, race relations, sexism, and policies that streamed working class and immigrant kids into dead-end basic level programs. Liaison committees were set up between the Board and different communities to bring their concerns forward and to push for change.

The decriminalization of homosexuality in 1969 meant that the 1970s also saw a steady growth in the size and profile of the gay and lesbian community in downtown Toronto. Education was an issue for this increasingly assertive gay community. Many remembered experiences of exclusion, isolation, and harassment during their school careers, and a new generation of young people reported that little had changed. The only political party that dared to champion gay rights at the time was the New Democratic Party (NDP), Canada's small but tenacious social democratic party. Coincidentally, a majority of reform trustees on the Board identified with the NDP. It was not surprising then that in 1980, a group of gay activists, seeking to take advantage of the progressive winds blowing across the Board and their NDP connections, proposed setting up a Lesbian and Gay Liaison Committee to mirror those established by other communities. In response, trustees added sexual orientation to the Board's general statement condemning bias, and set up a committee to study the advisability of establishing the new liaison committee.

Unfortunately, the timing was bad; 1980 was a municipal election year and homosexuality became a major issue. The election saw the defeat of Toronto mayor John Sewell, who had championed the rights of minorities, including gay people. After a mudslinging campaign by right-wing forces accusing progressive trustees of preparing to hand over children to homosexual predators, reform trustees narrowly lost their majority on the Board of Education.

The results of the election also seemed to embolden the police, who in February 1981, carried out a massive raid on the city's gay bathhouses, arresting over 280 men. In response, there were huge demonstrations and a surge in gay community organizing—the bath raids are often referred to as Toronto's Stonewall.

When the proposal for a liaison committee came back to a more right-wing Board in the middle of the post-election, post-bath raids hysteria, it was defeated. The newly elected Board also removed sexual orientation from its anti-bias statement on the grounds that gay people were not protected under provincial human rights legislation, and adopted a clause prohibiting the "proselytization" of homosexuality in Toronto schools, a motion that was interpreted as a blanket ban on lesbian or gay speakers. All in all, it was not a very auspicious start.

Stung by defeat, lesbian and gay community shifted their energies away from education issues and mobilized to defend those arrested in the bath raids, and then, shortly afterward, to meet the challenges of the beginning of the AIDS epidemic. It would take the murder of a popular educator by queer-bashing students to put homophobia back on the Board's agenda.

In the spring of 1985, Ken Zeller, a public school librarian, was beaten to death in a well-known cruising area by a group of high school students. In the subsequent trial, the defence argued that the defendants were just "normal boys" letting off steam. This interpretation encouraged gay activists and the teachers union to ask what was happening in schools that would lead "normal" students to act this way. Downtown trustee Olivia Chow, whose ward included much of the "gay ghetto," conducted an ad hoc inquiry and reported that anti-gay harassment and bias was rife within the school system. She convinced the Board to establish the Human Sexuality Program, with a counsellor to work with lesbian and gay students and their families, and to ask the Physical Education Department to develop a resource guide to help teachers deal with questions of sexual orientation.

These moves heralded the beginning of a sea change. In 1985, Canada's new Charter of Rights came into effect, and public awareness of the impact of anti-gay discrimination was heightened by the AIDS epidemic. After a long struggle by activists, sexual orientation was added to the Ontario Human Rights Code in 1986, prohibiting discrimination against lesbians and gay men in the province. When the Board's Equal Opportunity Office organized a student conference on the new Charter of Rights the following year, it invited speakers from various equality groups, including a gay activist. That invitation was promptly blocked by the Superintendent of Curriculum, who cited the Board's anti-proselytization policy. Yet withdrawal of the invitation now contravened the Human Rights Code. The impasse threatened to derail the event, until finally the Associate Director of Education intervened to say that the proselytization policy did not, in fact, ban gay speakers after all. With the policy in limbo, it became increasingly easy for schools and teachers to invite gay and lesbian speakers to conduct anti-homophobia work in classrooms.

In 1990, the next breakthrough came: the surprise election of a provincial NDP government, committed to such issues as employment equity. The new government's policies encouraged widespread discussion of issues associated with minority rights.

Taking advantage of this new atmosphere, a Lesbian and Gay Employees Group was established within the Board. The group included both teaching and non-teaching staff, and its presence inside the system strengthened the strategic capabilities of those pushing for change. The 1991 municipal elections produced a new Board, with a majority of trustees supportive of anti-homophobia initiatives; the employee group developed a list of demands for the Board's first openly gay trustee, John Campey. In the spring of 1992, Campey introduced a series of motions proposing the entrenchment of the positions in Human Sexuality Program (eroded by the addition of other responsibilities over time), the release of the long-awaited resource document on sexual orientation (still tied up in "consultations"), the creation of a new Consultative Committee on the Education of Lesbian and Gay Students, and the official rescinding of the anti-proselytization policy.

These motions met fierce opposition from traditional Christian fundamentalists and a new, ostensibly secular group calling itself CURE (Citizens United for Responsible Education), which espoused "curing" gay people from the "illness" of homosexuality. Speaking in favour of the motions, however, were students from the lesbian and gay student support group set up by the Human Sexuality Program, teachers and other employees from the employees' group, and lesbian and gay parent activists. Together, the students, parents, and teachers formed a powerful coalition, thereby putting a real face on the need for such initiatives, which convinced some of the more reluctant trustees to adopt the motions. Campey also had crafted his motions to be congruent with existing Board initiatives on behalf of other marginalized groups—for example, social workers specializing in work with particular communities, curriculum resource documents focussed on racial and ethnic groups, and the Consultative Committee, which was modelled on similar committees for black and aboriginal students. Finally, Campey worked hard to line up the votes of his colleagues. As a trustee assistant, he had been involved in the equity initiatives of many immigrant groups and therefore was able to summon wide support outside the LGBT community. All the motions passed.

In 1992, the Board launched a new sexual harassment policy that, for the first time, specifically prohibited harassment on the basis of sexual orientation. The Board's old policy had been largely aimed at protecting women from unwanted advances from men in positions of power. The new policy envisaged a much broader notion of harassment, including name-calling, teasing, threats, and other unwelcome behaviours among both students and employees.

By this time, a new Equity Studies Centre had been set up in the Curriculum Department, bringing together the former advisers on women's studies, multiculturalism, and race relations. The new centre assumed responsibility for the production of curriculum documents, student programs, support and training for teachers, and a mandate to deal with racism, sexism, homophobia, and class bias.[3]

Opposition to these initiatives continued, including death threats against Human Sexuality Program personnel. In 1993, hundreds of people, most of them bused in from out-of-district suburban churches, flooded down to the Board offices in what was called a "Whose Children Awareness Rally." In response, the Lesbian and Gay Employees Group joined with student and community groups to found a new organization, Education Against Homophobia, which organized, a few months later, an even bigger rally and teach-in in support of anti-homophobia initiatives.

In 1995, Tony Gambini, a Human Sexuality social worker, proposed setting up a special program for students unable to succeed in the regular school system because of sexual orientation discrimination. John Campey directed the proposal through the Board, in tandem with a parallel program for black students experiencing similar difficulties. The Triangle Program, as the LGBT classroom came to be known, provided a queer-focussed curriculum in an intimate, safe setting for at-risk students.

Thus, by 1995, the Toronto Board of Education had the major pieces in place to combat homophobia in its schools: a harassment policy, curriculum initiatives and resources for the mainstream school system, teacher training, social work and support services, specialized programs for youth at risk, and organized student, parent, and community involvement. The year 1995 was also, unfortunately, a watershed year in provincial politics, as an aggressively right wing neo-conservative government under Premier Mike Harris gained control. As well as rolling back progressive labour laws, equity legislation, social benefits, and immigrant and community services, the Harris government engineered a major crisis in public education. It completely took over education funding from local municipalities, created a new funding formula that stripped millions from public education, sharply reduced trustee authority, and centralized control of curriculum. In 1997, it abolished the Toronto Board of Education and amalgamated it with five other much more conservative suburban boards to form the Toronto District School Board.

It was a very dark time for activists involved in anti-homophobia work. None of the suburban boards had a comparable track record around equity issues. Most were actively hostile to anti-homophobia initiatives. Equity budgets went into free-fall. Personnel left and were not replaced. Programs faced increasing threats.

The question of how homophobia would be dealt with in the new TDSB came to a head in 1998, when it was proposed to restrict the Board's new equity policy to issues of race and culture—the minimum required by provincial legislation. The move would dissolve any mandate for equity work around homophobia, sexism, class bias, or disabilities. A huge outcry ensued, but the now suburban-dominated Board and conservative administrators in charge of the policy development process refused to consider a broader equity policy.

In response, a coalition of groups, including lesbian and gay organizations, women's groups, the

Labour Council, and several major ethnocultural organizations, was formed to fight for a broad approach to equity. Only after months of rowdy public consultations, when trustees and administrators faced sustained and vocal opposition to their plans, including threats of legal action, did the Board finally back down. An equity policy that included anti-racism and ethnocultural equity, anti-sexism and gender equity, anti-homophobia, sexual orientation and equity, anti-classism and socio-economic equity and equity for persons with disabilities was finally passed by the Board in December 1999.[4]

Although the TDSB has one of the strongest equity policies on the continent inclusive of sexual orientation, and a number of structures and programs left over from 20 years of struggle in downtown Toronto, the actual state of affairs is far from ideal. Although the provincial Conservative government was finally defeated in 2005, the damage done to the public education system has been incalculable. The present funding formula is grossly insufficient to run Toronto schools and to meet the needs of the city's hugely diverse populations. The Board lurches from one budget crisis to the next and there are constant cutbacks and threats of cutbacks. A much-reduced Equity Department struggles to meet the demands of a huge system of nearly 600 schools. Students are largely unaware of the procedures for countering harassment. Recent surveys of employees and students on a range of issues, including sexual orientation, have been poorly handled, and community consultation around equity initiatives often seems like an afterthought. Staff that provided essential services have been cut to the bone. The burden of such system-wide problems are inordinately shared by all the equity seeking groups whose needs were never properly served by the system—the poor, visible and racial minorities, new immigrants, women, the LGBTQ communities, and people with disabilities.

At present, the promises of the equity policy are not driving a process of institutional change. They can and do, however, provide a justification for individual initiatives by students, teachers, or administrators. In certain cases, they make possible what might be unthinkable in other jurisdictions. The Board's heritage of structures and policies is an important foundation for the construction of a truly equitable school system that will serve LGBTQ and other minority students. But further construction on that foundation will only come with the mobilization and unity of all equity seeking groups.

Notes:

1. Equity Foundation Statement and Commitments of Equity Policy Implementation (Toronto District School Board, 2000, p. 4).
2. For a more detailed account of this history, see: Tim McCaskell, *Race to Equity: Disrupting Educational Inequality* (Toronto, Between the Lines Press, 2005).
3. For a more detailed account of anti-homophobia programs in the Equity Studies Centre, see: Tim McCaskell and Vanessa Russell, "Anti-Homophobia Intitiatives at the Former Toronto Board of Education," in *Weaving Connections: Educating for Peace, Social and Environmental Justice*, Tara Goldstein and David Selby, editors (Toronto, Sumach Press, 2000).
4. For a more thorough analysis of this period, see: Doreen Fumia, "Competing for a Piece of the Pie: Equity Seeking and the Toronto District School Board in the 1990s," Ph.D. thesis, University of Toronto, 2003.

A LITTLE BIT TOO CLOSE TO HOME: A CASE STUDY OF A BEGINNING TEACHER'S STRUGGLE TO TEACH CRITICALLY

Andrew M.A. Allen

While reading this chapter, consider the ways in which teacher candidates can find support within school settings that seem intimidating. What have you done or seen done in schools to address controversial issues? Teaching about families is a natural entry point in elementary curriculum to talk about issues of sexual orientation and gender diversity. What have been your experiences as a student, parent, or teacher in discussing these issues in class? Do they ever receive enough support from a board if parents disapprove? Who has the final say in what the students are exposed to in school?

As a teacher educator teaching in a faculty of education in Ontario, I have tried to engage my beginning teachers in discussions about social difference and marginalization as an important part of the process of learning to teach. I want to help prepare them to begin thinking in more complex ways about the issues they are likely to deal with in schools and in the communities where they will be working. In doing so, I soon realized that the most contentious and perhaps the most difficult issue in our teacher education program had to do with talking about issues of sexuality. In addition, no matter how progressive and critical I thought I was, I found myself having to deal with my own baggage and my values, attitudes, and bias based on my heterosexual, Christian background. I, too, experienced discomfort in teaching about such issues because of my own experiences. Of course, it also could be said that individuals, like myself, who self-identify as "heterosexual" and yet raise critical issues around sexuality are sometimes also put at risk of taunts, ostracism, and sometimes violence. More importantly, I was concerned about the ways in which teacher candidates themselves were responding to our attempts at preparing them to become critical reflective classroom teachers who will take up critical social issues in their own classrooms.

I became particularly interested in the experiences of the gay and lesbian teacher candidates in our teacher education programs when I noticed that they were experiencing the program in different ways from other teacher candidates. I wanted to learn more about the consequences in the program for gay and lesbian teacher candidates and the ways in which the program could respond more effectively to their needs. I am most fascinated by the nature of the difficulty around teaching about potentially contentious issues in their practicum classrooms and the moments of discomfort that they experience as they try to teach critically about various issues in their year of learning to teach. Over the years, teacher candidates often reported that they experience a number of tensions and contradictions between the intent and philosophy of their critical teacher education program and their experiences in practice teaching. However, most of the literature on progressive or critical teacher education tends to focus on the difficulties of preparing white, able-bodied, middle-class, heterosexual teacher candidates to teach the "other" (Howard, 1999). What I present in this chapter are the experiences of one teacher candidate who identified herself as a lesbian woman and her experiences in trying to teach about sexuality.

Therefore, the purpose of this case study is to examine the classroom experiences of a beginning lesbian teacher, learning to teach in the practicum component of a critical teacher education program that was designed to address issues of equity, diversity, and social justice. How does a beginning lesbian teacher negotiate the tensions and contradictions she experienced between her attempts at learning to teach for equity, diversity, and social justice and the realities she encounters in her attempts to apply what she learned in the program into her practicum classrooms? What are some of the costs of "straining the spirit" (see Lam, 1996) that she pays in teaching from her own social location? How does she negotiate the practicum or deal specifically with the teaching of a potentially contentious issue in her practice teaching? What are the implications for critical inclusionary teacher education programs?

Research Setting and Study Design

As a way of exploring these issues, I have pulled out excerpts detailing the experiences of this one particular teacher candidate from a larger study about the experiences of 30 teacher candidates in a critical antiracism teacher education program in Ontario. Participants from that study were teacher candidates in a one-year teacher education program specifically articulated to address issues of equity, diversity, and social justice. I collected data through individual interviews, focus group discussions, classroom and in-school observations, and analyses of participants' lesson plans and personal reflections in E-mail and online discussions. During the process of collecting that data from the entire group of 30 teacher candidates, I became mainly intrigued by this particular respondent, who spoke specifically about her experiences as a lesbian woman and her moments of discomfort in her attempts at teaching about her "own" issue. I found her story quite compelling, because it gave me insights into the consequences of preparing teacher candidates to teach critically.

Teacher Education and Social Justice

Recent literature on teacher education has identified a number of challenges facing teacher educators as they attempt to prepare prospective teachers to be critical reflective parishioners. The issue of critical teacher education is of great importance, because schools traditionally tend to perpetuate the status quo by serving the purpose of preparing students to become workers that fit into predetermined roles in society (Giroux & McLaren, 1986). Some specific initiatives have been adopted that recognize the need for teachers-in-training to actively name and contest the sources of inequality inherent in the school system as an integral part of their teacher education programs (James, 1994a, 1997; James & Mannette, 2000; Solomon, 1995, 1998; Solomon & Levine-Rasky, 1996b, Solomon & Rezai-Rashti, 1997). For example, some critical program initiatives involve the infusion of an inclusive or transformative teacher education curricula and the institutional adaptations to support implementation of such programs (Flynn Foyn, 1998; Gresson, 1997; Shapson, 1994; Solomon, 1996, 1998; Solomon & Levine-Rasky 1996; Yeo, 1997). However, recent studies and ongoing monitoring of teacher candidates in various critical teacher education programs have identified many tensions and contradictions faced by the student teachers because of issues raised around equity and diversity in these programs (James, 1994a, 1995a, 1997; James & Mannette, 2000; Solomon, 1995, 2000; Solomon & Allen, 2001). Second, the academic discourses surrounding the implementation, the effectiveness, and particularly the consequences of such programs suggest that the issues involved are more complex than was originally anticipated. For instance, antiracism pedagogy as a form of critical discourse in teacher education may raise questions about the nature of the teacher education curriculum and program content (James, 1994a, 1995a, 1997; James & Mannette, 2000). In some cases, teacher candidates encountered contradictions between the proposed aims of their teacher education programs and the ways the programs were actually implemented (James, 1994a). They experienced tensions because of the mixed messages they received from the school and university settings (Solomon & Allen, 2001). In other cases, their own social identities were called into question when issues of social difference became a focus for teacher education (James, 1997; James & Mannette, 2000).

The Experiences of Teacher Candidates

A number of studies have further identified the contradictions that teacher candidates experience in their practice teaching classrooms. For example, Levine-Rasky (1998) argues that in their attempt to teach for social justice, some teacher candidates tend to avoid the explicit teaching of overtly contentious issues—for example, issues around race, gender, and sexuality—for what they considered "safe" issues [like poverty] that required less critical reflective inquiry. They avoid talking with students in their practice teaching classrooms about equity, social justice, social difference, the silencing of voices, power relations, and the oppression and marginalization of various groups in society. Often times, even introducing or taking up issues with students may cause unexpected tensions in their classroom, because of the potential conflicting views or perspectives held by students and other school personnel. In such cases, teaching also can become potentially contentious, particularly for teacher candidates, because of the difficulty of dealing with these tensions. It requires painful introspection for teacher candidates to question their power as teachers and their social position in society and may precipitate a sense of vulnerability (Jakubowski & Visano, 2002). This is primarily because the teacher candidate's own social and institutional identities, beliefs, knowledge, and privilege are implicated and called into question by the issues of equity and social justice being raised with their students. Teacher candidates also experience difficulty because of their own positions as students learning to teach for the first time formally and because of learning to teach in very new and challenging ways. They find themselves learning to teach in a critical teacher education program in ways they perhaps had not come to expect. For teacher candidates in these situations, the process of constructing their teaching identities reveals emerging conflicts and dilemmas in the relationships between any critical theory, their practice teaching, and the teacher education pedagogy they are working with.

Angie's Classroom: Creating Space To Teach Critically

Angie [a pseudonym] is a teacher candidate in an urban teacher education program that is specifically articulated to prepare teacher candidates to teach for equity, social justice, and activism. In her practicum placement, Angie practice taught in a 4th-grade class that is in a very diverse school in the Greater Toronto Area. The classroom was laid out in clusters of student desks, grouped together in small groups of four to six desks. The room contained a number of books and posters that were connected to the themes and topics of study for the class. Students' artwork and writing also were displayed around the room. When I visited her practicum classroom, Angie was working at a table in the back of the room with one small group on a group project. She had designed a unit of study for the 4th-graders on family, and she focused the discussion for that day on alternate family constellations. Angie struggled to resolve the discomfort she experienced as she attempted to engage in any form of critical teaching practice and activism in her practicum.

"I did take on some difficult issues in my classroom. . . . It was a hard thing for me to do because it was a little bit too close to home."

Even before she began discussing different kinds of family constellations, Angie experienced some of the personal consequences for trying to create space to teach critically. As a lesbian teacher, Angie began to feel vulnerable teaching for social justice in her elementary classroom and talking about sexuality. Angie realized that this type of activism required more preparation and support and came at a greater personal cost than she had expected. In her case, creating space to teach critically came at a cost, related to her own personal background.

> *Angie: I did take on some difficult issues in my classroom. When I did a unit on families, I did an in-clusive unit on families. It was a hard thing for me to do because it was a little bit too close to home. I thought I would have had an easier time if it hadn't been so personal because this is my issue. So it adds a lot of passion. It's a matter of letting the kids come to it the way they are, dealing with what they bring and starting from where they are. But I found that there were a few scary moments when, of course, the boys came up with all kinds of negative comments like, "Euuh! Gross, this is horrible stuff." When we got to the part about two moms and the two dads as part of the family unit and talked about how lesbian moms have kids and gay dads have kids . . . that it is done a little bit differently, and sometimes there are legal things that are involved and often they adopt kids and so on . . . and they sometimes did decide not to have kids.*

Angie had not expected that she would need to deal with the students' responses. She was surprised and disappointed with the students' reactions to her attempts at teaching them.

> *Angie: But once you got past the "Eeu" stuff, I got them refocused. This isn't about that. It is not about what they do behind closed doors, I don't know what your parents do behind close doors. It is about family and people who love you. What I found was, once we got past that, there were some lights that went on. It was very exciting, because some of the boys who we reprimanded for calling each other "fags" stopped. I didn't hear it come from them for the rest of the time I went through my block. Because they realized that is a person. There are people that label themselves that. It became clear to me that it wasn't so much that they were homophobic as much that this was a word that was derogatory. So that was really neat and that was a piece of this whole issue I would not have known otherwise. The kids, when they say those words, often don't know what they are saying and don't know that it is actually a person. That gave me a little inroad about some other words that kids use or are talking about. We got into some major issues with some other words.*

Angie speaks of the issues being close to home, being a lesbian teacher and talking with her students about homosexuality as part of her unit on families. She describes the teaching of such issues as being personally difficult, being emotionally loaded and coming at a higher price for her as a lesbian.

> *Angie: Yeah, sure, you have to tell yourself to calm down, it is not about you, it is not about your friends, it's a piece of learning that has to happen here and this is what you are trying to do; then again, it is about you. I think it is a higher price for me, the teacher, than teaching about anything else. I think that was my hardest lesson that I had to teach . . . because it was so emotionally loaded; not just for me, but for the kids, too. Because there was a lot of stuff that came up. . . . I was thinking, I'm changing the construct of what*

they think and the construct is built on insecurity. There's still some emotional stretching that's happening for them and for me. I don't think that it is ever going to be safe.

Angie's teaching stretches the limits of her own comfort level; in order to cope with teaching at this level of discomfort, Angie sought out the support and assistance of colleagues or a mentor within the school.

"I felt that it was important that someone knew that I was going to do that difficult lesson that day."

As we will see in the following account, Angie thought that it was important for her to be able to tell someone about her teaching, particularly when she was teaching issues that caused moments of tension for her and her students.

Angie: I felt that it was important that someone knew that I was going to do that lesson that day. If I needed to talk to [someone] about my experience doing it, I could. There is another teacher in the school who actually sat in with me because my mentor teacher was not there that day. She knew I was going to be teaching, she was okay, but she was in a meeting. You need to be able to debrief. You need support. I found that very valuable. I needed her to give me feedback on, "Did I stay calm? How did the kids respond?" To have another pair of eyes in the room . . . . It was just another teacher in the school and not necessarily my mentor teacher or adjunct professor. It was great to have her there. She was not giving me a mark. I told her I was going be doing the lesson and I would like her support. I don't think I could have done it without her. She could support me in what I was saying, too. If I was saying something and the kids were still coming back, she could be supportive and give her point of view, too. Yes, I was a little bit worried about losing control, especially when I started, because classes are pretty wild. I don't think I could have lost control completely. Perhaps they just would've put up a wall and just not want to go there, and just want to keep what they originally thought.

As Angie pointed out, it was important that the person she chose for support and to help her to debrief and reflect on the lesson was a colleague or peer who was not in an evaluative role. Angie needed to talk to someone freely about her vulnerabilities without the fear of being marked negatively.

"I was not worried about parents and how they would react."

Another real concern for Angie was parents' reactions to her lessons with the students. I was quite curious to learn from Angie if the fear of negative reactions from parents was a factor she had considered in teaching the lesson.

Angie: I was not worried about parents and how they would react. I might have thought about it afterwards if I had parents come back, but there was a little bit of fear of parental backlash, especially from some of the more right-wing religious communities that had spoken out against the Toronto Board. They say that this is something that should not be talked about in schools. Because that is a group of people that you're dealing [with], not just one parent. The matter of knowing that the school board is behind what you are doing here because they have a document that supports it, but with not much teeth. The kids can tell when you're vulnerable because they start feeling insecure too. They are not feeling that solidness in you that they are used to and they want that, so they challenge you.

Angie has expressed limited apprehension about parents' reactions to activism in her elementary classroom, and particularly dealing with issues around sexuality. Although the lesson posed a particular challenge to her classroom teaching, she was also aware that this was one area that had the potential to cause further conflict with parents. Teacher candidates' comfort level concerning parental reaction to their teaching of potentially contentious issues was an important consideration. Angie believed that the teacher education program left her unprepared to apply her learning from the faculty of education seminars and course discussions.

"I find myself coming away feeling very tense after some days in our classes here."

Angie indicated that she felt marginalized when her identity was implicated in course discussions of race, class, gender, and sexuality. For example, she felt that, at times, candidates used opportunities during course presentations to raise the level of discussions in course content to further examine certain issues.

> *Angie: I try to take on the homophobia and gender issues. Well, for me, I've lived a very out kind of life and I will refuse to not do that, no matter what kind of things people throw at me. This has been a very receptive group to that. Our presentations on the issues . . . we try to help people feel what it would be like to have to be closeted and gay, and not been able to speak about assembly or home life and so on. But even as we were doing the exercise, I thought the majority of the people—by the way they were speaking—there were some subtle kinds of heterosexism and some subtle homophobia. But, it is not overt. I have not found a lot of overt homophobia within the program.*

It would seem that teacher candidates each approach and experience the program differently and bring different degrees of awareness of issues and commitment to activism. Consequently, as Angie argues, for those teacher candidates who come to the program without certain experiences and backgrounds, the challenge of learning to teach critically might be greater.

> *Angie: It is interesting that in every one of the "isms" [racism, classism, sexism, heterosexism, etc.], there is a lot of tension. I find myself coming away feeling very tense after some days in our classes here. This is just about you [being] constantly bombarded with all these issues. If I look at myself, there are things that we do that were programmed in me when we were very young, and I am finding myself [trying] to rework all the wiring. It is a lot of work and it's exhausting work. . . . People don't have the energy to be with yet another issue because that's all we do all the time. The [issues] are all coming at you. . . . I think [people] feel completely overwhelmed. . . . Because I feel completely overwhelmed myself and I've been dealing with issues for a long time.*

Although Angie brought a great deal of passion and commitment for engaging in social activism, the form and content of curriculum, instruction, and support in the program could potentially facilitate her activism or even work against it. Although she was accepted to the program and later discovered the antiracism or critical philosophy and approach to the program, she was attracted to the types of critical issues that were taken up in her courses.

> *Angie: Well, I didn't know what exactly this program was about, or when I got my acceptance back and there was that questionnaire and it had several diversity issues on the questionnaire. I was accepted to*

three universities and that is why I came here, because of that questionnaire. I thought this is a school that is thinking about these things. And because of my background, I wanted a program like that, because I am constantly in the face of these things. That is why I chose this university. But if someone doesn't know and is thrown into the situation, that would be the ideal person that you want here. You don't want the converted. You want people that have something to learn.

The "converted" that Angie refers to here are those teacher candidates who have themselves confronted oppression or marginalization. Angie alludes to the idea that her lived experiences were an important factor to her engagement in critical activism in the program. However, she believes that the program should work to move the thinking of those who lacked the awareness or the lived experiences of oppression. She believed that the experiences provided in the practicum are ideal for helping those teacher candidates better understand their privilege and provide an environment for them to work through difference.

Angie: I don't know if you can, in one year, change a person's lifetime of thinking. But I think you can plant a seed in a year. I don't think it's enough time for a person to unravel that stuff. [There are] people who had a head start because they have had to unravel those things in the lives. I don't think that you can expect in one year that those people will necessarily be where some people were when they got in. They're going to leave with something.

As Angie suggests, the program attempts to move teacher candidates of varying degrees of awareness and commitments to a point where they will all begin to engage in activism. Some of the consequences of trying to move teacher candidates' thinking through a one-year program pose a certain challenge to teacher education. The movement in teacher candidates' thinking is affected by their lived experiences and personal investments coming into the program, and therefore requires an assessment of individual teacher candidates' experiences, backgrounds, commitments, and needs within the program. The next point illustrates the ways in which the support in the practicum classroom also could affect Angie's attempt at teaching for social justice.

As we have seen, Angie welcomed the program initiatives as a way to actively engage in liberatory, emancipatory practice or change agency. However, although she found herself in a classroom where her supervising teacher was open to such practice, Angie soon realized this type of teaching was difficult and personally taxing. For instance, teaching for social justice involves taking certain risks and engaging in contentious situations. As a result, teacher candidates needed more preparation and support going into those lessons. Continual mentorship and support from peers, school staff, and faculty instructors were important in helping candidates deal with some of the anxieties, fears, vulnerability, and pain in teaching about certain issues, particularly when the candidates' personal or professional identities are called into question.

"We are living difficult lies . . . under a microscope for a year and it's an awful feeling of constantly been watched."

In another instance, Angie spoke about the struggle to make sense of the contradictions of her experiences in the practicum. In the next section, she describes the resulting coping strategies that teacher candidates adopt. In our discussions, Angie coined the term "difficult lies" to describe the pain of living in silence and pretending in order to appease the various potential or perceived evaluators, denying her own beliefs. For teacher candidates like Angie, who are very strongly committed to activism in their classroom, the silence becomes difficult to live with. This is particularly difficult in a program that seeks to open up discussions of social activism, which are shut down in the practicum.

Critical teacher educators need to be more aware of this discourse of teacher candidates living with these "difficult lies" in the program. One way of responding to or addressing this issue is to open up the discussion with teacher candidates about the contradictions and mixed messages they encounter in the program. Teacher educators must be aware of the barriers to critical teaching in the school setting and the possibility of having unsupportive classrooms and mentor teachers. In addition, teacher candidates need time within the program to reflect upon their experiences and to openly engage in group discussions, particularly around issues that might hinder the intents of the program.

Angie was also concerned with receiving negative evaluations and reports in the practicum if she did not adhere to the expectations of the mentor teacher. Although she was aware that her evaluations and grades were supposed to be determined only by her practicum supervisor, she was still apprehensive about potentially offending the participating teacher in the classroom. Her classroom teacher was not responsible for direct evaluation or practicum grading of the teacher candidates. However, Angie was still aware of the power those mentors may have had over her and the types of informal evaluations and discussions that can take place between mentors and the direct evaluators, supervising teachers, or course directors.

> *Angie: I don't feel pressure from the course directors to be equitable in the classroom. I feel it within myself that "Yes, I want to be that way, regardless of whether they are watching me or not." The struggle for me is I want to be that way, I want to plan my lessons that way, I do plan my lessons [that] way, and I am met with a non-receptive mentor teacher who says, "Well, no, we can't talk about that." And I say, "Yes we can. The board [equity policy] says yes we can and we should talk about this issue." That is the person who is grading me, the mentor teacher who is grading me. She tells me this after I have done the lesson. Then, that's where the difficulty is. We are living difficult lies. We are under a microscope for a year and it's an awful feeling of constantly being watched, constantly being graded about what to say, about what you write, how you teach. Once that microscope is gone, I feel a lot freer to be an equitable teacher. But right now I have been put in a powerless position by constantly being watched and graded.*

Angie's concern about living under a microscope in the teacher education program will probably continue into her teaching as a classroom teacher. In these times of accountability, the surveillance continues as teachers need to be continuously evaluated by their school administrators. Angie admitted to being unaware of the continued surveillance she would have to undergo as a teacher. She responded by asking, "When will we be really free to take up the kind of issues we want to?"

Angie also sees the point of conflict in the program centering around the relationship with the mentor teacher and the pressure to please the mentors, particularly when mentors do not support the critical initiatives of the teacher education program. Often, teacher candidates run the risk of developing adversarial relationships with their mentor teachers because of the discontinuity between the mentor teachers' commitments to issues of equity and diversity and the commitment of the teacher candidates. Angie suggests that because mentor teachers play a vital role in the teacher education program, more selective measures should be taken in selecting mentors for the program to make sure that mentors are in agreement with the program's initiatives.

Angie: There needs to be a lot more care in selecting host or mentor teachers. We need someone who has been observed or screened by the faculty and that they feel is a good role model for us teacher candidates. I was very lucky that my second-term placement was amazing. My first-term placement was a disaster.

Angie admits that her current second semester mentor teacher has been quite supportive of her effort to be more equitable and inclusive in her lessons. However, she recalls feeling frustrated with some of the difficulties she experienced in the first semester and by her observations of, and discussions with, other teacher candidates in her practicum school.

Some Suggestions for Teacher Education

I propose that one central theme to find in the accounts of Angie's experiences in her teacher education program and her responses to the program is her emerging philosophy about teaching for social justice and social activism. How Angie responded to the various, often contradictory, messages about equity and social justice/activism discourse that she received (both in the course work and in her practicum school) offers insights into the ways she began to formulate her own theories about teaching critically. At the beginning of the study, Angie was frustrated by the restrictive environment in which she tried to integrate issues of social difference into the curriculum. In order to cope with the uncertainties of adopting an inclusionary practice, Angie began to adopt various coping strategies: During our interview sessions and online discussions, Angie sought support from her peers in the program, from faculty members, and from other supportive teachers in the school in order to refine and reformulate her own thinking. Such decisions yield important implications for teacher education programs. Teacher candidates need more time in the program to collectively work in cohort groups and reflect on, make sense of, and formulate their teacher identities.

Perhaps an important missing element in critical teacher education is acknowledging the existence of tensions and contradictions. Teacher educators need first to understand that the process of negotiating tensions in learning to teach involves uncertainty, rationalizing, and compromise (Dudley-Marling, 1997) before they can begin to help their teacher candidates to negotiate these tensions. Levine-Rasky (1998) argues that teacher candidates need to understand that teaching is a continual process of coming to terms with tensions and living with unresolved issues, or developing a rationale for accepting the prevailing incongruencies and consequences in teaching. Hartnett and Carr (1995) suggest that it is also important that teachers start grappling with complex moral and political issues at the initial stages of learning to teach. For example, an essential starting point should be helping teacher candidates examine the limitations of their own education and experiences, and question the way these limits may negatively affect other groups in society. As mentioned earlier, teacher candidates' knowledge, experiences, and backgrounds are sometimes in conflict with those of the students they teach. The teacher education program should help them to start examining their own location in the classroom and how this might affect the children.

Summary and Conclusion

For teacher candidates, teaching about sexuality can mean learning how and when to attempt to teach critically in their mentor's classroom. As we have seen from Angie's experiences, she sought support from sympathetic mentors and she learned to compromise in favor of their teaching approach, holding off on teaching critically in order to appease conservative mentors. She felt that, at times, she was being discouraged from taking a critical approach to her teaching. She even feared that her mentors and evaluators might penalize her in those situations and that this might inhibit her chances of being evaluated fairly. Angie felt discouraged from employing activism in her teaching, and so she waited until she completed the program and became a classroom teacher before she could begin to teach critically. It became apparent that open discussion and support needed to be an important element of the teacher education program. Providing space for Angie to prepare for her lessons and to debrief afterwards might help her to resolve some of the inherent conflicts in her attempts to confront deep personal issues in the program. Consequently, these conflicts will become the starting point to help Angie reframe her thinking within the program.

References

Dudley-Marling, C. (1997). *Living with uncertainty: The messy reality of classroom practice.* Portsmouth, NH: Heinemann.

Flynn Foyn, S. (1998). A troika of programs: African Nova Scotian education at Dalhousie University. In V. D'Oyley & C. E. James (Eds.), *Re/visioning: Canadian perspectives on the education of Africans in the late 20th century* (pp. 178-199). Toronto: Captus Press.

Giroux, H., & McLaren, P. (1986). Teacher education and the politics of engagement: The case for democratic schooling. *Harvard Educational Review, 56*(3), 213-238.

Gresson, A. (1997). Identity, class, and teacher education: The persistence of "class effects" in the classroom. *The Review of Education/Pedagogy/Cultural Studies, 19*(4), 335-348.

Hartnett, A., & Carr, W. (1995). Education, teacher development and the struggle for democracy. In J. Smyth (Ed.), *Critical discourses on teacher development* (pp. 39-53). Toronto: OISE Press.

Howard, G. (1999). *We can't teach what we don't know: White teachers, multicultural schools.* New York: Teachers College Press.

Jakubowski, L., & Visano, L. (2002). *Teaching controversy.* Halifax, NS: Fernwood Publishing.

James, C. E. (1994). *"Access students": Experiences of racial minorities in a Canadian University.* Paper presented at the Society for Research into Higher Education's Annual Conference, 1994—The Student Experience, at the University of York, York, England.

James, C. E. (1995). "Reverse racism": Students' responses to equity programs. *Journal of Professional Studies, 3*(1), 48-54.

James, C. E. (1997). Contradictory tensions in the experiences of African Canadian in a faculty of education with an access program. *Canadian Journal of Education, 22*(2), 158-174.

James, C. E., & Mannette, J. (2000). Rethinking access: The challenge of living with difficulty knowledge. In G. Dei & A. Calliste (Eds.), *Power, knowledge and anti-racism education: A critical reader.* Halifax, NS: Fernwood Publishing.

Lam, C. (1996). The green teacher. In D. Thiessen, N. Bascia, & I. Goodson (Eds.), *Making a difference about difference: The lives and careers of racial minority immigrant teachers.* Toronto: Garamond Press.

Levine-Rasky, C. (1998). Teacher candidates and the negotiation of social difference. *British Journal of Sociology of Education, 19*(1), 89-112.

Sears, J. T. (1994). Challenges for educators: Lesbian, gay and bisexual families. *High School Journal, 77*(2), 138-156.

Shapson, S. (1994). Emerging images for teacher preparation. In V. D'Oyley (Ed.), *Innovations in black education in Canada.* Toronto: Umbrella Press.

Solomon, R. P. (1995). Why to teach from a multicultural and anti-racist perspective? *Race, Gender & Class, 2*(3), 49-66.

Solomon, R. P. (1996). Creating an opportunity structure for blacks and other teachers of colour. In K. S. Brathwaite & C. E. James (Eds.), *Educating African Canadians* (pp. 216-233). Toronto: James Lorimer.

Solomon, R. P. (1998). Reconstucting teacher education for educational equity and diversity. *Caribbean Journal of Education, 19*(1), 31-51.

Solomon, R. P. (2000). Exploring cross-race dyad partnerships in learning to teach. *Teachers College Record, 102*(6), 953-979.

Solomon, R. P., & Allen, A. (2001). The struggle for equity, diversity and social justice in teacher education. In J. P. Portelli & R. P. Solomon (Eds.), *The erosion of democracy in education critque to possibilities* (pp. 217-244).

Calgary: Detselig.

Solomon, R. P., & Levine-Rasky, C. (1996a). When principle meets practice: Teachers' contradictory responses to antiracist education. *Alberta Journal of Education, 42*(1), 19-33.

Solomon, P., & Levine-Rasky, C. (1996b). Transforming teacher education for an antiracism pedagogy. *CRSA/ RCSA,* 33.3.

Solomon, R. P., & Rezai-Rashti, G. (1997). *School-university partnership in teacher education for educational equity and diversity.* A paper presented at the Canadian Society for the Study of Education Conference. St. Johns, Newfoundland.

Yeo, F. (1997). *A vested interest in failure: Teacher preparation and inner-city schools.* New York: Garland Publishing.

LESSONS FOR ELEMENTARY TEACHER EDUCATORS: A CONVERSATION WITH GAY AND LESBIAN TEACHERS

April Whatley Bedford

*A*s you read this chapter, reflect on the messages you might send to students in your classroom through your language, choice of instructional materials, and actions about what you consider "gender-appropriate" behavior. How do you respond to incidents of teasing and/or bullying related to gendered behaviors involving students? Did your teacher education program address issues of sexual orientation? If so, how? Have you participated in any professional development focusing on sexual orientation? How do you feel about this? How do you involve the families of the students you teach in their children's education? What is your comfort level in working with family members in general and nontraditional families in particular? At what age or grade level do you believe teachers should begin discussing issues of gender orientation with students? Why? Do you discuss issues of gender orientation with the students you teach? Why or why not? Are you aware of any colleagues with whom you teach who are GLBT? If so, how open are they about their sexual orientation in the school setting?

Snapshot One: In a casual conversation with my son's 7th-grade teacher, she mentions her concern that the children at the K-8 parochial school where she teaches call each other "gay," "fairy," "fag," and "queer" as the most degrading insults they can think of. She is sure that the younger children don't know what these words mean but recognize them as powerful put-downs. She also voices her fear that the parents of these students who hold strong homophobic views themselves would not be upset knowing that their children make such remarks to other children who behave in ways not considered gender-appropriate.

Snapshot Two: When teaching a graduate class in elementary social studies methods and discussing a variety of family structures, a teacher with 20 years of teaching experience loudly proclaims that she would never be able to accept a student with gay or lesbian parents and that she would have no choice but to tell such a child that, according to the teachings of the Bible, his family's lifestyle is wrong. While discussing my distress about this situation with teacher educator colleagues, a few confide that they do not bring up issues of sexual orientation in their college courses because they do not want to deal with their students' hostility.

Snapshot Three: While observing a preschool classroom during the fall of a recent school year, I notice a 4-year-old boy dressing up in a princess costume during learning center time and dancing around the room with a wand, asking all of the other children whether he looks pretty. His teacher admits to me that this behavior makes her uncomfortable and she has tried to discourage it, but to no avail. When I visit the classroom again six months later, the same boy is still as happily engaged in the same dress-up behavior as before; this time, however, the teacher smilingly tells me that the entire classroom community has realized how much joy this imaginary play brings the child, and they support it.

These opening snapshots have all happened to me, a teacher educator, during the last five years. As each event occurred, I became more and more convinced that I needed to do a better job of addressing issues of sexual orientation in the classes I teach to preservice and inservice teachers. By all accounts, relatively little research has been conducted with elementary or preschool educators investigating how they address issues of sexual orientation in the classroom. The little research that does exist suggests that while teachers often express the belief that such issues should be addressed with young children, they rarely actually do so, for a variety of reasons, including religious beliefs, protecting childhood "innocence," and equating discussions of gender difference with discussions of sex (Colleary, 1999; Robinson, 2002). My own experience as a teacher educator for the past eight years presents a more disturbing picture. Instead of expressing openness, many of the preservice and inservice teachers I have taught exhibited anger, hostility, and intolerance when I broached the topic of sexual orientation in my elementary methods classes. Given these two situations—openness but inaction, as described in research findings, and the hostility and intolerance experienced in my own classroom—I became curious about how gay and lesbian elementary teachers, in particular, address issues of gender and sexual orientation in their classrooms.

Beyond my personal feelings, other rationales exist for undertaking a study of gay and lesbian elementary teachers. As Bickmore (1999) points out, "Elementary schools are places where young people's identities are formed, as individuals and as citizens," and "Elementary teachers have the capacity to help children learn how to share public spaces with people similar to, and different from, themselves" (p. 15). Obviously, elementary teachers can do much to shape how *all* children will grow up feeling about sexual difference. Like Colleary (1999), I believe in "the power of teachers' voices to increase our understanding" (p. 159) of issues of sexual diversity in elementary education; gay and lesbian elementary teachers, in particular, are a group whose voices have not often been heard. My hopes for this study were to learn from lesbian and gay elementary educators themselves about what is happening in their own classrooms and what their hopes are for elementary education, so that I can better prepare future teachers to reduce prejudice in their elementary classrooms.

Participants and Methodology

For this chapter, I interviewed two self-identified lesbian and two gay male elementary teachers about their classroom experiences. Finding teachers to interview proved more problematic than I first anticipated. I began by asking colleagues around the country if they were acquainted with any gay and lesbian elementary teachers who might be willing to be interviewed by me. While teacher educators from Georgia to Arizona to Michigan all agreed to ask teachers they knew to participate in the study, few responded positively. This experience was, to me, indicative of the fear many elementary teachers feel toward talking openly about their sexuality. Although I initially hoped to interview elementary classroom teachers solely, I widened my search somewhat to include teachers who had some elementary teaching experience; two are now physical education teachers rather than classroom teachers, one in a middle school. I finally found the four teachers who did actually talk with me through a variety of ways: one is a former student of mine, one is a teacher I met at an academic conference, one is a personal friend, and one I met through an introduction from a colleague. Because I promised them strict confidentiality, I assigned each participant a pseudonym and I will not describe where they live or teach in great detail. One participant lives in the Midwest, one in the Southeast, one in the Southwest, and one in the Deep South region of the United States.

Based on my own past teaching experiences and my reading of the current, albeit limited, research on sexual orientation issues in early childhood and elementary classrooms, I constructed an interview protocol that included open-ended questions focusing on areas I found particularly interesting. From my reading, I learned of a variety of strategies recommended by education researchers for opening up safe classroom spaces for sexually diverse teachers, students, and families. However, I also learned that these strategies were not actually being put into practice in many instances. The studies, strategies, and statistics described in the literature, coupled with my own experiences as a teacher educator, led me to investigate the following areas:

- Memories of elementary school experiences regarding gender
- Teasing and name-calling related to gender
- Inclusion of sexual orientation in the participant's teacher education program
- Teacher responsiveness to all families, including gay, lesbian, bisexual, and transgendered parents
- Inclusion of issues of sexual orientation in curriculum, instruction, and classroom materials
- Whether or not the teacher is "out" in the school setting and how this affects her/his teaching, relationships with colleagues, administrators, students, and parents, and overall career satisfaction
- Recommendations for teacher education programs on ways to prepare teachers for including issues of sexual orientation in their classrooms.

I have attempted to synthesize my readings in the seven areas I explored in my interviews and to add the voices of my participants, as well as my own voice, to the conversation of educators interested in exploring issues of sexual identity in elementary schools.

Teachers' Elementary School Memories

According to previous studies, teachers of young children typically believe that the children whom they teach are not sexual beings and that defining sexual identity prior to adolescence is unlikely, if not impossible (Casper, Cuffaro, Schultz, Silin, & Wickens, 1996; Robinson, 2002). However, in one study of 200 young people living in Chicago, most recalled same-sex attractions prior to their tenth birthdays, and some were aware of their identities as gay or lesbian even as early as age 4 or 5 (Herdt & Boxer, 1993). Clearly, the age of awareness of sexual orientation requires further study, but the research that has already been conducted demonstrates that teachers at all of the elementary grades need to realize that the children they teach can, and do, experience sexual feelings, regardless of how uncomfortable teachers may be in acknowledging this fact.

While I did not specifically ask the participants in this study the ages at which they first remember being aware of their same-sex attractions, I asked them a more general question: "What are your memories of elementary school experiences regarding gender?" They responded with wide-ranging descriptions of events that occurred both in and out of school during their elementary years. Brandon immediately responded that he does not remember having any male teachers until he was in middle school. He commented that, being a male elementary teacher himself, he has given this issue a lot of thought, because he believes that the sexuality of male elementary teachers is often questioned. None of the other participants mentioned their elementary teachers.

Three of the four participants reported forming friendships with children of the opposite sex during their elementary days. Robin commented, "I was teased a bit in 5th grade for playing mostly with the boys." Both Brandon and Joe described having more female friends than male in elementary school, getting along better with girls, and feeling more at ease around them. Brandon shared the following vignette:

> At home, I had my younger sister (one year younger), and I remember letting loose at home more and doing things I would never do at school or out in public. For example, we would play songs like "Girls Just Wanna Have Fun" or "Let's Hear It for the Boy," and we would take turns lip-syncing, and I would always pick a girl's song.

The same three participants demonstrated an awareness of which of their behaviors were considered gender appropriate during their childhood years, and they remember experiencing negative consequences when their behaviors did not match the expected norms. Like Brandon, Joe enjoyed creative role-playing, as he described in the following scene:

> I seemed to be overly dramatic when I was younger and gravitated more to the creative play type of activities that most of the boys avoided. I remember a shed that we used to have in our yard when I was in 6th grade, and we would do a whole reenactment of The Wizard of Oz with me playing the male role of Dorothy and all of the neighborhood kids joined right in.

Both men also have been interested in cheerleading throughout their lives, and this interest led to mixed reactions from others. Joe described in detail his "obsession" with cheerleading, including watching the cheerleaders at college football games through binoculars when he was a young boy—"I think my father thought I liked looking at cute girls, so that is probably why he thought nothing of it." Both Joe and Brandon cheered in high school and college; Brandon went on to coach cheerleading camps and judge cheerleading competitions. Joe tried playing Little League baseball and football in elementary school and Brandon played tennis competitively, but both men described cheerleading as the sport in which they experienced the most success.

Both men remembered receiving praise as well as taunts for their cheerleading abilities as well as teasing for their other behaviors that were deemed gender-inappropriate. Brandon remembers being teased every day in 5th grade and being called a sissy by a boy who was a better soccer player than he; he also described himself as "very skinny" and "not athletic" in middle school and again being called a sissy by other boys. Joe feels that his gender-atypical behavior, and particularly his interests in cheerleading, made his parents "a little uneasy."

Joe also went on to describe his adult conversation with his sister about how she protected him from teasing:

> A big memory I have is in talking with my sister, who is 11 months younger than me. She told me that she would stand up for me when others were cruel. I think she did a good job of shielding me because my only memories of being bullied were in junior high . . . by two creepy twin brothers. That was the first time I had heard the word "queer" and had no idea what it meant, but I knew it had to be terrible or something. It was probably the most depressing time of my life, and if it weren't for being the oldest of eight siblings, I am not sure if I would have made it through. It was the idea of having younger brothers and sisters who idolized me that kept my chin up. . . . I think the words they used scared me and I didn't want my parents or family to find out.

Conversely, Robin was both praised and ridiculed for being interested in and good at more typically male-dominated sports. In elementary school, she remembers sometimes being teased by other children for playing baseball, kickball, and tackle football. However, she recalled, "I was praised often for being athletic by my PE teacher and many of my teachers—with the addition of, 'for a girl'."

Unlike the other participants, Cali stated, "I really do not have too many memories of my elementary school experiences in regard to gender." She added, "I don't remember being told I can't do anything because I am a girl." Robin, however, became aware that she had violated an expectation of gender behavior when she was "scolded by a neighbor mom for not wearing a shirt in 3rd grade." Joe remembers that, "The roles of gender didn't seem to matter until I reached the 4th grade and the differences became quite apparent." Brandon, on the other hand, seemed to always be aware of which behaviors were considered gender-appropriate and which weren't, and he associated these with a public/private dichotomy. For example, the lip-syncing play in which he engaged at home with his sister was something he would never have performed anywhere else, as he related:

In school, I did much better being gender-appropriate. I don't know how I learned that, where I learned that, but I was always very conscious of who was around, from a very early age. But also, I was a different kid at home—I knew how to act in public.

Teasing and Name-calling

As I have already mentioned, the name-calling and teasing related to sexual orientation occurring at my son's school was one of the initial events that led to the present study. Earlier researchers have found that such teasing is ubiquitous in elementary schools (King & Schneider, 1999); that most of even the youngest children in elementary schools have heard words like "gay" used as taunts or put-downs (Bickmore, 1999); and that, in particular, most males who grew up gay remember childhood as a time of taunting (Kissen, 1999). The experiences of the four participants in the present study lend support to these prior findings.

According to King and Schneider (1999), "The instance of abusive talk based on presumed sexual orientation in schools is astoundingly common. The follow-up and correction by teachers who hear such talk is troublingly rare" (p. 126). These researchers go on to suggest that simply punishing such derogatory language is not enough. While punishing such language might silence it, the victims of this verbal abuse still suffer. Instead, advocates of including issues of sexual orientation in the elementary school recommend openly addressing instances of verbal bullying. Cahill and Theilheimer (1999) state that if teachers hear students use "homophobic slurs," behavior that should be in violation of the classroom rules, then teachers should:

Hold individual or community meetings that engage children in solving the problems at the root of the behavior. Children may be repeating homophobic comments with an understanding of their power, but not of their meaning. Good teaching practice unpacks the meaning of children's comments with the children and recognizes the power of which children, too, are aware. (p. 45)

Although this is undeniably difficult work, teachers must not tolerate taunts about less-visible but equally valid components of identity like sexuality, just as they would not tolerate teasing or name-calling based on race or religion (Kissen, 1999).

Based on these findings from previous studies, I asked each of the four participants how they addressed issues of teasing and name-calling as lesbian or gay teachers in their own classrooms. Robin could not remember hearing students engage in such talk. She elaborated:

The worst gender-related problem I have had at my school has been not wanting a particular girl in a cooperative group because she is a girl. I go into my lecture about how everyone is different and we must get along with everyone because that is real life.

Joe, however, has witnessed his 4th-grade students tease each other using derogatory terms related to sexual orientation. He stated:

I address name-calling as an act of a bully and deal with it accordingly. . . . I will not tolerate it and I think myself having experienced it makes me more sensitive to protecting those who won't or are unable to [protect themselves]. I teach my students to respect differences and that means we accept everyone.

He went on to describe an instance that had occurred just before our interview while a substitute teacher was present in his classroom. Since the substitute did not address the occurrence as Joe would have, he added, "I am addressing it in our community meeting."

Brandon discussed how he has witnessed teasing and name-calling related to sexual orientation at his school, especially since he began teaching 4th grade. Although he stated that he didn't hear as much of this verbal behavior while he was teaching 1st grade, Brandon added, "Actually, I did hear the word 'faggot,' but they [the students] didn't know what it meant when I questioned them about it." When Brandon does hear this type of unacceptable language, he always addresses it, questions students about their understandings of the meanings of the words they are using, and helps the children he teaches examine the effects of their words.

He also described an incident during the last school year when, in addition to discovering an episode of written teasing of particular children, he himself was the object of name-calling by a group of students at his school. Children at his school who attended the after-school program there wrote and distributed a newsletter titled *ASP Gossip News,* in which they published a list of children they labeled as "gayfer" or "faggot." When a parent who was very upset that her own daughter was one of the writers of this publication brought it to the attention of teachers and school administrators, they conducted an investigation. Students who were questioned admitted to calling Brandon names for once wearing a pink shirt to school and for wearing what they termed "short shorts" when he was running on the school track after school. All of the students involved were 5th-graders. Since this happened during Brandon's first year at the school, while teaching 4th grade, none of the children involved had been his own students. Brandon, the only male adult employee of the school, felt fully supported by his principal in not tolerating such remarks, and he addressed the incident with his own students in class meetings. Since then, no further situations have arisen, to his knowledge.

Cali, too, feels that she herself has been a target of students' teasing. When she was teaching elementary school, several students asked her if she was a boy or a girl. She responded:

I would just answer their question. When it became clear they were asking it in a teasing way, like the same kids asking the same question every day, I would tell them they already know the answer to the question and a person might think you were teasing when you ask the same question over and over again. They really didn't want me to have my feelings hurt, so they would apologize.

Like the other participants, Cali never lets gender-related teasing go unchallenged. Unlike Robin, she has witnessed students being "very cruel" to one another. She handles these situations in the following way:

I usually deal with name-calling and teasing one-on-one. I talk with the student about the impact words can have on a person. Usually, if you talk to students intelligently, with respect, they respond. It is important to be consistent and not let anything slide by. I often hear students say, "that's gay" or "this is gay." If I hear that, I just say that is not an appropriate use of the word and to choose a word that makes sense, like "I don't like this" or something like that.

In addition to talking with the perpetrators of teasing and name-calling, Cali also addresses the situation with victims of such incidents. She described the following:

When students are the receivers of the name-calling or bullying, I usually meet with them individually and tell them that people tease and make fun of us because they are feeling bad about themselves and that usually the name-calling has nothing to do with them. In extreme cases, I will call parents.

Issues of Sexual Orientation in Teacher Education Programs

The four participants in this study all attended teacher preparation programs within the past two decades, with Joe's college attendance in the early 1980s being the most removed and Brandon's in the late 1990s being the most recent. In answer to the question of how, or if, issues of sexual orientation were addressed in their teacher education programs, Robin, Brandon, and Joe all affirmed that such issues were never discussed. While not speaking directly about his teacher preparation program but about the university he attended in general, Joe did add that he had observed some improvement recently:

I happened to go back to campus last fall and was amazed that in the same building where I had had my teaching courses were now offices for diversity for gay/lesbian students and faculty. Unfortunately, it was a Saturday and all the offices were closed, but man, I wanted to just shake their hands and say, "It's about time." We had no outreach for gays and lesbians on the campus, so it was a pretty underground, isolating experience when I did my undergraduate work.

Cali was the only participant who remembers issues of sexual orientation being mentioned at all in any of her teacher preparation classes. She stated:

In my teacher education program, I took a couple classes on diversity. In my opinion, it was more a class in being politically correct. "Exceptional People" and "Teaching Diverse Populations" were both generic diversity classes that brushed upon the topic of sexual orientation.

Responsiveness to GLBT Families

According to Hulsebosch, Koerner, and Ryan (1999), while "elementary teachers have become increasingly aware of the need to respond to the diversity of their students," they "do not necessarily consider sexual orientation as part of that diversity" (p. 183). There are currently an estimated 6 to 14 million children who have gay or lesbian parents; this is a sizeable population that many preservice and inservice teachers may not know exists. Because they believe that "even teachers who are passionately committed to issues of inclusion and social justice in elementary classrooms are uncertain when encountering lesbian- or gay-headed families in their classrooms" (p. 183), Hulsebosch, Koerner, and Ryan interviewed five elementary teachers and one principal who had been identified by lesbian parents as being particularly "responsive" to their children. In their study, they found that these educators really did nothing more than treat lesbian-headed families kindly or "normally," and they "protected" the children in these families by not making their family structures visible to the other students in the classroom. Both the researchers and I were disappointed by these findings. On the other hand, Cahill and Theilheimer (1999) caution that not all gay or lesbian parents want to be seen as "resources" by teachers and that teachers should do their best to get to know all families and be sensitive to their individual needs. To understand more about this complex issue, I asked the four teachers I interviewed about their own responsiveness to gay, lesbian, bisexual, or transgendered families. This was a question to which they all seemed eager to respond.

Brandon stated, "One 1st-grader I taught had a parent I'm pretty sure was a lesbian, but neither the mother nor the child ever told me. I didn't reach out to her in any way." While he didn't treat this parent any differently than any other parent, which might have been what the parent wanted, he indicated that he wished she had confided in him. He was hesitant to be the one to broach the subject, though. Robin asserted, "I do not have any [g/l/b/t parents] at my school that I am aware of. I am always hoping I will!"

Joe discussed how all families need teachers who are responsive to their needs:

I would say I am pretty responsive to the needs of all parents. I have yet in my teaching career had a parent come to say to me that they are gay. I have tried to talk some of my gay friends who are parents into sending their children to our school. We are pretty diverse and support parents who are going through some gut-wrenching times.

Cali is the only teacher I interviewed who knows for certain that the parents of two of her students are lesbians. She discussed speaking with both mothers of a 6th-grade boy who was having a problem with another student and of speaking with the nonbiological mother of a girl who had been injured in PE class. In both of these conversations, she stated, "I treated them just as I would any other parent." Like all the educators I interviewed, Cali believes that "it is important to treat all families with respect. . . . Many kids today live in nontraditional families, whether it is with a grandparent, aunt, or two mothers; it is important to be sensitive and not make any assumptions."

Including Sexual Orientation in the Classroom

For many educators, the goal of including issues of sexual orientation in elementary curriculum, instruction, and classroom materials is to challenge the assumption that all children, adults, and families are heterosexual "until proved otherwise" (Cahill & Theilheimer, 1999, p. 41). As Bickmore (1999) points out, "The first reason to discuss sexuality in elementary school is that it is already present in students' lives" (p. 15). Yet, this is not easy. Colleary (1999) states:

Of all the complicated discourses that take place (or don't take place) each day in schools between teacher and teacher, teacher and student, student and student, teacher and parent, the rare discussion around sexuality of any kind or homosexuality in particular is usually a very uncomfortable and sometimes frightening one. It is, on one level, so much easier to remain silent rather than face the discomfort. (p. 158)

I asked the teachers I interviewed how (or if) they include issues of sexual orientation in their curriculum, instruction, and classroom materials. Both Robin and Cali described their roles as elementary and middle school teachers of health and physical education. Robin indicated that she would be unable to broach such issues unless they were part of the mandated curriculum. She stated, "My district just adopted a set of health books for the elementary schools, and there is no mention of sexual orientation in them." Cali said, "The only way I have included issues of sexual orientation is through a sex ed/STD unit. However, that was only one component [of the unit]."

Cali went on to discuss what she called the "informal curriculum" with the following example:

One of my students who has a gay mother once got upset in a game. He didn't like his team. He announced to his team, "Man, this game is gayer than my moms." It was actually pretty funny and bold. It was interesting to see the students' reactions. After class, one of his teammates asked me what he meant. I told him that families come in all shapes and sizes and if he was really curious, he should ask Sam (the boy).

Both Brandon and Joe seem to address issues of difference, in general, rather than overtly focusing on issues of sexual orientation. Brandon stated:

I don't specifically do things like reading books with two moms or two dads. But I do on purpose, intentionally, sneak books in that get kids to look at things differently, like a guy dancing or a girl playing ball. I let the kids know that I take ballroom dancing and that I was a cheerleader.

He did state that he "couldn't" explicitly include issues of sexual orientation in classroom curriculum, instruction, or materials, although he said:

I would love to be able to. I think I would be doing a good thing. I honestly think the principal would back me up, but I wouldn't attempt it because I think I would be putting myself in danger because of parents' reactions. If I were a heterosexual male, I would do it.

Like Brandon, Joe also mentioned books when asked this question. He responded:

I don't actively seek out books that deal specifically with gender or sexual identity issues. I focus more on developing a curriculum that reflects the diversity of our world and the need to understand and not be judgmental when it comes to looking at people.

He went on to describe the reactions of another teacher to discussing issues of sexual orientation with elementary students:

She was so adamant in her argument that it made me realize how touchy this subject was or is for many people. I think in the years ahead it won't be such a big deal, but it seems to strike a raw nerve with many people.

To Be or Not To Be Out: Teachers Out at School

As I discovered from attempting to find teachers to interview for this study, coming out in the school setting can be a dangerous decision for gay and lesbian teachers to make. This may be truer for male elementary teachers than for female teachers or male secondary teachers. King (1997) identifies three reasons that male elementary teachers may be reluctant to reveal their sexual orientation:

> First, elementary teachers are constructed as selfless and gay men as self-indulgent. Second, elementary teachers are seen as virginal and gay men as promiscuous and sybaritic. Third, elementary teachers are seen as nurturing and gay men as predatory. (p. 245)

The four teachers I interviewed expressed a range of experiences with regard to this particular question and had a lot to say in response. Brandon, the youngest of the participants, seemed to support the arguments made by King. He stated:

> *I'm out to certain people. In my school, I'm out to four people, other teachers, three of whom were at my previous school. I'm also out to their spouses (all hetero) who are also all educators or administrators. No administrators or parents. At my previous school, I was out to an administrator because she was a lesbian.*

Brandon added that in his school district, "there's no policy protecting us [gay teachers]," while a nearby urban district does have such a policy. "I don't know why they have one, being more minority and low-income," he added. "I can't imagine who lobbied for it."

Brandon definitely feels he has to keep his sexual orientation a secret to keep his job and also "just to keep it comfortable." His long-term partner, a teacher in another district, never goes to school functions; Brandon does go to functions at his partner's school, where they are known as a couple. When I asked about whether he would be more satisfied in his career if he were able to be out at school, he elaborated:

> *I don't know what it would be like to be able to do that. I'm extremely happy teaching. It's hard sometimes when I'm in a group setting and people are sharing what they did over the weekend and I can't join in that conversation. It does take extra effort to always be conscious of keeping it a secret. I know if I want to do what I want to do for a living, I have to make sacrifices. I know I should be able to be out, and I think I would have a completely different life, on a different level.*

When I asked him specifically how he thinks his life would be different, Brandon conjectured, "I wouldn't have to worry about kids or parents asking me if I have a girlfriend or if I'm married." When I asked what he thought parents assumed about his sexuality, he responded that some probably never think about it, some probably think he's gay and don't care, and some parents probably think he's gay and have a problem with it. While, to his knowledge, no parent has ever openly expressed an objection to Brandon's perceived sexual orientation, one father told the principal that Brandon "wasn't masculine enough to deal with his son."

Cali has mixed feelings about disclosing her sexual orientation at school. She said:

> *I am in my third year teaching at my current school. I am basically out to most of my colleagues and my administration. It was a slow process that occurred as I felt comfortable and after I proved myself to my administra-*

tion. I am the only female PE teacher at a middle school of approximately 1,000 students. Therefore, I am in charge of the girls' locker room as well as my classes. I was concerned about coming out because of the locker room liability.

She continued, "My school and colleagues are very supportive. My partner attends out-of-school social functions and is welcomed among most. The teachers who may have any negative feelings keep them to themselves."

When I asked her about students, however, her responses were different. She said, "I am not out to my students. I feel that teachers should keep their personal lives personal. I know that many students may be suspicious or curious." A part of her wishes that she could be more open with her students. She stated:

Middle school is the time when students really first start dealing with emotions associated with sexual orientation. Sometimes, I feel that it would be nice if students had a positive gay role model, someone they can go to when they are trying to figure things out. But in our current social climate, I am not comfortable being that person.

Cali went on to describe an incident with two middle school students who "liked each other," but one was uncomfortable with making their relationship public. Cali feels that "they could have benefited from having someone to talk to, but I did not come out to them. It was too scary."

Robin expressed similar sentiments. She stated, "I am out to my school co-workers but not to students. . . . I am out to only two sets of parents." She feels that "being out at school does not affect my teaching or my relationships with my administrators." She did add that since her principal sent an E-mail to the school faculty in remembrance of her partner's mother's death, "I noticed several teachers have kept their distance and several other teachers have brought up 'gender/gay' issues more frequently to me." Overall, she stated, "I feel very satisfied being out at work and do not worry about how my sexuality may affect my career."

Of the four teachers I interviewed, Joe is the most open about his sexuality in his school environment. He stated:

I am very fortunate to be in a school where I can be out. I am not the type of person that flies the rainbow flag in the classroom, but I do not back away when someone asks me about my marital status. My partner will attend school functions with me and it is only the new students to our school who ask if I have a girlfriend. [I respond] "Yes, she is six feet tall and hairy . . . hee hee."

Joe added that he has received no negative responses from school staff, but they have expressed curiosity and asked questions about his sexuality. He also described a positive encounter with a parent:

I even had parents of a kindergarten student come up to me last year who said how glad they were that I was here at [our school]. They were noticing that their son was showing gay traits . . . singing and dancing to show tunes . . . and asking mom and dad if boys can marry boys in our state. They are pretty open-minded parents and answered his question quite honestly . . . go to Massachusetts.

However, Joe also recounted a negative experience earlier in his teaching career:

I was hired as a 5th-grade math teacher in [a different school district] around 1993. My first year, I had excellent evaluations. The second year, same principal, my first semester evaluation was the complete opposite. It read that I had no idea what I was doing and was the worst teacher to ever work in her building. This was my seventh year of teaching. I was tenured in my previous school in my second year. I was totally taken aback and proceeded to ask her if she wanted me to leave. She said that would probably be best, so being the dramatic person that I am, I said, "Fine. I will be gone in two weeks." This was right before Christmas break. She thought I would stay for the end of the year. The students were devastated and even threw me a party and collected cash because they knew I would be unemployed. I ended up taking off six years and worked a variety of customer service positions. . . . The next year after I departed, I was in a conversation with a friend who had said that he knew my former principal. During the time I was there she was taking continuing ed classes with my friend and had confided in him that she suspected she had a gay teacher and wanted to know how to handle it. It then dawned on me why this all happened, because I [had been] totally clueless. I also was deeply offended that my friend didn't offer any advice to her that would have saved my job. He is a gay principal. So this was my first experience with the whole gay discrimination. . . . It took a long time to get over the anger I felt when I would just see her smug face. The fact that she wasn't honest with the real reason and leading me to believe that I was not a good teacher is something that is hard to forgive.

Recommendations for Teacher Educators

The current literature includes a number of recommendations for including issues of sexual orientation in teacher education classes, many of which formed the basis for the questions I asked the teachers. As a teacher educator myself, I was particularly interested in what recommendations these lesbian and gay teachers would make for programs like the one in which I teach.

Robin offered few suggestions, although she does believe that issues of sexual orientation should be raised in teacher preparation programs. She mentioned a specific documentary, *Middle School Confessions*, that she feels "would be beneficial for all ages." Cali communicated stronger opinions when she said:

Overall, I think teacher education programs fail future teachers by not dealing with the realities of education. We don't have a perfect system. There are many flaws that future teachers are not made aware of. I think future teachers should be prepared to deal with nontraditional families and students who are struggling with their sexual orientation. Future teachers should be made aware of the informal curriculum that happens in the classroom. Often times, that has a bigger impact than the formal curriculum. I also think that curriculum should be changed to include issues of sexuality and gender identity.

Although Robin teaches health and physical education herself, she added, "I think the easiest ways to include these issues are through literature and history."

Brandon mentioned the oft-cited disconnect between teacher education programs and "real world" school environments. He said:

School districts have to change first. It [sexual orientation] needs to be put into the curriculum. We can talk to students in teacher ed programs about it, but why, if they can't do anything about it when they're actually teaching?

When I asked him where in the elementary curriculum he thought issues of sexual orientation would best fit, he stated, "Sex ed starts in 5th grade at my school—a two-week course. That would be a great place to put it into the curriculum." He added, "Even if it came from a counselor, it would be a great start, but it doesn't happen there."

When I asked Brandon about specific places in the teacher preparation program to discuss issues of sexual orientation, he first mentioned children's literature. He added, "Almost any teacher ed class, because we would always look at so many different topics from different perspectives." Remembering his own teacher education program, he said, "When we looked at gender, sexual orientation was never mentioned."

Finally, Joe offered advice directly to teacher education faculty:

I think the biggest recommendation I can have for a teacher ed faculty member is to be supportive of [a gay] student, no matter if you agree or disagree with being gay. These students need someone they can talk to and [who they] know . . . will care for them. Don't push the subject away, and stand up for these kids when they are being belittled or bullied [in the college classroom]. I recently talked to a 23-year-old who said he came out his senior year in high school. The response from the school counselor was to hand him a pamphlet on suicide prevention. The student had never once mentioned the thought of killing himself. He just needed someone to listen to him and to help him find acceptance for himself as a gay youth. These are situations that should never happen in this day and age.

Discussions and Implications

These teachers' comments gave me much to ponder. In recalling their own childhood experiences related to gender, they clearly demonstrated that expectations for gender-appropriate behavior were strictly reinforced as they were growing up, and that they were definitely aware of feeling "different" from their same-sex peers as early as elementary school. The name-calling related to sexual orientation that they have witnessed with their own elementary students in recent years suggests that a lack of tolerance for gender nonconformity is still present in elementary schools in many regions of the United States. Fortunately, these teachers do not let teasing or name-calling go unchallenged, but address it directly with individual students—both perpetrators and victims—as well as in class meetings. As Joe mentioned, these teachers are likely to be more sensitive to issues of name-calling and bullying because of their own backgrounds, but all teachers should take similar approaches to disrupt such harmful behaviors by students.

The teachers I interviewed also seemed eager to work with families headed by gay, lesbian, bisexual, or transgendered parents, but only Cali has actually encountered such families in her teaching. In these instances, she asserted that she treated these parents as she would any other parents, but she certainly acknowledged her awareness of their sexual orientation by speaking to both mothers on speaker phone in one instance, and by speaking to the nonbiological mother of a child just as she would the biological mother. Hulsebosch, Koerner, and Ryan (1999) found that some educators who taught children with nontraditional family structures intended only to help the children "go unnoticed and, therefore, unharmed" (p. 189). I hope that in the context of classroom communities like those created by the teachers I interviewed, where bullying and name-calling related to gender are not tolerated, all types of families would be embraced. The sensitivity to the needs of all families expressed by these four participants leads me to believe that this would be the case.

However, there are likely many teachers who are unaware that they are teaching children from GLBT families. For example, Brandon taught a student whose mother he thought might be a lesbian, but neither the mother nor the child confided in him. If he felt able to be open about his own sexual orientation, would this mother perhaps have felt more comfortable in being open about hers? As a teacher, Brandon did not want to be the one to broach the subject with her—and rightly so, I believe—but could he have done something to make this parent more comfortable in sharing her family structure with her child's teacher? Considering alternative family structures as part of the curriculum might have helped, for example.

Bickmore (1999) writes:

> In the name of comfort and accessibility for the (imagined) typical young student, standardized and increasingly outdated notions of "family" are reintroduced to children—unheralded—not as topics to question but as quiet corollaries to lessons on mathematics, geography, or literacy. (p. 16)

This attitude needs to change. Elementary teachers often make the study of families a large part of the curriculum, and they need to become more comfortable in introducing a variety of family structures, and thereby possibly encourage more families to view schools as places of acceptance.

All four of the teachers I interviewed said that they consistently try to encourage acceptance of all types of differences by their students. As classroom teachers, both Brandon and Joe said they look for children's literature and other classroom materials that help convey this message. Even they, however, do not include materials that overtly focus on sexual orientation. This is probably typical of American elementary teachers. Bickmore (1999) asserts that most teachers self-censor any curricular material that might be challenged as inappropriate. "Prejudice against gays and lesbians is simply not confronted as curriculum in most classrooms" (Cahill & Theilheimer, 1999, p. 39). Brandon made a poignant comment when he stated that he would be more likely to address issues of sexual orientation in the elementary classroom if he were heterosexual; as a gay man, he truly believes his job would be in danger if he were to do so. All elementary teachers, gay or straight, need to take up this challenge.

"Questions of sex, gender, and homosexual identity," according to Bickmore (1999, p. 18) "do fit into the elementary curriculum in a number of places"; as teacher educators, we can help preservice and inservice teachers identify these entry points for talking about such questions. We can introduce them to children's literature with positive portrayals of a variety of family structures, and we can nudge them to examine the language they use. We can raise their awareness that "the materials teachers select and the words they use may actively communicate a norm of heterosexuality. What teachers do not provide and say also gives a powerful message to children" (Cahill & Theilheimer, 1999, p. 43). We can encourage elementary educators to *create*, rather than wait for, opportunities to address issues of sexual identity (Colleary, 1999).

Of course, as teacher educators, we must create these same opportunities in our own courses. We must be sensitive to the language we use and the messages we send when speaking to students. Joe talked about the isolation he experienced in his teacher preparation program because his sexuality was never acknowledged in any way. He urged teacher educators to be open to the idea that they may well have GLBT students in their classes and to communicate their own acceptance of these students as well as promote acceptance by classmates.

Sensitivity alone is not enough, however. There is a lack of a teacher knowledge base at all levels for combating homophobia (Colleary, 1999) and for promoting "the contributions of homosexuals to the arts and sciences, military and politics, sports, and technology" (Sears, 1999, p. 4). Sears argues that we need to challenge school curricula that remain silent about these issues and contributions, and Cahill and Theilheimer (1999) state that, "If children who are developing same-sex affectional and sexual orientations do not know that gays and lesbians are among those they look to as role models, their sense of being alone is further reinforced" (p. 40). As teacher educators, we must first increase our own knowledge base so that we can share that knowledge with preservice and inservice teachers. For example, I wonder how many of my students know about the specific contributions of gay individuals to society. Sadly, when I asked Brandon about his own knowledge on this topic, he stated that there is not a need for him to know much, because it would be "useless knowledge" since he feels prohibited from sharing it with students. Just as I have attempted over the years of my teaching career to infuse my teaching with examples of contributions to society made by individuals from diverse racial, ethnic, linguistic, religious, and socioeconomic backgrounds, in order to demonstrate to my students the importance of all students to both see themselves represented in the curriculum as well as to learn about difference (Style & McIntosh, 1988), I realize now that I must begin educating myself to learn more about specific contributions made by GLBT individuals in order to share these with my students.

In terms of being "out" or open about their sexual orientation in the school setting, only Joe described feeling totally at ease with being out to colleagues, administrators, students, and parents—and this came at the cost of an early teaching job and lingering questions about his ability to teach. Both Robin and Cali stated that they were out to their colleagues and administrators and, while they sensed some disapproval from some colleagues, they reported overall satisfaction with being out in the work setting. However, neither is out to many parents nor to any students; Cali admitted that while she would like to be able to be out to students, this would just be "too scary." She also stated that "teachers should keep their personal lives personal." But each time a straight teacher mentions a spouse in the classroom, or talks in the faculty lounge about going on a date over the weekend, is this type of conversation considered too revealing of a "personal life"? I would wager that precisely the types of conversations that heterosexual teachers have about marriage and family, dating and romance, in both the classroom and the teachers' lounge, are the topics from which gay and lesbian teachers feel most excluded. Certainly, Brandon would like to join in such conversations, but he feels extreme pressure to keep his sexual orientation a secret in order to keep his job. He is also aware that there is no school board policy that protects him from discrimination, and as Bickmore (1999) points out, "A school board equity policy that does not protect sexual preference creates a chilly climate for antihomophobia instruction" (p. 17). It is exactly this "chilly climate" that Brandon fears. Yet, I wonder how many straight teachers actually know their school board policy on any issues related to sexual orientation.

Conclusions

From my readings and from my conversations with these four educators, I learned how much I still have to learn and how far I have to go to teach in ways that promote social justice and advocacy for all students. Specifically, I was struck by two compelling lessons I gleaned as a teacher educator from listening to the voices of the teachers with whom I spoke. First, we must be willing to risk discomfort (Howe, 2005). Bringing up issues of sexual orientation in teacher education courses can undeniably lead to "potentially risky discourses" (King & Schneider, 1999, p. 128), but as Bickmore (1999) admonishes us, "If we want children to be safe in the long run, and if we want them to learn, then the risky road of facing conflict and sensitive issues must be taken" (p. 21). As teacher educators, acknowledging our own discomfort with "touchy subjects" may ease students' discomfort somewhat; regardless, we cannot let our fear of students' resistance or hostility prevent us from having important discussions of sexual identity and equity with practicing and future teachers. If we do not demonstrate such risk-taking behavior for them, then we cannot expect them to take risks in their own classrooms, where students potentially face harm.

Second, we all must realize that issues of sexual orientation in education are important to *all* of us, not just to those who are gay, lesbian, bisexual, or transgendered. In many cases, such as Brandon's, the risks of a gay or lesbian teacher addressing such issues are simply too great. They need allies. They—and their students—need heterosexual educators who will be advocates on their behalf until that time when addressing issues of sexual identity in the elementary classroom is seen as commonplace, as no longer dangerous. Part of being an advocate is seeking knowledge that we lack. Narayan (1988) asserts that "abstract good will does not make one an ally; allies actively seek out and acquire . . . knowledge" (p. 37). Such advocacy work is not easy, but it is necessary. Like many other teacher educators whose work I have read, I firmly believe that taking a strong antibias position on issues of sexual orientation is as important as taking a public stand against any other form of prejudice or discrimination (Cahill & Theilheimer, 1999).

As I have pondered these issues, my overriding question for students I teach, both preservice and inservice teachers, has become: "Do you believe schools should be places of physical and psychological safety for *all* children?" I opened this chapter with snapshots of two events that clearly demonstrated the lack of psychological, if not physical, safety children have experienced in schools in my own community. The third snapshot, however, gives me hope. Teachers and students preparing to be teachers must become aware of the damage done by the omission of, or negative discourses surrounding, issues of sexual orientation in elementary schools. From such awareness can come change. As teacher educators, we must be willing to risk discomfort, our students' and our own, for such change to occur. From now on, these are the lessons I will be more conscious of taking to my students.

References

Bickmore, K. (1999). Why discuss sexuality in elementary school? In W. J. Letts & J. T. Sears (Eds.), *Queering elementary education: Advancing the dialogue about sexualities and schooling* (pp. 15-25). Lanham, MD: Rowman & Littlefield.

Cahill, B. J., & Theilheimer, R. (1999). Stonewall in the housekeeping area: Gay and lesbian issues in the early childhood classroom. In W. J. Letts & J. T. Sears (Eds.), *Queering elementary education: Advancing the dialogue about sexualities and schooling* (pp. 39-48). Lanham, MD: Rowman & Littlefield.

Casper, V., Cuffaro, H., Schultz, S., Silin, J. G., & Wickens, E. (1996). Toward a most thorough understanding of the world: Sexual orientation and early childhood education. *Harvard Educational Review, 66*(2), 271-293.

Colleary, K. P. (1999). How teachers understand gay and lesbian content in the elementary social studies curriculum. In W. J. Letts, & J. T. Sears (Eds.), *Queering elementary education: Advancing the dialogue about sexualities and schooling* (pp. 151-161).

Herdt, G., & Boxer, A. (1993). *Children of horizons.* Boston: Beacon Press.

Howe, J. (2005, November). *A master class in teaching children's literature: From resistance to acceptance—introducing books with gay and lesbian characters.* Paper presented at the meeting of the National Council of Teachers of English, Pittsburgh, PA.

Hulsebosch, P., Koerner, M. E., & Ryan, D. P. (1999). Supporting students/responding to gay and lesbian parents. In W. J. Letts & J. T. Sears (Eds.), *Queering elementary education: Advancing the dialogue about sexualities and schooling* (pp. 183-193). Lanham, MD: Rowman & Littlefield.

King, J. A. (1997). Keeping it quiet: Gay teachers in the primary grades. In J. J. Tobin (Ed.), *Making a place for pleasure in early childhood education* (pp. 235-253). New Haven, CT: Yale University Press.

King, J. R., & Schneider, J. J. (1999). Locating a place for gay and lesbian themes in elementary reading, writing, and talking. In W. J. Letts & J. T. Sears (Eds.), *Queering elementary education: Advancing the dialogue about sexualities and schooling* (pp. 125-136). Lanham, MD: Rowman & Littlefield.

Kissen, R. M. (1999). Children of the future age: Lesbian and gay parents talk about school. In W. J. Letts & J. T. Sears (Eds.), *Queering elementary education: Advancing the dialogue about sexualities and schooling* (pp. 165-175). Lanham, MD: Rowman & Littlefield.

Narayan, U. (1988). Working together across difference: Some considerations on emotions and political practice. *Hypatia, 3*(2), 30-47.

Robinson, K. H. (2002). Making the invisible visible: Gay and lesbian issues in early childhood education. *Contemporary Issues in Early Childhood, 3*(3), 415-434.

Sears, J. T. (1999). Teaching queerly: Some elementary propositions. In W. J. Letts & J. T. Sears (Eds.), *Queering elementary education: Advancing the dialogue about sexualities and schooling* (pp. 3-14). Lanham, MD: Rowman & Littlefield.

Style, E. & McIntosh, P. (1988). *Curriculum as window and mirror* ([Monograph]. Summit, NJ: Oakknoll School.

Surviving the Pain and Widening the Circle: Celebrating Lesbian and Gay Pride Week in an Elementary Classroom

John J. Guiney Yallop

This chapter originally appeared as a module in an online course offered by the University of Oulu (Guiney Yallop, 2004) and includes sections from a paper presented at the GLEE Project Pilot Schools Network Meeting in Oulu, Finland, on August 2-6, 2000 (Guiney, 2000).

This chapter details an experience of homophobia and heterosexism, an unsuccessful attempt to celebrate Lesbian and Gay Pride Week in an elementary classroom, and a subsequently successful unit on Lesbian and Gay Pride Week that was written about by the elementary school students who planned and presented the unit (Guiney, Bonnick, Millington, Mohla, & Routledge, 2001). While the piece is written about a particular experience and from the perspective of the author, readers are encouraged to reflect on how this event could have taken place in the educational environment in which you learn or teach. In your reflections as you read this piece, you may wish to answer the following questions: How can graffiti be a form of violence? Who is (are) the victim(s) of violence? What are some of the possible responses to violence? How have you responded (or witnessed a response) to violence? Does a multicultural/anti-bias curriculum support queer celebrations of diversity during specific days/weeks/month? Why or why not?

The Incident: Graffiti as an Act of Violence
In the late 1990s, while I was a grade 5 teacher in an elementary school in Canada, twice within one week threatening and homophobic graffiti was written on the outside of our classroom. (I was teaching in a portable.) The first piece of graffiti said, "We Will, We Will, Get You." The second, stretching the length of one outside wall, read, "Fuck you Mr. Guiney. Suck your gay dick. Remember me." My students and some colleagues, as well as a parent who was present, were visibly disturbed by the graffiti. Not wanting to appear intimidated, I initially responded in an almost dismissive manner to the graffiti.

Celebration: A Restorative Response
Following a discussion with my students, in which I invited them to share how they felt about the graffiti, it became clear that a more restorative response was necessary. My students expressed a feeling of being invaded and violated. They said that the graffiti had been done to *their* classroom and *their* teacher. I decided that celebrating Lesbian and Gay Pride Week would be a way for my students to reclaim their classroom and their teacher. When I suggested this to the students, they responded with considerable enthusiasm. I asked for volunteers to serve on the planning committee; at least nine students raised their hands. The planning began. In an open letter to staff, I outlined what had happened and the restorative action my students and I were taking.

Individual and Institutional Blocks: Other Forms of Violence

Celebrating Lesbian and Gay Pride Week with my students did not happen that year, because my principal was "uncomfortable" with the idea. Although I outlined why this was needed, what I would do, and why we didn't need a "Heterosexual Pride Week," I did not achieve any positive results. I persisted, however, and my principal requested a lesson plan for what I was intending to do, a lesson plan that would have to be approved by my superintendent. Although I had never been asked for such a plan in any of my previous equity/diversity work, I agreed to provide it. "And," my principal said, "it has to be good for students. It's not good enough that it's good for you; it has to be good for students." At that moment, something changed in my professional and emotional landscape. While it took hours to process it, I experienced that statement as discriminatory. As a teacher who was also an "out" gay man, I believed that statement suggested that I may be planning the celebration of Lesbian and Gay Pride Week with my students because it might be *good for me* and not because of the educational and, in this case, *healing* value for students. My motivations for my work as a teacher had never been questioned before.

I wrote a letter expressing my view and concerns to my principal. I attended school the following week, but found it increasingly difficult to function as a teacher. What followed were a series of events that indicated to me a further entrenchment of the principal's heterosexism and homophobia, supported by the superintendent who, in a meeting with me, the principal, my teachers union local president, my worksite union steward, and the human rights officer for the board, said, "Let's not beat around the bush; it's not going to happen." Appeals to the next level of administration also met with no acceptable results.

Retreating and Challenging: Simultaneous Responses to Violence

My doctor provided me with a letter for a medical leave for the remainder of the year. My teachers union, on my behalf, filed a grievance against the principal, the superintendent, and the board. In a more than 60-page document, supported by another 75 pages of attachments, I chronicled the story in much more detail than I present it here.

Reflection: A Method of Understanding Pain and Power

To date, I do not recall an experience in my life that was more traumatizing than that one. It should be noted, however, that I had considerable resources and supports at my disposal when this happened. I had a grounded sense of self and a well-developed self-esteem. I was approaching the 14th anniversary with my partner in life, who has always supported me. I had circles of friends and communities around me. I had a solid reputation as a capable teacher who cared deeply about and was highly skilled with students; I was even being encouraged by administrators to consider seeking leadership positions within the board. Finally, I was 40 years old and aware of people and processes that would help me fight for my rights. Despite all of that, my self-esteem suffered a major blow. I questioned my ability to teach, not just my teaching skills, which we all question and can always improve. I questioned my very capacity to be before a group of students and to know that my motivation for being there was my commitment to their learning. If that was the impact on me, with all of my resources, all of my experiences, all of my power, imagine the impact of homophobia and heterosexism, and the resultant discrimination, on a youth or a child—on one of your, of our, students.

Healing: A Response to Love

Because I had received so many heart-wrenching get-well cards from my students, which included expressions of hope that I would be able to attend their graduation, what was called the *Farewell to Grade Fives*, I, with the support and encouragement of my partner and my doctor, made myself able to attend, although I did not feel safe enough to be on stage or to present their diplomas. After I had watched the formalities from the audience with my partner, the students came towards me. I was surrounded by smiles, laughter, tears, handshakes, and hugs. Because of the number of people around me, I was able to move within a radius of no more than one or two metres. One parent commented to me, "Can you feel all that love around you, Mr. Guiney?" I smiled back and responded that I could. Reflecting on that love formed a significant part of my healing throughout the summer.

The following September, I returned to teach with the same board, in the same superintendency, but at a different school. I should add that this new teaching position was the result of an interview process that had happened prior to any of the above-mentioned events. It was the first year of a new school—an enviable assignment and I was proud to have been hired as one of the inaugural staff. I was, however, now working for a board against which I was party to a grievance and about which I had filed a human rights complaint.

The following February, a settlement for both the grievance and the human rights complaint was reached. The settlement had a number of clauses. A few of them were remedies for me, including financial remedies. Some of the clauses addressed student needs. Other clauses addressed training for staff and administration.

Changing the Ending: An Act of Self-Respect and Professional Integrity

I had made a decision prior to returning to teaching that September. I would either continue to be the educator I was, one who included as many equity/diversity issues as possible, or I would not address a single equity/diversity issue in my classroom. I decided on the former. Quite frankly, I am uncertain that I would have been able to maintain the latter. In my long-range plans, submitted to my principal and vice-principal in September, I outlined what, and how, I would be teaching my grade 6 class during that school year. Included was the statement, "Throughout the year, as much as possible, celebrations of diversity/inclusive curriculum/equity issues will be addressed, such as Festivals of Light, Martin Luther King Jr. Day, Black History Month, International Women's Day, and Lesbian and Gay Pride Week."

In June, as the end of the year approached, my students formed end-of-the-year planning committees. Among those committees was the Lesbian and Gay Pride Week Committee, composed of three boys and three girls, all volunteers. Each committee was responsible for researching, planning, and delivering their topic to the rest of the class. The work began. I served as a consultant to the committees.

More Stumbling Blocks: Systemic Homophobia and Heterosexism

Shortly after the students began planning for Lesbian and Gay Pride Week, an article appeared in the local newspaper about a grade 4 teacher from another school who had "come out" as a lesbian to her students and the board's response following the complaints of some parents. What I, and many others, judged to be an unenlightened and reactionary response from the board could have jeopardized, rather than enhanced, the educational value of the experience for that teacher's school community.

I brought a copy of the article to class for discussion. I asked my students what they would like me to do if our principal received a complaint about our activities for Lesbian and Gay Pride Week, or about the fact that I am "out" in the same way that many of my colleagues who are heterosexual are "out." Their response was very clear. They wanted these activities. They considered them part of their learning. If anyone complained, I was asked to invite them to come and talk directly with my students. One girl shared that these activities were particularly important for her, because she had a relative who is gay; before this activity, she had not been comfortable with her relative. Now she is comfortable. One boy said that being in this class helped him understand that gay people were not off somewhere else, but were around other people and could even be a teacher in the school. Interestingly, a comment was made, and seemed to receive general agreement, that students should be able to ask teachers about their sexual orientation and expect a truthful answer; they saw it as part of getting to know their teacher. I told my students that I would fight any attempt by others to stop them from having this learning experience. "Of course," I said, "I will fight with my words and not with my hands."

In light of the incident reported in the paper, I sent an E-mail to my principal as a reminder of my long-range plans. My principal and my vice principal met with me to find out what I would be doing. I provided a copy of my students' plans. My principal was "comfortable." There was a "request," however, for some communication to parents. I suggested that I could attempt to get our regular class newsletter out before Lesbian and Gay Pride Week. I was clear that I did not wish to treat this unit any differently than any other equity/diversity issue. In particular, I did not want to send out a permission form. I would, nevertheless, respond to specific parent requests.

The week before Lesbian and Gay Pride Week, an associate producer of *Metro Morning*, a widely listened-to radio show of the Canadian Broadcasting Corporation, contacted me. I was asked if I would agree to an interview regarding the activities my students were planning for Lesbian and Gay Pride Week. In the discussion that followed, I expressed that I was certainly open to an interview, but I wanted it to happen in the middle of the week. I did not want another reaction by the district school board to jeopardize this experience for my students.

The Student-Planned Unit on Lesbian and Gay Pride Week

Monday. Two rainbow banners were displayed on our chalkboard. Some information about gay and lesbian people, and their history, was presented by the committee. A skit, based on *Gloria Goes to Gay Pride* (1991) by L. Newman and R. Crocker, was prepared and presented by the six committee members. Following the skit, students were provided with art materials to make their own rainbow flag. Some students asked to make a second one, and were allowed to do so if time permitted.

Tuesday. The committee had asked that we have a speaker. At first, I resisted this because I wanted them to be the "experts." I realized, however, that they were asking for the same type of experience they had with the other equity/diversity work we did. I suggested they contact a woman whom I had met at a recent equity conference. She was also a teacher, and one who had done a lot of work in equity/diversity education. She and her partner had recently had a baby boy, and I said that this year Lesbian and Gay Pride Week may have a special meaning for them. Once I responded that, "Yes, she is a lesbian," the committee wanted to invite her and her family. My principal was less comfortable with this idea, and requested to be notified of the content of the guest's presentation. When our guest did arrive with her partner and child, they were taken to a private room by my principal and asked about what they would be saying. I know that our guest speaker was particularly offended by my principal's actions. She felt, and I believe rightly so, that this would not have been done to any other visitor speaking on any other equity issue. These measures were not taken with any other visitor to our classroom that year, and we had several.

Nevertheless, the experience for my students was a positive one. While a little quieter than usual, they did have some great questions for our guests. They impressed the visitors with their knowledge of gay and lesbian realities. By way of thank-you, the committee again performed their wonderful skit. The infant, as all infants are, was adorable and a big hit with my students.

Wednesday. The Interview. As with everything else, I had informed my principal of the interview. He offered some advice, based on his experience with the media. I accepted it, and expressed my appreciation for the input. I received the scheduled call at 5:55 a.m. The interview was recorded and broadcast at 6:50 a.m. My partner and I listened to it on our way to work. The response was primarily positive. The broadcasted responses the next day were all positive. I received some congratulatory comments and calls. My principal also congratulated me. I sensed that there was some relief that I had not used the interview as an opportunity to comment on the board's poor handling of gay and lesbian issues. I am aware of one negative call to my principal and one "concerned" letter to the superintendent. The interview fulfilled its purpose—to inform. For me, an at least equally important purpose was to celebrate my students. At the end of the week, I told my students that I had been interviewed because they had done something that, to my knowledge, was unprecedented for this board, possibly for this province, and maybe even for our country. I was very proud of them.

Thursday. I had noticed that a basket of rainbow ribbons that I had placed in the staff room on Monday morning with an invitation to wear one had, for the fourth time, been placed on the window ledge with the invitation facing away from view. I sent an E-mail to my principal expressing my concern that this had happened and had the potential of creating a "poisoned environment." While I was certainly inviting my colleagues to wear a rainbow ribbon, I was not judging their decision to wear or not to wear one. I was, however, quite prepared to judge and condemn anyone's attempt to prevent me from issuing that invitation. I also considered the relocation of the rainbow ribbons to be a cowardly act. I accepted my principal's judgment that the relocating of the basket was probably not deliberate. It was not relocated on Friday. Two colleagues, on a staff of more than 40, wore rainbow ribbons that entire week.

Friday. The committee had prepared a question-and-answer game based on what had been presented that week. The questions and answers for the game were shown to their consultant (their teacher) prior to the game. As usual, the game was a good learning tool, especially for review. The committee then gave each student a rainbow sticker. Two students did not take a sticker because they said that their parents did not allow them to do so.

The Week

The week was not without its negatives. There was no announcement on the school public announcements system of Lesbian and Gay Pride Week, even though I had requested it. There was no public administrative acknowledgement, within the school or outside it, of the work that my students had done. Outside of our classroom, there were no visible signs in the school, I thought, of Lesbian and Gay Pride Week.

The week also had a lot of positives. Many of them are already detailed above. No matter what the response, however, nothing can take away from my students' experiences. For them, the words *gay, lesbian, bisexual,* and *transgender* will not be name-calling words. *Different* will not equal *wrong* or *bad.* Nor will *different* equal *alone.* Difference, in fact, will be a shared experience, something to be celebrated along with our sameness. Despite obvious discomfort, my principal was comfortable enough, and confident enough, with my ability and my commitment to provide a positive environment and facilitate a learning experience for my students, or maybe just thought it best to stay out of our way.

Finally, I was wrong when I thought there were no visible signs of Lesbian and Gay Pride Week throughout the school. One of my grade 7 students, who came to me for French once a day, asked about the rainbow ribbons because he noticed that "all of the teachers were wearing them." That showed me just how powerful the actions of those two staff members who wore a rainbow ribbon had been.

Pride Week: My Family and Community Celebration

Pride Week that year was, I felt, a particularly special one. On a personal note, it was the 15th anniversary that my partner and I were celebrating together; we had met at a Pride Week Dance. On a professional level, I felt that a circle had been closed—a circle of pain caused by ignorance, homophobia, and heterosexism. As well, a circle may have been opened—a circle of inclusion; a circle where students and educators might feel free to include all realities of equity/diversity education; a circle where educators and those they serve might feel free to be themselves; a circle where people might be supported, cared for, and valued because of their differences rather than despite them; a circle where *tolerance* may be seen as a beginning and not as an end; a circle where acceptance may be seen as a stage of growth; a circle where true equity could involve celebrating the realities of all of our communities; a circle where you and I would be needed; a circle that you and I would be invited to join; a circle that you and I are invited to create.

Conclusion

The event that my students planned, implemented, and experienced was a positive one. Some other steps within the boards in which I have worked, and in some other boards of education, might since then have been taken with the stated intent to create welcoming, safe, and equitable learning environments for all. Despite refrains of *but we've come a long way* or *it's much better than it used to be*, however, schools remain places where I believe the event described at the beginning of this chapter is more likely to happen, places that are unwelcoming, unsafe, hostile, and violent environments for many of those who are, or appear to be, different from the majority, particularly those who have a different sexual orientation or gender identity from the majority, or whose parents identify as members of one or both of those two "communities." Much work still needs to be done. Educators with the courage and the commitment to do the work are needed. Supports for those educators are also necessary. Systemic change is long overdue.

References

Guiney, J. J. (2000, August). *Lesbian and gay pride week in an elementary classroom: Widening the circle.* Paper presented at the GLEE Project Schools Network Meeting, Oulu, Finland.

Guiney, J. J., Bonnick, C., Millington, S., Mohla, R., & Routledge, A. (2001). Lesbian and gay pride week in an elementary classroom. *etfo VOICE*, 21-24.

Guiney Yallop, J. (2004). Surviving the pain and widening the circle: Celebrating lesbian and gay pride week in an elementary classroom. *Increasing Teacher Trainees' Awareness of Sexualised and Gendered Violence—International Course on Sexualised and Gendered Violence 2004, Course Module.*

Newman, L., & Crocker, R. (1991). *Gloria goes to gay pride.* Boston: Alyson Publications.

DIVERSE THREADS IN SOCIAL FABRICS: AUTOBIOGRAPHY AND ARTS-INFORMED EDUCATIONAL INITIATIVES FOR SOCIAL JUSTICE

Kristopher Wells

*T*his chapter explores how I engage with reflexive autobiographical practices and arts-informed research strategies as part of a multi-faceted inquiry into the discourses and discursive practices that construct LGBTQ teachers and students as sex, sexual, and gender outlaws. Two anti-oppression educational projects are highlighted as forms of an arts-informed public pedagogy of hope and resilience.

As you read this chapter, ask yourself: How do silence, invisibility, and exclusion impact the learning and work environments of LGBTQ students and teachers? How can arts-informed educational strategies be utilized to open up spaces of hope and possibility for all identities to become recognized and respected in our classrooms, schools, and communities? What will you do to challenge oppression in all of its many forms?

Introduction: Teaching Li(v)es

In 1999, I walked away from my job as a public school teacher in Alberta. I left feeling tired, beaten, and broken after having spent the better part of my short teaching career living a life in the closet. I silently watched as students under my care struggled to come to terms with their own sex, sexual, and gender differences. I felt as though I could do nothing to help them without casting the ever-present gaze of suspicion onto myself. I had heard the words in the hallways and staffrooms—*faggot, queer, freak*. Those same teachers who were my nine-to-five colleagues were also my silent tormentors. None of their hateful comments were ever directed at me, but the scars still remain etched into my flesh from the violence of their words.

To this day, I can vividly recall the pack of junior high boys who circled my car at the local video store. I watched as they motioned for my partner to roll down the car window. I was trapped inside the store with fear caked in my throat. Watching the scene unfold beyond the glass window, I thought to myself, "What would my partner say if they asked?" or "Did they already know?" The students hovered like vultures waiting to rip into his flesh. I retreated quickly to the car, forgetting about the video at the counter. Holding my breath, I asked, "What did they say?" My partner replied, "They asked if I was your boyfriend." Still waiting I said, "And?" "I told them no! Don't be disgusting," my partner replied. I sighed in relief as I glanced out the window and reached for my partner's hand, yet I was crying on the inside. "What kind of life am I living where my partner has to deny his love for me?" "It's disgusting" . . . we've learned to internalize the messages all too well as we degrade and defile ourselves just so I can continue to work for another day in "my" community. The costs finally became too high and I left teaching.

I still remember that last day of my school life. I reached for the handle and opened the door to an uncertain future, not knowing where, or even if, I would be able to find another job. I left hoping that I could find a place, any place, where I could finally, just maybe, be myself. As the door closed,

I refused to look back down the hallway. I couldn't bear to see their faces again. It wasn't the faces of my tormentors that frightened me. It was the faces of the other students, the ones who needed me to be there for them. I couldn't stomach the thought that I'd let them down with my silence. It's the same silence that I had needed broken as a queer kid struggling to come to terms with my sexuality in a sea of invisibility and hatred. I was the queer student and later I became the queer teacher who was still running scared, never knowing when they might finally find out the truth.

Today, as I sit in my office at the University of Alberta reflecting on my experiences, I can still taste the fear, anger, and sorrow that I experienced as a closeted teacher. Eight years after I walked out of my last school, I finally have the strength to reflect back on those experiences. Through my research, I've learned to channel my anger and hurt into a burning rage that fuels and focuses my personal and professional ambitions as a university educator. With the support of my university colleagues, I've finally found a "safe space" that has supported me in being and becoming the kind of educator that I've always wanted to be. Now, when I walk into a classroom, I enter as a proud teacher who works to create a recognized and valued space and place for lesbian, gay, bisexual, trans-identified, and queer (LGBTQ) students and teachers in Alberta schools. I work closely with the Alberta Teachers' Association to develop educational resources and professional development opportunities to help preservice and practicing teachers engage in a capacious understanding of their professional, ethical, and legal responsibilities to create safe, caring, and inclusive classrooms and schools for *all* students and *all* teachers (Grace & Wells, 2004; Wells, 2001/2007, 2006).

As society becomes increasingly more accepting of LGBTQ persons, more and more teachers and students are finding support and coming out in their schools (Grace & Wells, 2005). A whole new generation of young teachers—"Generation Queer," as some have called it (Paris, 1999)—have spent most of their adolescence and young adulthood out of the closet and they are not willing to go back in when they re-enter the classroom as beginning teachers. What new challenges will this generation face? Will they still hear homophobic slurs in the staffroom? Will the vultures still circle, watching and waiting for any sign of difference or weakness? I'm hopeful that it will be easier for Generation Queer, but even though these individuals are coming out at younger and younger ages, with their visibility also comes the increased risk of violence and victimization. Queer students and teachers still need to remain vigilant, always watching and waiting, trying to decide if the next person they come out to will be a source of support or a specter of fear.

In my teaching, research, and community service work, I frequently draw upon my own lived and learned experiences as a queer person, as a method of autobiographical narrative inquiry (Clandinin & Connelly, 2000; Grace, 2006; Grace & Benson, 2000; Wells, 2003). In this reflexive space, I use critical theorizing and arts-informed educational techniques to engage in a "lusty [and] rigorous" (St. Pierre & Pillow, 2000) deconstructive inquiry space that challenges normativity and the forces of oppression that too often subjugate LGBTQ lives. In the pursuit of turning theory into meaningful and tangible practice, I highlight two arts-informed educational projects that work with LGBTQ youth through the media of photography and textiles to narrate a public pedagogy of resistance, hope, and the possibility for a more just and humane world.

A Picture Is Worth a Thousand Words: Utilizing Photography as a Research Method

In 2003, I worked with four Alberta youth (ages 17 to 22) to explore their experiences with and resistances to heteronormativity in their schools, families, and communities. As part of this multifaceted research inquiry, I utilized visual (photographic) narratives and collage (Bach, 1998; Collier & Collier, 1987; Harper, 1998; Pink, 2001; Weiser, 1993). The intent of these visual research techniques was to provide the youth participants with an opportunity to become the "image makers of their stories" (Bach, 1998, p. 14). In this visual narrative process, the participants composed photographic representations that focused on images, symbols, and metaphors emerging from our earlier, unstructured interview conversations.

To begin our research collaboration, I provided each of the four research participants with disposable photographic cameras. I then asked each participant to take photographs that represented various aspects of their formal and non-formal educational experiences and lives. After I distributed the cameras, I provided initial guiding themes to assist the research participants in the early stages of their photographic project. All of the research participants were provided with the opportunity to expand on the suggested themes, and they were invited to take as many or as few photographs as they wished. Possible photographic themes suggested included identity, safety, school experiences, family, community supports, homophobia, heterosexism, secrets, dreams, hopes, and desires. I hoped that the research participants would create photographs that *talked back* (hooks, 1994) to certain aspects that represented their sex, sexual, and gender differences. Clover (2006) describes this process as participatory photography, "whereby marginalized or disadvantaged people are provided cameras and the opportunity to document, analyze and make meaning of their own experiences and realities through images and symbols of their choosing" (p. 276).

Queer Youth Visual Narratives

Of the four research participants, only Alex and Jordana ultimately felt comfortable enough to take photographs that represented their experiences. Keith and Jamie opted to create photo collages as an alternative (and perhaps less threatening) way to express their experiences. Taking photographs can become a very personal experience that may leave research participants feeling vulnerable and exposed as they revisit difficult and potentially painful memories of what it was like to be a queer youth in an often hostile and uninviting world. Alex had this to say about his involvement in the photographic process:

I got to learn a lot about myself and how these pictures reflect me. Each one of them reflects how I felt at the time and what I have been through. . . . I'm really happy that I got to take the photographs. I'm going to sort them out first. The ones that don't reflect my life right now, I'm going to put them away in a box. I'm not going to throw them away. That's like ripping a part of your history away.

Jordana viewed the photographic experience this way:

I love photography. I love taking pictures. I wouldn't mind taking pictures of myself if I looked a bit better. The photos are how I see the world and the moments that are really precious to me. . . . Everything in the pictures has meaning to me. They all have a really interesting story. . . . I feel like I'm even attached to those pictures. They are pictures that I will never forget. I really liked doing this project.

As these comments suggest, "visual images have their own biographies" (Pink, 2001, p. 95). The creation of these visual narratives can provide for a conscious (and at times unconscious) reflection on how the personal thoughts, experiences, and feelings of queer youth are lived out in public and private spaces. These visual narratives serve as an active resistance to normalizing pedagogies that seek to devalue, defame, and demoralize non-heterosexual lives. The research participants' photographs and collages also can become a tangible way to visualize and live out the tenets of a critical pedagogy that seeks to empower youth to become active agents in the critique, reflection, and, ultimately, reconstruction of their daily realities.

In the construction of this critical public pedagogy, key questions should be asked as youth take up the creation of visual narratives:

- What are the risks involved in these acts of visual resistance? Are these visual narratives merely aesthetic, or do they have deeper and multiple meanings for the participants?
- What implications do these visual narratives have for the regulatory discourses that are present within formal educational institutions?
- Are these narratives acts of resistance, forms of cultural negotiation, or attempts at social transformation?
- How is the creation of these visual narratives more than what Giroux (1993) calls "hip pedagogical posturing" (p. 48)?
- How might these visual narratives be read by viewers from different backgrounds?
- How do these visual narratives take up and question notions of power, privilege, and possibility?

Queering the Gaze

The following photographs and collages were created by the four youth who participated in our arts-informed research inquiry. As you view the images, I encourage you to reflect upon and revisit the question: What is life like for queer youth in schools, families, and communities?

I took pictures of a flower. One picture is of it in the morning, when the flower is open and alive as it tries to adapt to the day. The other picture is at night, when the flower is closed and adapting to the darkness. I just thought it was beautiful. It's red and red is my favourite colour. The flower is trying to adapt to day and night, like we all do. . . . When you need energy you always open yourself up and you feel free and safe. When you are closed you feel kind of dark and scared.

Everything is constantly changing and you have to learn how to adapt. . . . I'm like the open flower now. There is so much more that I am going to learn and be open to share, just like the flower. She is open to beauty, but also drawing energy from the sun. That's how I feel. I'm the red.

—Jordana, age 19

There's a lot that my pride flag says. I bought it when I came out.
I've had it ever since I've been free. Every colour has a meaning for me.
I haven't figured out what green and yellow mean yet.
Purple means reliability and trust.
Blue means purity and innocence.

Red is my favourite colour. For me, it is not a colour of passion. For me, it is the colour of blood.
I have a lot of scars. I've seen a lot of blood because of my scars and slashing myself.
It has a lot of meaning for me.
Red tells me I am alive. Red means life to me.
Orange is the colour of youth.
It reminds me of nourishment and nurturing.
I'll figure out what green and yellow mean to me in the future.
I hope that I have a long life to live.
This pride flag will always be with me. It has seen a lot.
It has always been hanging there on my wall.
I talk to her every night.

—Jordana, age 19

After we discussed all of Jordana's photos, I handed her a blank photograph and asked her if there were any pictures that she avoided or was fearful of taking.

[This would be] the outside of my parent's house. . . . Although I'm closer to my parents, I couldn't share any of these pictures with them. They don't want to see it. . . . I love them and their house. It's the first house that they bought since they moved to Canada. It's a house I never really got to live in. Once they did buy it, I was in the hospital, and then I did live in it for a month and then I got kicked out when they found out that I was a lesbian.

This is a traditional Chinese environment—Dim Sum. Because it is very traditional, I didn't feel safe as a gay youth there. . . . If they found out that my mom had a gay son, we would not be worthy enough to talk to. Having face or prestige is more important than anything else in a Chinese setting.

—Alex, age 18

Rather than taking photographs, Kevin and Jamie opted to make the following collages.

Kevin's collage, age 17

Jamie's collage, age 22

In this project, I have used photography as a research method that seeks to promote a critical consciousness-raising that encourages the research participants to document aspects of their lives in the ways that they see them. These photographs and collages represent a form of self-reflexive autobiography that is often in sharp contrast to the ways that many educators and policymakers view the lives and experiences of LGBTQ youth. Concomitantly, Clover (2006) describes participatory photography "as an educational tool to record and reflect people's needs, promote dialogue, build confidence, and encourage activism, or inform policy" (p. 277). Accordingly, these photographs and visual images serve as a way to reflect the experiences of queer youth back upon their communities as they reveal their everyday hopes, dreams, and struggles to be, become, and belong as full and valued members of their schools, families, and communities.

Diverse Threads in Social Fabrics

Another arts-informed educational project that I engaged in involved members from Youth Understanding Youth, which is Edmonton's LGBTQ social/support group for sexual minority youth under the age of 25. Collectively, the youth group decided that they would participate in creating a quilt that would reflect images and symbols representative of their experiences as LGBTQ youth. To begin thinking about what this project might look like, we discussed the metaphor of the quilt and how it has become an important symbol within a variety of historically disenfranchised communities. We spoke of the history of women's "sewing circles" as a place to build communities of dialogue and support. We discussed the history of quilt making in the African American and African Canadian communities during the American Civil War. Youth group members were surprised to learn that these quilts often contained hidden messages identifying safe waypoints along the Underground Railroad to freedom. Of particular interest to the youth group members was the history of the AIDS Memorial Quilt. I read aloud to the youth group the children's storybook *A Name on the Quilt: A Story of Remembrance* (Atkins, 2003). This story illustrated how a family came together to remember "Uncle Ron's" life when he passed away from HIV/AIDS. For many of the youth group members, this was the first time they had heard of the AIDS Quilt. They were surprised to learn that each panel on the quilt is 3 x 6 feet, which symbolizes the standard size of a coffin. We discussed the meaning and history of the AIDS Quilt as more than a story of remembrance, but also as an important story of queer activism and the celebration of queer lives. As we shared more and more stories about the quilt, the youth group decided that they wanted their quilt to be woven together with stories of hope and resilience.

We worked on our quilt project over a series of several months. We began with each youth group member brainstorming ideas about what they wanted their individual panel to represent. We worked on designs and colours for the quilt panels. We talked about the rainbow flag being recognized as an international symbol of the LGBTQ community. We discussed the rich symbolism of the flag and how each colour has a different meaning. (Red is for life. Orange is for healing. Yellow is for sun. Green is for nature. Blue is for art. Purple is for spirit.) Together, we wove time spent creating our quilt into more than just pieces of felt and cloth. The quilt became a space to talk about the past and about the possibilities for our future. We created our own sewing circle, as the quilt became a place for us to share our storied lives. When all the patches were completed, Marjorie, one of our youth group facilitators, took on the special responsibility of stitching together the panels. After many weeks and long hours of sewing, the day finally came when the quilt was ready to be brought back to the youth group. A powerful silence overcame the group as we unveiled the quilt. We were all awestruck by the beautiful tapestry. Youth group members rushed over to touch their panels, and we gathered in a circle as each member began to tell their stories from the quilt.

I'll never forget that night. No one knew what the quilt would finally look like. At times, we had wondered if we would even be able to finish it. Seeing the quilt held up by the youth group members and hearing their stories was a very special moment. It made me think back to when I was 15 . . . age 15 and so deep in the closet that I would wait eight more years until I would take my first steps out of the darkness. I'm so hopeful when I look around the room and see so many young faces. For me, the quilt not only represents the stories of the youth who created the panels, it also represents a story to live by—a story based in the hope and possibility that exists in communities of difference.

Each of the youth who created a panel on the quilt also provided an artist's statement explaining what their panel represented. The quilt panels and statements below are representative of the many stories from the quilt.

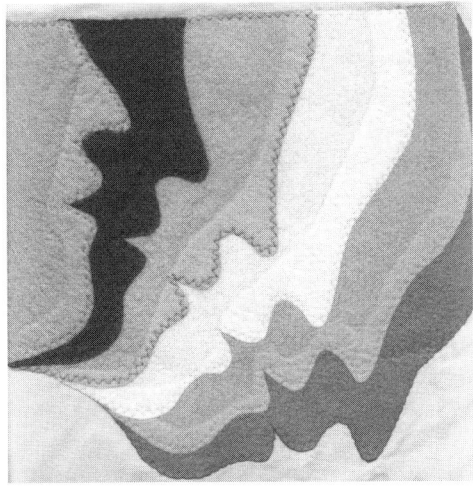

Questions
      —Kenny
Love? Lust? Kindness?
Selfishness? Peace? Which
ones are you? We all have
each other, filled with pride
as we live life each day.

Ribbon Off the Streets
      —Clinton
The red AIDS ribbon is torn at ends
as though it had been picked up
off the streets. The colours of the
gender symbols show that we are
present in every race; the order of
the interlocking combination
indicates that any combination is ok.

Pride Boi
—John

Screams Into a Dark Night
—Jen

My panel means diversity and
discovering your sexual orientation.
It also represents a form of equality,
even a love for straight people
despite their lack sometimes of love.

It mostly represents
openness even though sometimes that
is not always the best thing to be.
It stands for love of all and PRIDE!

This panel shows two women yelling,
surrounded by a heart. They are
yelling out hearts (love, defending
each other) that are going into a black,
dark, and unaccepting world
for gay people.

The stories from the quilt continue to take on a life of their own. In 2005, the Alberta Teachers' Association (ATA) and The Society for Safe and Caring Schools and Communities created a *Safe Spaces Initiative*[1] that features the patchwork from the quilt on a Safe Spaces poster, sticker, and brochure. The ATA has sent a copy of the poster, sticker, and brochure to every school in Alberta.

Stories To Live By: Expanding the Horizons of Hope and Possibility

As part of a reflexive autobiographical research practice, I have attempted to situate my experiences as a queer educator who engages with narrative inquiry and arts-informed educational techniques as an analytic method to help reveal the dominant discourses and discursive practices that construct LGBTQ teachers and students as sex, sexual, and gender outlaws (Grace & Wells, 2001, 2004; Tierney, 1997; Wells, 2004). This multifaceted arts-informed inquiry is rooted in deconstructive strategies that strive to enable the youth participants and me to become the story makers and storytellers of our own experiences. These deconstructive lines of inquiry seek to open up new positions in an effort to reveal and resignify the radical potential to uncover new possibilities for being, belonging, and becoming in educational, familial, and community contexts (Butler & Scott, 1992). From this vantage point, a self-reflexive approach to arts-informed inquiry is not a standpoint or fixed theoretical perspective that seeks to add to or participate in theory building or the canonization of knowledge production. Rather, this inquiry space strives to critique and question the very grounds upon which theoretical perspectives, research methodologies, knowledge, and subjectivities have come to be naturalized (Butler & Scott, 1992; St. Pierre & Pillow, 2000). This line of inquiry refuses to name in advance what possibilities might be revealed or opened up through our collective efforts in storying and restorying experience. Instead, this liminal space attempts to engage arts-informed anti-oppressive educational practices that "speak beside" our experiences as LGBTQ persons as we ask "what is possible," "what is livable," and "what is imaginable," given the "horizon of possibilities" that exist within the matrix of (hetero)normalizing discourses that are in constant circulation and production (Butler, 2004, p. 355).

Note:

[1] The Safe Spaces materials can be viewed by visiting the Alberta Teachers' Association's Sexual Orientation and Gender Identity Web page: www.teachers.ab.ca/Issues+In+Education/Diversity+and+Human+Rights/Sexual+Orientation/Safe+Spaces+Initiative/Index.htm

References

Atkins, J. (2003). *A name on the quilt: A story of remembrance.* Toronto, ON: Aladdin Paperbacks.

Bach, H. (1998). *A visual narrative concerning curriculum, girls, photography, etc.* Edmonton, AB: Qual Institute Press.

Butler, J. (2004). Changing the subject: Judith Butler's politics of radical resignification. In S. Salih & J. Butler (Eds.), *The Judith Butler reader* (pp. 325-360). Malden, MA: Blackwell.

Butler, J., & Scott, J. W. (1992). Introduction. In J. Butler & J. W. Scott (Eds.), *Feminists theorize the political* (pp. xiii-xvii). New York: Routledge.

Clandinin, D. J., & Connelly, F. M. (2000). *Narrative inquiry: Experience and story in qualitative research.* San Francisco: Jossey-Bass.

Clover, D. (2006). Out of the dark room. Participatory photography as a critical, imaginative, and public aesthetic practice of transformative education. *Journal of Transformative Education, 4*(3), 275-290.

Collier, J., Jr., & Collier, M. (1987). *Visual anthropology: Photography as research method.* Albuquerque, NM: University of New Mexico Press.

Giroux, H. A. (1993). *Living dangerously: Multiculturalism and the politics of difference.* New York: Peter Lang Publishing.

Grace, A. P. (2006). Writing the queer self: Using autobiography to mediate inclusive teacher education in Canada. *Teaching and Teacher Education, 22,* 826-834.

Grace, A. P., & Benson, F. J. (2000). Using autobiographical queer life narratives of teachers to connect personal, political and pedagogical spaces. *International Journal of Inclusive Education, 4*(2), 89-109.

Grace, A. P., & Wells, K. (2001). Getting an education in Edmonton, Alberta: The case of queer youth. *Torquere, Journal of the Canadian Lesbian and Gay Studies Association, 3,* 137-151.

Grace, A. P., & Wells, K. (2004). Engaging sex-and-gender differences: Educational and cultural change initiatives in Alberta. In J. McNinch & M. Cronin (Eds.), *I could not speak my heart: Education and social justice for gay and lesbian youth* (pp. 289-307). Regina, SK: Canadian Plains Research Centre, University of Regina.

Grace, A. P., & Wells, K. (2005). The Marc Hall prom predicament: Queer individual rights v. institutional church rights in Canadian public education. *Canadian Journal of Education, 28*(3), 237-270.

Harper, D. (1998). On the authority of image: Visual methods at the crossroads. In N. K. Denzin & Y. S. Lincoln (Eds.), *Collecting and interpreting qualitative materials* (pp. 130-149). Thousand Oaks, CA: Sage.

hooks, b. (1994). *Teaching to transgress: Education as the practice of freedom.* New York: Routledge.

Lather, P., & Smithies, C. (1997). *Troubling the angels: Women living with HIV/AIDS.* Boulder, CO: Westview Press.

Paris, B. (1999). *Generation queer: A gay man's quest for hope, love and justice.* New York: Warner Books.

Pink, S. (2001). *Visual ethnography: Images, media and representation in research.* Thousand Oaks, CA: Sage Publications.

St. Pierre, E. A., & Pillow, W. S. (2000). Introduction: Inquiry among the ruins. In E. A. St. Pierre & W. S. Pillow (Eds.), *Working the ruins: Feminist poststructural theory and methods in research* (pp. 1-24). New York: Routledge.

Tierney, W. G. (1997). *Academic outlaws: Queer theory and cultural studies in the academy.* Thousand Oaks, CA: Sage.

Weiser, J. (1993/1999). *PhotoTheraphy techniques: Exploring the secrets of personal snapshots and family albums.* San Francisco: Jossey-Bass.

Wells, K. (2001). Where is the hope? *Journal of Among Teachers Community: Experience and Inquiry, 30,* 15.

Wells, K. (2001/2007). *Sexual orientation and gender identity.* Retrieved June 18, 2007, from www.teachers.ab.ca/Issues+In+Education/Diversity+and+Human+Rights/Sexual+Orientation/Index.htm

Wells, K. (2002). *Sexual orientation and gender identity: A professional development website for Alberta teachers.* Retrieved February 9, 2005, from www.teachers.ab.ca/Issues+In+Education/Diversity+and+Human+Rights/Sexual+Orientation/Index.htm

Wells, K. (2003). *Understanding difference differently: Sex-and-gender OUTlaws in Alberta schools.* Unpublished master's thesis, University of Alberta, Edmonton, Alberta, Canada.

Wells, K. (2004). Safe in my heart: Found poetry as narrative inquiry. In J. McNinch & M. Cronin (Eds.), *I could not speak my heart: Education and social justice for gay and lesbian youth* (pp. 7-18). Regina, SK: Canadian Plains Research Centre, University of Regina.

Wells, K. (2006). *Gay–straight alliances in Alberta schools: A guide for teachers* (2nd ed.). Edmonton, AB: Alberta Teachers' Association.

Acting Out:
Using Augusto Boal's Theatre of the Oppressed Techniques To Teach About Homophobic Incidents in Catholic Schools

Tonya Callaghan

*A*s part of a presentation for a graduate course about contemporary issues in Canadian education, I teamed up with a classmate, Frankie Billingsley, to produce four dramatic skits to address the institutionalization of homophobia in secondary schools. The content of the dramatic skits comes from my own personal experiences with homophobia in Catholic schools and is directly related to the topic of my master's thesis.

The skits were designed according to a theatre technique called "Theatre of the Oppressed," also known as "Popular Theatre," developed by Brazilian Augusto Boal in the 1960s. Boal's Theatre of the Oppressed (1974/1979) method involves enacting everyday challenges faced by ordinary people and practicing new, creative, and non-violent ways of confronting these challenges.

For Boal, Theatre of the Oppressed was a weapon for oppressed people to use in the hope of changing their social reality (Conrad, 2004). It was a theatre for the people, by the people—what Boal (1974/1979) called "a rehearsal of revolution" (p. 155). Of course, Brazil at the time Boal was writing was under military rule and was suffering from political struggles stemming from both the military regime and the Brazilian elite. While the homophobia that I am highlighting in this chapter is in no way comparable to the political oppression that Boal was hoping to address, I believe that Boal's Theatre of the Oppressed techniques can be applied to all kinds of oppressive situations.

Boal's Theatre of the Oppressed technique is a dramatic skit involving an oppressive character and an oppressed character. Actors (or non-actors) perform an initial run of the skit in front of the audience, trying as much as possible to underscore the tension between the two characters. Once the audience is familiar with the problem being portrayed, any member of the audience who feels that he or she could reduce the tension by acting differently can come into the scene and take the place of the oppressed character. By taking part in the skit, or by simply watching the scene unfold, audience members can explore and evaluate their own and others' perceptions of the problem.

When the dramatic skits are set in the hyper-heteronormative and homophobic environment of the Catholic school, audience members learn to recognize homophobia and find ways to stop it. Ideally, audience members see that, like drama, our social reality is constructed and can be reconstructed (Conrad, 2005). What follows is a brief overview of the Theatre of the Oppressed method, descriptions of the settings of each scene that were provided to the audience before each dramatic skit, a series of scripted descriptions of the process, and a discourse analysis of some of the scripts to help me make sense of our process. It is my hope that readers will understand how Theatre of the Oppressed can be successful in tackling controversial issues.

Theatre of the Oppressed

I first encountered this form of participatory theatre at the third annual "Agape Education and

Culture" conference. Agape is a focus group for the study of sex, sexual, and gender differences in education and culture, and is designed to meet the needs of lesbian, gay, bisexual, two-spirited, trans-identified, queer and questioning (LGBTQ) and allied staff, faculty, and students in the Faculty of Education at the University of Alberta. I was particularly drawn to this form of expressive problem solving, because I had become frustrated by the number of times straight family members, friends, and colleagues had told me they could not see the subtle and overt forms of homophobia operating all around them. I felt that if certain scenes could be acted out in front of them, they would start to see what form of oppression homophobia could take.

To learn more about the Theatre of the Oppressed method, I consulted Diane H. Conrad, who is well-known at the University of Alberta for her use of Popular Theatre as a qualitative research method that is both participatory and performative. Popular Theatre is the term Conrad prefers to use to talk about a politically motivated type of participatory theatre alternately referred to and/or closely allied to Augusto Boal's seminal text, *Theatre of the Oppressed* (1974/1979). According to Prentki and Selman (2000), Popular Theatre is "a process of theatre which deeply involves specific communities in identifying issues of concern, analyzing current conditions and causes of a situation, identifying points of change, and analyzing how change could happen and/or contributing to the actions implied" (p. 8).

Popular Theatre both grew out of and developed alongside the popular education movement that was taking place in the 1960s and 70s under the direction of Brazilian Paulo Freire, who is now commonly recognized as one of popular education's most powerful proponents (Conrad, 2004). Freire wrote his influential and oft-cited text, *Pedagogy of the Oppressed* (1970), during a time of extreme political repression in Brazil. His ideas of liberatory literacy education involved not only reading the *word*, but also reading the *world* through the development of critical consciousness, or what he called "concientization."

Augusto Boal believes that "theatre is a form of knowledge [that] can also be a means of transforming society. Theatre can help us build our future rather than just waiting for it" (Boal, 1992, p. xxxi). As an English teacher within a Catholic school system, I witnessed a destructive heterosexist culture that I felt needed to be changed. In preparation for the theatrical presentation, I set out to write a series of ethnographic vignettes (Saldana, 1999) based on homophobic situations in Catholic schools. The first scene depicts a highly publicized homophobic response on the part of a Catholic high school in Ontario toward a grade 12 student who wanted to take his boyfriend to his high school prom, and the last three scenes are from my own experiences.

The scenes represent what I consider to be significant moments of homophobia in Catholic schools that I thought would best assist the audience in understanding this often-unrecognized problem. In terms of the order that the scenes would be presented, I thought it would be best to start off with the situation that did not actually happen to me, so that the audience could see that these types of incidents can occur anytime, anywhere, and are not simply the product of a personality clash, or of one person simply being "oversensitive" to the homophobia around her.

At the beginning of our presentation, Frankie and I gave the following directions to the audience so that they would know how to participate, if they so desired:

How it works: As a member of the audience, you are invited to stop the action of the improv if you see someone being disempowered or oppressed. The skit will go through once first, uninterrupted, so you can get a sense of the issue. If you see a problem in the improv and think that by reacting differently you could break the oppression or solve the problem, simply yell "Stop!" When you yell "Stop!" you come into the scene, take the place of the oppressed person, and try out your idea through improvisation. In the end, whether or not the new direction introduced is successful in solving the problem at hand is not the point. It is more important to achieve a good discussion than a good solution. The theory behind this exercise is that the oppressed and disempowered have the potential to become empowered through their own initiatives and actions.

A few simple rules to remember:

1) When you choose to yell "Stop!" you come into the play and assume the role of the oppressed, not the oppressor.
2) Try to limit your involvement to one or two phrases so that other members of the audience can have a chance to try out their ideas.
3) It is more important to achieve a good discussion than a good solution.

Background to the First Dramatic Skit

In 2002, the principal of a Catholic secondary school in Oshawa, Ontario, refused to allow 17-year-old Marc Hall, a gay Catholic student in his senior year at the school, to take his boyfriend to his high school prom (Grace & Wells, 2005). As early as his grade 11 year, Marc had begun to take steps to secure official approval to take his boyfriend to prom; his attempts were met with several months of stalling tactics by his principal, Mr. Powers. When Mr. Powers finally said "No," first to Marc himself and then later to Marc's parents, he explained that interacting with a same-sex partner at the prom would constitute a form of sexual activity that was contrary to Catholicity (MacKinnon, 2002).

Marc's story aired on the March 18, 2002, edition of CTV National News. On March 19, 2002, the Durham Catholic District School Board publicly supported Mr. Powers' decision in a press release that proclaimed its constitutional right to administer its schools in a manner consistent with church teachings (Grace & Wells, 2005). The issue being forced by proactive and resilient queer youth like Marc Hall is one of institutional rights versus individual rights. Individual rights, and the responsibility of publicly funded institutions to respect the Canadian Charter of Rights and Freedoms, were upheld on May 10, 2002, when Justice Robert MacKinnon granted Marc Hall an interlocutory injunction allowing him to attend his high school prom with his boyfriend.

Students who were enrolled in the graduate course, for which this scene was going to be enacted, were aware of the facts and the issues surrounding the Marc Hall case because of an article on the required reading list. In order for the audience to make immediate sense of the mise-en-scène and the dialogue of the dramatic skit about to be performed in front of them, the following information was placed on an overhead projector for the audience to read while the actors got prepared for the scene offstage.

Theatre of the Oppressed Scenario One: Marc Hall's Prom Request

Background: Marc Hall is a grade 12 student who has been asking to meet with his principal in order to formally request permission to take his boyfriend to the prom. Marc first approached his English teacher for advice on how to proceed, and she assured Marc that she would speak to the principal on his behalf. Since learning of the matter from the English teacher, the principal has been evasive and has found excuses not to meet with Marc when approached by the student in the hallways. Knowing that he would have to act on this sooner or later, and not wanting to be waylaid by Marc in the hallways again, the principal decides to call Marc out of English class and down to his office for the discussion.

Setting: It's 2:30 in the afternoon as Marc is ushered into the principal's office by the secretary. The principal is seated at his desk, working on the computer. As Marc enters, the principal turns towards him and gestures with an open hand to one of the two chairs opposite his desk.

Some possible arguments that the principal could make:

- Your request is against school policy and Catholic teachings.
- The high school prom is a rite of passage into normal adulthood where boys are clearly boys and girls are clearly girls . . . there is no room for your sort of deviant behaviour at the prom.
- We can't have homosexual acts taking place right here in our school for all to see!
- What you're proposing is abnormal, unnatural, immoral . . . it's morally disordered. It's not the kind of message we can condone as a school.
- If you really want to celebrate your high school graduation with your boyfriend, why can't you just meet up with him later in private?
- Why don't we settle on a compromise? You can ask one of your female friends who doesn't have a date to the prom to go with your boyfriend as his "date," and then you could ask another one of your female friends to accompany you as your "date." Then the four of you could all sit together and that way your boyfriend can attend prom with you. That sounds like a fine solution to me.

The two presenters play out an improvised skit for the audience, with the oppressed character having very few creative ideas in terms of how to respond to the oppressive character's overpowering and authoritative statements.

The excerpt below depicts what I consider one of the more significant and memorable impromptu dramatic skits that developed after one of the audience members yelled "Stop!" and came into the improv scene in the role of the oppressed character. In this scene, the oppressor is the Principal, and the initials MH indicate Marc Hall, the oppressed character.

Marc Hall's Prom Request

Principal: As I was saying, the high school prom is a rite of passage into normal adulthood where boys are clearly boys and girls are clearly girls. There is simply no room for your sort of deviant behaviour at the prom.

MH: But, sir, it's my prom, too! I'm on the honour roll and on the student council. I'm not involved in any kind of "deviant behaviour."

Principal: Well, you know what I mean. You're a homosexual. We cannot have homosexual acts taking place right here in our school for all to see!

MH: What are you talking about, homosexual acts? All I want to do is bring my boyfriend to prom. We will arrive together, sit at the same table together, maybe hold hands, and dance a bit. What's wrong with that?

Principal: What you're proposing is abnormal, unnatural, immoral . . . it's morally disordered. It's not the kind of message we can condone as a school.

MH: It's not any different than what straight people do at prom, but they're not considered immoral.

Principal: It's immoral because it's deviant homosexual behaviour. The official Catholic stance on homosexuality is that it's OK to be gay, just don't act on it. It's because you're acting on it that you are being immoral.

MH: But, how can I not be myself? I don't understand. I learned in religion class to love my neighbour and to treat others as I would like to be treated. It feels like you are contradicting those teachings when you won't allow me to be myself and take my boyfriend to prom.

In this scene, the oppressed character, MH, presents several creative ways to deconstruct the statements made by the authoritative and oppressive character of the principal. Slowly, the oppressed character of MH becomes more empowered and gives the principal a lot to consider through the strength of his arguments. Specifically, MH points out that homosexual people would not behave any differently at a prom than heterosexual people, and he thus exposes the double standard of the immorality charge.

On a broader scale, MH successfully reveals the contradiction inherent in the official Catholic position on homosexuality, which contends that, it's OK to be gay, yet requires homosexual persons to deny their sexuality. This skit effectively reveals to the audience the types of homophobia that homosexual persons can encounter. People in the audience who may be harbouring the types of homophobic beliefs expressed by the character of the principal may feel compelled to re-evaluate their beliefs after reflecting upon some of the ideas contained in the skit. People in the audience who may not have known how to effectively respond to the kinds of homophobic statements made in the skit may now have some new ideas that they can use later on.

Theatre of the Oppressed Scenario Two: The Banning of Homosexual Books

Background: The Coordinating Teacher for St. Mary's English Department has just come back to the school from a Bob Edwards literary luncheon where the distinguished guest speaker, Canadian novelist Timothy Findley, spoke openly about his life with his long-term partner, Bill Whitehead. She expresses her disgust at how a perfectly civilized luncheon could be so easily ruined by this "homosexual outburst." She, for one, is never again going to teach Findley's novel *The Wars*. In fact, she's tired of having to field phone calls from upstanding Catholic parents who want to know why the novel is on the reading list. She can't think of a good reason why it's there and proposes that the entire department stop teaching it along with "that other homosexual novel," *Fried Green Tomatoes at the Whistle Stop Café*.

Setting: It's 3:10 and the last class of the day has just been let out. English teachers are returning to the English Department with their materials to file away and begin the process of packing up for the end of the day. The Coordinating Teacher whirls in, embroiled in a heated discussion with one of the other English teachers who accompanied her to the luncheon. Five out of the six members of the department are now present in the second floor English department office.

Some arguments that the Coordinating Teacher might make for excluding *The Wars* from the department's reading list include:

• It's just SICK! What makes him think he can go on publicly about his disgusting lifestyle? I shouldn't have to be subjected to that at a literary luncheon, for God's sake!

• I don't care if he's an internationally celebrated Canadian author who has won numerous literary awards! This kind of material is just not suitable for children, even if the International

Baccalaureate says it is.

- Our Catholic parents have a right to question what their children are reading. Heavens, I even question it. It's against our Catholic teachings to have a book on the curriculum that has a homosexual character and homosexual sex scenes in it.
- I don't care if the Alberta Ministry of Education sanctioned it, I don't approve of this book and I don't want any one of you teaching it anymore either. That goes for that other homosexual book with those two gay women that some of you are teaching, *Fried Green Tomatoes at the Whistle Stop Café*—I don't want any of you teaching that any more. In my capacity as Coordinating Teacher, I forbid it!
- If any of you decide to teach it anyway and a parent complains, you're on your own. This department won't support you, the administration won't support you, and without those two vital supports, downtown will never support you. It's just not worth it to teach such controversial books in our Catholic schools.

As in the first dramatic skit, the two presenters play out an improvised skit for the audience, with the oppressed character having very few creative ideas in terms of how to respond to the oppressive character's overpowering and authoritative statements.

The excerpt below depicts what I consider one of the more successful impromptu dramatic skits that developed after one of the audience members yelled "Stop!" and came into the improv scene in the role of the oppressed character. In this scene, the oppressor is the Coordinating Teacher (CT), and the oppressed character is the Teacher.

The Banning of Homosexual Books

CT: It's just SICK! What makes him think he can go on publicly about his disgusting lifestyle? I shouldn't have to be subjected to that at a literary luncheon, for God's sake!

Teacher: Well, you know, Timothy Findley is an internationally celebrated Canadian author who has won numerous literary awards. That's probably why he's on the reading lists sanctioned by both the International Baccalaureate and the Alberta Ministry of Education.

CT: I don't care if he's an internationally celebrated Canadian author! This kind of material is just not suitable for children, even if the International Baccalaureate says it is.

Teacher: Clearly, the master teachers who sat on the selection committee for literary reading lists did not think his books were unsuitable for children. What, exactly, is unsuitable?

CT: Well, I don't remember. It's not important. There's a gay character in that book, and it's just not right. Our Catholic parents have a right to question what their children are reading. Heavens, I even question it. It's against our Catholic teachings to have a book on the curriculum that has a homosexual character and homosexual sex scenes in it.

Teacher: But Alberta Education has sanctioned it and, since we are mandated to teach the curriculum prescribed by the provincial government, I guess that means we can teach *The Wars*.

CT: I don't care if the Alberta Ministry of Education sanctioned it; as a Catholic school, we don't have to adhere to everything that Alberta Education puts out there. I don't approve of this book and I don't want any one of you teaching it anymore, either. That goes for that other homosexual book with those two gay women that some of you are teaching, *Fried Green Tomatoes at the Whistle Stop Café*—I don't want any of you teaching that any more. In my capacity as Coordinating Teacher, I forbid it!

In this scene, the oppressed character, the Teacher, calmly counters the emotional arguments put forth by the oppressive character, the Coordinating Teacher. The success of this scene lies not so much in what the Teacher says but what she doesn't say. The Teacher manages to stay calm and make a few pointed statements, while the CT gets increasingly more flustered and ends up making some unsupportable statements. The fact that the CT cannot provide an example from any of Findley's books that she deems unsuitable for children shows that calls to censor texts are sometimes based on hearsay and not on actual knowledge of the text itself.

When the CT states that Catholic schools do not have to adhere to everything the provincial government prescribes for the curriculum, she is drawing attention to the selectiveness with which some publicly funded Catholic schools deliver the curriculum. This skit effectively enacts a more subtle form of homophobia than the first dramatic skit and invites the audience to review their own beliefs about censoring texts that are taught in schools. The skit also underscores the problem of how some Catholic schools simply sidestep certain details of the provincial curriculum when those details run counter to Catholic beliefs.

Theatre of the Oppressed Scenario Three: Lesbian Student Gets Bullied

Background: Jamie is a 17-year-old student who is trying to be out as a lesbian in her Catholic high school. She wears boys' clothes, sports a spiky haircut, keeps her wallet in her back pocket attached to a chain on her belt loop, has her lip pierced, carries around her skateboard, and wears lesbian-identified buttons on her military jacket lapel. She has been enduring weekly and sometimes daily bullying about her sexuality for the past two months. The bullies call Jamie names and whisper sexual things they would like to do to her when they see her in the school hallways and have lately taken to following her around after school, taunting her and even occasionally throwing rocks at her. She has finally had it when the bullies run up to her after school, shove her, grab her skateboard, and throw it in the river. Jamie decides to go to the principal to report the bullying.

Setting: It's 3:30 in the afternoon and Jamie has finally got up enough courage to go in to speak to the principal about what has been happening. Luckily for Jamie, the principal is available. Jamie is ushered into the small office; mounds of paperwork slightly obscure the principal, who is leaving a message for someone on the phone.

The principal looks at the student and can't recall ever seeing her before. She senses immediately that this student is upset and waves Jamie over to the table in the corner as she finishes leaving her message.

Some statements the principal might make:

- You say you've been experiencing this sort of bullying for two months or so. Why have you waited so long to do anything about it?
- It sounds to me as though the majority of your experiences at the hands of these bullies have taken place off of school property . . . I'm afraid I cannot act on your behalf because the school does not have any authority off of school property.
- You say that these bullies have been calling you names like "dyke" and "queer" and that they tell you that you are going to burn in hell. Can you think of any reason why they might be saying this?
- Have you thought of maybe changing your appearance so that you fit in a little bit more to our school climate and perhaps don't incite this kind of harassment?

- Do your parents, for example, know that you come to school dressed in this way?
- Jamie, are you a practicing lesbian? You know the Catholic Church says that homosexuals do have a right to exist but that you are called to celibacy, and since you've told me you are living with your . . . "girlfriend" . . . I'm afraid you are not honouring your Catholicity. If you are choosing not to honour your Catholicity, I'm afraid there's nothing I can do for you.

As in the previous two dramatic skits, the two actors/presenters play out an improvised skit for the audience, with the oppressed character not having much of a response to the oppressive character's domineering presence and overpowering statements.

The excerpts below depicts what I consider two of the more successful impromptu dramatic skits that developed after audience members yelled "Stop!" and came into the improv scene in the role of the oppressed character. In this scene, the oppressor is the Principal and the oppressed character is the Student.

Lesbian Student Gets Bullied (I)

Principal: As I was saying, I'm afraid I cannot act on your behalf, because the school does not have any authority off of school property.

Student: But last week you wrote an article for the newsletter about the dangers of stalking, after one of our students followed around another student from our school, after the last dismissal bell, well beyond the limits of school property.

Principal: Well, I can't discuss the details of that case. It was a pretty particular case. But normally, we don't handle matters that take place off of school property. Anyway, you say that these bullies have been calling you names like "dyke" and "queer" and that they tell you that you are going to burn in hell. Can you think of any reason why they might be saying this?

Student: Maybe because I'm a lesbian?

Principal: Have you thought of maybe changing your appearance so that you fit in a little bit more to our school climate and perhaps don't incite this kind of harassment?

Student: Have you thought of maybe changing your policies so that you can make my school experience just a little bit safer?

Lesbian Student Gets Bullied (II)

Principal: Do your parents, for example, know that you come to school dressed in this way?

Student: Why should it matter how I dress? Our student handbook says that we are not allowed to wear any clothing with offensive language or messages and, since I hate clothes with messages, I never wear such things. What does what I wear have to do with me getting bullied?

Principal: Jamie, are you a practicing lesbian?

Student: Well, ma'am, I used to be practicing, but now I'm close to perfect.

In the first of these two scenes, the oppressive character, the Principal, engages in evasive stalling practices common to administrators who would rather avoid, than solve, a problem at hand. When the principal subtly suggests that the student might have brought the bullying on herself because of the way she dresses, we see an instance of the classic "blame the victim" tactic. This scene echoes what family and friends often tell lesbians and gay men who are just coming out: "If you could just tone down the gayness of your appearance, no one would have to really know you're gay, and then you would be safe from homophobic treatment."

The second scene contains the student's clever rejoinder, which caused the audience to erupt with laughter. I chose these two scenes because both contain increasing levels of sarcastic humour on the part of the oppressed character, the Student. This suggests that the audience was becoming more and more emboldened by the *Theatre of the Oppressed* skits, and they started to suggest new, creative, and even humorous ways to confront the challenges posed by the oppressive character.

Theatre of the Oppressed Scenario Four: Lesbian Teacher in Catholic School Refused Permission To Participate in Pro-Gay Safe and Caring Schools Project

Background: A high school English teacher has been invited by the Society for Safe and Caring Schools to write a series of lesson plans designed to combat discrimination on the basis of race, gender, and sexual orientation. She learned of the opportunity to write the lesson plans from the Sexual Orientation and Gender Identity committee for the Alberta Teachers' Association, where she is out as a lesbian. She was invited to write the lesson plans expressly because she is a lesbian. Unfortunately, the workshop for the lesson plan writing is scheduled for a Friday, which will require missing a school day in order to attend. The English teacher approaches the Guidance Counsellor in her school, who is responsible for their local high school Society for Safe and Caring Schools, to see if she can get some support for the leave. The Guidance Counsellor is impressed and even offers to provide funding from her budget to send the English teacher to the workshop. The Guidance Counsellor phones some administrators at the downtown school board office to get their approval for this expense, but finds out that the Board is no longer interested in supporting this endeavour. The Guidance Counsellor now has to find a way to tell the English teacher that she will have to withdraw her support.

Setting: It's the 32-minute lunch "hour" in the staff room of Father Lacombe High. The Guidance Counsellor spots the English teacher at the sink as 30 or so teachers mill about, having their lunch. The counsellor approaches the English teacher and begins to tell her of the new turn of events.

Some statements the Guidance Counsellor might make in this situation:

- Even though I offered you funding before, the administrators downtown will not approve of this type of expenditure.
- I cannot provide you with any of the names of the people involved, as that was a private conversation.
- I am able to contact certain administrators in my capacity as a Guidance Counsellor. However, you do not have the same access to these people as a teacher.
- While the Catholic board acknowledges that gay students are at a high risk of violence, either from themselves or from others, it cannot support a workshop that condones and normalizes homosexuality.
- The Catholic Church does not accept homosexuals.
- While I am aware of the Alberta Teachers' Association initiative to create safe and caring schools for *all* students, we, as a Catholic school board, are not necessarily part of that project. We are developing our own Catholic response to these sensitive issues.

As in the earlier dramatic skits, the two actors/presenters play out an improvised skit for the audience, with the oppressed character being at a loss as to how to respond to the statements made by the oppressive character. The reason the scene is played out in this way is so that the audience can have time to imagine some more productive ways for the oppressed character to respond.

The excerpt below depicts what I consider one of the more illuminating dramatic skits that developed after an audience member yelled "Stop!" and came into the improv scene in the role of the oppressed character. In this scene, the oppressor is the Guidance Counsellor (GC) and the oppressed character is the Teacher.

Lesbian Teacher in Catholic School Refused Permission To Participate in Pro-Gay Safe and Caring Schools Project

Teacher: But this doesn't make any sense. Just yesterday, you were impressed with this opportunity and thought it would be great to have a teacher from our school participate.

GC: Well, yes, but now we can't go through with it because the administrators downtown will not approve of this type of expenditure.

Teacher: Did you tell them it is for the Society for Safe and Caring Schools and that you are behind our own mini Safe and Caring Schools project here in this high school, and that you support the idea of sending one of our teachers to develop anti-discrimination lesson plans?

GC: Yes, but it's out of my hands, I'm afraid.

Teacher: It's because the anti-discrimination lesson plans would also deal with homophobia, isn't it?

GC: Well, they didn't offer a reason as to why they would not approve of this expenditure. You do know, of course, that the Catholic Church does not condone homosexuality.

Teacher: The Safe and Caring Schools project should be for all students, not just those accepted by the Catholic faith. Are you aware that the Alberta Teachers' Association protects students from discrimination on the basis of sexual orientation?

GC: Well, yes, that may be so, but we, as a Catholic school board, do not necessarily adhere to every aspect of the ATA. In fact, we are developing our own Catholic response to sensitive issues, such as homosexuality in our schools.

Teacher: I don't understand how you can have a selective membership in the Alberta Teachers' Association and why you would want to develop your own workshops about homosexuality when that work has already been done by the ATA.

GC: We have a special responsibility as a Catholic school board to ensure that what we do reflects the doctrines of the faith. It is clear that you are very interested in this matter. Perhaps you would like to join the committee that is developing our unique Catholic response to sensitive issues in our schools?

This scene underscores one of the more subtle forms of homophobia in Catholic schools—the faceless institutional control over what teachers may and may not do in the fight to reduce discrimination on the basis of sexual orientation. It reveals the classic "pass the buck" tactic that various officials in Catholic schools may employ when questioned about why they will not support anti-homophobia work in the schools. It also reveals the contradiction inherent in the way that many Catholic schools may support the safe and caring schools project in theory but not in practice, especially if that means ensuring the safety of homosexual students, who are arguably the group most at risk of harm, either from themselves or from others in the school. As in the second skit, in which a Coordinating Teacher said that Catholic schools do not have to teach everything that is in the provincial curriculum, this skit sheds light on another example of selectivity on the part of Catholic schools when faced with progressive policies that may be at odds with the Catholic faith.

In presenting a description of the process behind the performance of these four dramatic skits, it is not my intention to suggest that all Catholic schools are always homophobic. Rather, I offer these dramatic skits as a Foucauldian (1977) counternarrative that unsettles the common understanding that homophobia does not exist or, at the very least, is difficult to see. The dramatic skits are presented in the order of the most overt example of homophobia to the least overt example, so that by the time the audience encounters the most subtle skit, their eyes and minds may be better trained to perceive the homophobia that is operating in the skit. I employ Augusto Boal's *Theatre of the Oppressed* (1974/1979) techniques in the broadest sense, recognizing that the political oppression he was addressing is not the same as homophobia, the form of oppression I am highlighting. Nevertheless, Boal's techniques can be effectively applied to all kinds of oppressive situations with a view to providing an avenue of expression for oppressed peoples.

Prentki and Selman (2000) suggest that "in the moment of improvisation or performance, there is a sense in which anything can be risked, in which the 'unsayable' can be said, the 'undoable' done and then, if necessary, undone" (p. 146). Feldhendler (1994) also agrees that there is potential in the improvisation of situations for transformation, for something to happen that can "symbolically change [one's] relationships both on the stage and in one's life" (p. 86). By engaging in Boal's *Theatre of the Oppressed* techniques, audiences can explore and evaluate their own and each other's perceptions and understandings of the world. In such performance, there is the potential for change. When these four dramatic skits were performed before an audience of graduate students, many later said that they did not know such examples of homophobia existed. Those who actively took part in creating the drama saw that, like drama, our social reality is constructed and can be reconstructed. Underlying each performance is the potential for change. Indeed, for Boal (1974/1979), drama was a rehearsal for future action.

References

Boal, A. (1979). *Theatre of the oppressed*. (C. McBride & M. McBride, Trans.). London: Pluto Press. (Original work published 1974).

Boal, A. (1992). *Games for actors and non-actors*. (A. Jackson, Trans.). London: Routledge.

Conrad, D. (2004). *"Life in the sticks": Youth experiences, risk & popular theatre process*. Unpublished doctoral dissertation, University of Alberta.

Conrad, D. (2005). Rethinking "at-risk" in drama education: Beyond prescribed roles. *Research in Drama Education, 10*(1), 27-41.

Feldhendler, D. (1994). Augusto Boal and Jacob L. Moreno: Theatre and therapy. In J. Cohen-Cruz & M. Schutzman (Eds.), *Playing Boal: Theatre, therapy, activism* (pp. 73-92). London: Routledge.

Foucault, M. (1977). *Language, counter-memory, practice: Selected essays and interviews*. (D. Bouchard & S. Simon, Trans.). Ithaca, NY: Cornell University Press.

Freire, P. (1970). Pedagogy of the oppressed. (M.B. Ramos, Trans.). New York: Continuum Publishing Corp.

Grace, A. P., & Wells, K. (2005). The Marc Hall prom predicament: Queer individual rights v. institutional church rights in Canadian public education. *Canadian Journal of Education 28*(3), 237-270.

MacKinnon, Justice R. (2002, May 10). *Smitherman v. Powers and the Durham Catholic District School Board* (Court File No. 12-CV-227705CM3). Whitby, ON: Ontario Superior Court of Justice.

Prentki, T., & Selman, J. (2000). *Popular theatre in political culture: Britain and Canada in focus*. Bristol, UK: Intellect Books.

Saldana, J. (1999). Playwriting with data: Ethnographic performance texts. *Youth Theatre Journal, 13*, 60-71.

The Silenced Family:
Policies and Perspectives on the Inclusion of Children's Literature Depicting Gay/Lesbian Families in Public Elementary Classrooms

Theresa M. Bouley

"*Those of us raised in alternative families, especially gay and lesbian families, have grown up feeling invisible without knowing why. As the next generation grows up, they must have resources in which they can see themselves reflected and therefore validated.*"—*The Co-directors of COLAGE (Children of Lesbians and Gays Everywhere), 2001.*

Think of the classroom you are in, the books you share with your students. Who do they represent? Whose story are they telling?

Leslea Newman, author of *Heather Has Two Mommies*, has been called the most dangerous writer living in America today. Daphne Muse, the editor of *The New Press Guide to Multicultural Resources for Young Readers* (1997), notes, "*Heather Has Two Mommies* has caused entire school districts to issue culturally restrictive and intellectually repressive guidelines" (p. 6). When she wrote the book in 1988, Newman had no idea it would ever get published, let alone become one of the most challenged books of the 1990s. Newman (2000) stated, "Though I have been repeatedly accused of having a militant, political agenda, my goal in writing the book was, simply, to tell a story" (Afterword). In fact, the American Library Association (2000) reported *Heather Has Two Mommies* and *Daddy's Roommate* (Willhoite, 1990) as being two of the most challenged books in the United States.

As a result, numerous children of gay/lesbian parents spend each day in classrooms without access to a single book that tells their story. The organization Children of Lesbians and Gays Everywhere (COLAGE, 2001) estimates that there are approximately 6 to 10 million children of gay, lesbian, or bisexual parents in the United States. Others estimate the range to be greater, that there are anywhere from "2 million to 8 million lesbian and gay parents who have between 4 and 14 million children" (Casper & Schultz, 1999, citing Patterson, 1992, 1995).

Emerging from the research in reading is the understanding that reading is not a passive activity. Rather, readers are constantly activating their schema, or prior knowledge, to interact with text and transform ideas about themselves and the world (Smith, 1985). Applying a critical literacy perspective, Mason described literacy as a process of "coming to self-consciousness," in which one not only discovers but also creates oneself (as cited in Mc-Gill-Franzen, Lanford, & Adams, 1997). In *Envisioning Literature* (1995), Langer discussed how students can learn to better understand themselves and their world through literature:

Inherent in the act of literacy understanding is the promise of touching the many-sidedness of human sensibility. It is through the envisionments we develop as we explore new horizons of possibility that we can at least begin to imagine the perspectives of others—in other circumstances, eras, and cultures—and be moved to make new sense of ourselves, our times, and our world. (p. 145)

Langer's perspective has been extended to encompass children of all backgrounds. Harris pointed out: "When students of diverse backgrounds read literature that highlights the experiences of their own cultural group, they learn to feel pride in their own identity and heritage" (as cited in Au, 1993, p. 177). Clearly, students of diverse backgrounds benefit from the inclusion of multicultural/multiethnic literature into their classrooms (Walker-Dalhouse, 1992). Giving students opportunities to link literature to personal experience can have a positive impact on both their view of themselves and their reading. It has been suggested that the inclusion of such literature can motivate students to engage in the reading process (Wigfield & Guthrie, 1995). Furthermore, students' increased motivation to read can heighten their belief that they are competent and efficacious at reading (Baker & Wigfield, 1999).

Children of gay and lesbian families must attend schools with administrators, teachers, and materials prepared to meet their individual academic needs. Yet, the heterosexist assumptions of administrators and teachers in elementary schools have resulted in curricula and pedagogy that fail to know and therefore meet the needs of gay/lesbian families (Kozik-Rosabal, 2000). As a result, a pervasive systematic silencing of gay/lesbian families exists in American schools. In our efforts to provide the best learning environment possible for all children, we must break the silence, bring visibility to all families, and open up the discourse relating to the inclusion of gay/lesbian issues in elementary schools.

The most age-appropriate way to include gay/lesbian families in elementary classrooms is through children's literature. Children's literature depicting gay/lesbian families must be both accessible to children, and used for instruction by classroom teachers. Yet, teachers must first examine their own beliefs and have opportunities to discuss them with their principals and superintendents.

It is my intent in this chapter to share my research investigating the availability and use of children's literature depicting gay/lesbian families in elementary classrooms. In addition, I will also share teacher, principal, and superintendent attitudes, beliefs, and biases towards the inclusion of such literature. Most important, I will demonstrate, through a review of the literature, that to allow for an equitable access to literacy, all children must have the opportunity to view themselves accurately depicted in the literature.

As Francis Day in *Lesbian and Gay Voices* (2000) said, "We owe young people and ourselves nothing less than the best possible world we can imagine. Let us take energetic action to get these wise and compassionate books into the hands of young people everywhere" (p. xxi).

An Equitable Access to Literacy

Multicultural education is a means for positively using cultural diversity in the total learning process. The goals of multicultural education, as suggested by Gollnick and Chinn (1990) are: "1) to promote the strength and value of cultural diversity; 2) to promote human rights and respect for those who are different from oneself; 3) to acquire a knowledge of the historical and social realities of U.S. society in order to understand racism, sexism, and poverty; 4) to support alternative life choices for people; 5) to promote social justice and equality for all people; and 6) to promote equity in the distribution of power and income among groups" (p. 301). In order to effectively develop educational services in our pluralistic society, curriculum, materials, and methodology must include consideration of students from various backgrounds. Teaching multiculturally calls for teaching that starts from students' life experiences, not from the experiences of the teacher, nor the experiences necessary to fit into the dominant school culture (Shor, 1986). When applying a multicultural teaching perspective, classroom teachers both personalize the curriculum, by relating curriculum materials to the students' interests and experiences, and humanize the curriculum, by attributing human characteristics to concepts and principles (Gollnick & Chinn, 1990). The ultimate goal of multicultural education is to meet the individual learning needs of each student so that all students can progress to their fullest capacity.

A teacher practicing critical pedagogy takes multicultural education beyond acceptance to affirmation. Irwin (1996) suggests that it is only at this level of multiculturalism that an environment is truly antibias and antidiscriminatory. Christensen (1992), in her description of building a multicultural community, emphasized empathy as being "a key in community building" (p. 14). Her multicultural curriculum draws on the strengths and experiences of her students. This example of affirming students' cultural capital defies modernistic classroom environments, where the value is placed solely on the practices of the dominant culture. A result is the prevention of the culture shock that most students of subordinate groups experience in school. In this non-hierarchical environment, racism and other forms of discrimination are openly discussed and problematized. Christensen (1992) eloquently explained the ideology behind what has been referred to as fear of naming: "Topics like racism and homosexuality are avoided in most classrooms but they seethe like open wounds. When there is an opening for discussion, years of anger and pain surface" (p. 14). In her classroom, students are taught how to communicate with each other about a range of real-life matters.

In order to teach such a pervasive multicultural program, it is critical that teachers self-examine their own ideology or biases and attempt to experience the thoughts and feelings of others. This raising of consciousness is critical for all individuals. Irwin (1996) purports that the process of becoming nonsexist, multicultural persons is lifelong and entails "learning by listening, asking and being open to others' perspectives" as well as admitting to our "unconscious biases and the unwitting mistakes that we have made" (p. 136).

In an attempt to personalize curriculum and relate materials to students' interests and needs, teachers must both familiarize themselves with multicultural/multiethnic literature as well as its use. Multicultural literature has been defined as literature that focuses on subordinate groups, such as "people of color (i.e., African Americans, Asian Americans, Hispanic Americans, and Native Americans), religious minorities (i.e., the Amish or Jewish), regional cultures (i.e., the Appalachian and Cajun), gay/lesbian/bisexual/transgendered individuals, the disabled and the elderly" (Harris, 1992). Au (1993) discussed the particular advantages to the use of multicultural/multiethnic literature, as opposed to literature written from a mainstream perspective:

> Multicultural/multiethnic literature can be used in the classroom to affirm the cultural identity of students of diverse backgrounds, and to develop all students' understanding and appreciation of other cultures. This view of literature is one of the new patterns of instruction that can help to support the school literacy development of students of diverse backgrounds. (p. 176)

For a number of reasons, students of diverse backgrounds may be empowered by multicultural/multiethnic literature. Being able to identify with characters and events in a story and viewing the members of their own cultural group can have a significant effect on students' affect and self-efficacy towards reading (Purves & Beach, 1972). Allington and Cunningham (1996) concurred as they emphasized the importance of stocking schools with books that represent the diversity in our culture and suggested that by doing so, teachers can enhance minority students' reading achievement. Sims (1982) used the term "culturally conscious literature" to define literature that authentically reflects a group's "culture, language, history, and values." A piece of "culturally conscious literature" would have characters who are of the culture or ethnic group represented and a story that is presented from the perspective of that particular group. Au (1993) described "culturally conscious literature" as including "characteristics that are not present as stereotypes but as complex human beings" (p. 76). It is crucial that teachers show students how to detect racism in literature. Books provide opportunities to convince students to question society's attitudes, stereotypes, and myths. Once students learn how to detect racism in literature, they can "proceed to transfer the perception to wider areas" (Muse, 1997, p. 17). It is critical that teachers not only have multicultural/multiethnic titles available in their classroom, but that they use these titles pervasively and effectively. Allington and Cunningham (1996) suggested that a classroom framework that emphasized the reading of several texts daily for the purpose of read-alouds, instruction, and independent reading is highly beneficial to all children. It is critical that multicultural/multiethnic literature be introduced to students and used for instruction, read-alouds, and available for self-selection.

Many teachers are aware of the importance of including multicultural literature in their curriculum. Titles that address diversity with respect to culture, ethnicity, economics, linguistics, and special needs are fairly accessible in public elementary classrooms. Furthermore, many teachers personalize curriculum relating to families by including children's literature that depicts diverse family backgrounds. One-parent homes, divorced-parent homes, grandparents as caregivers, and adoptions are often reflected in the chosen titles. Yet, children's literature depicting gay/lesbian families appears to be nearly non-existent. While there are very few studies on the use of gay and lesbian literature with elementary-age children, those conducted have found very little evidence of the inclusion of such literature. In fact, researchers have found that these titles are not only left out of elementary classrooms, but that teachers often feel they should protect children from knowledge of gay/lesbian issues (Casper, Cuffaro, Schultz, Silin, & Wickens, 1996). Schall and Kaufman (2003) found similar results when they introduced books with gay/lesbian characters to preservice teachers: "The majority of preservice teachers rejected the idea of children reading these books in the classroom, saying that books with gay/lesbian characters were inappropriate because children couldn't deal with books 'like that' " (p. 36). Other studies emphasized the reasons why such an impenetrable, systematic silencing of gays and lesbians occurs, especially in elementary schools. Nieto (2002) suggests that a perception of parents' discomfort is one of the reasons why teachers and administrators avoid mentioning gay/lesbian families. She states that teachers and administrators expressed a general lack of confidence that parents would be open and accepting of including gay/lesbian literature. Newman (1997) discusses the viability of this suggestion and adds that parents' fear of the unknown may result in their lack of support:

> It seems to me that a disproportionate number of parents live in fear of their child reading just one book with a gay character in it, for such exposure will, in these parents' minds, cause their child to grow up to be lesbians or gay. It is usually useless to point out that the vast majority of lesbians and gay men were brought up by heterosexual parents and spent countless hours of their childhood reading books with heterosexual characters. Fear is irrational. (p. 152)

Many teachers may worry about support from administrators, parents, or the community at large.

Schneider, in *No Blood, Guns, or Gays Allowed!: The Silencing of the Elementary Writer* (2001), found a common concern among teachers when discussing controversial writing topics: "Whether it was parents, newspapers, or administrators, the teachers felt the scrutiny of outside others who are in position to judge their teaching, intentions, and lives" (p. 421).

Regardless of the reason, children growing up in gay/lesbian families very rarely or never feel the level of acceptance or validation that others receive when their families are read about, discussed, and affirmed. As a result, the obvious conclusion is that the love they witness in their homes is neither legitimate nor healthy (Kozik-Rosabal, 2000). To gay and lesbian parents, "One message comes through loud and clear: Schools are breeding grounds—intentionally or not—for a heterosexist ideology that actively works against even the marginal legitimacy of gay families" (Kozik-Rosabal, 2000, p. 382).

Conversations With Teachers, Principals, and Superintendents

As part of my research investigating the availability and use of children's literature depicting gay/lesbian families in elementary classrooms, I had numerous planned and spontaneous conversations with elementary school teachers, principals, and superintendents. I conducted the ethnographic interviews with three Connecticut school principals on their knowledge, use, and beliefs regarding the implementation of such curricula and materials, two Connecticut school district superintendents on district policies regarding curriculum or materials (children's books) addressing gay/lesbian families, and 10 teachers regarding their beliefs about and awareness of literature depicting same-sex families. I also had numerous impromptu conversations with teachers and school librarians. In addition, I developed and administered a survey to teachers in 1st through 4th grade to determine their awareness and use of children's books portraying gay/lesbian families. All of the teachers who were interviewed completed the survey, but not all of the 70 teachers who completed the survey were interviewed. Qualitative analyses were conducted of all interview/conversation/survey data and included 70 teacher surveys and 30 interviews/conversations.

Results and Implications

Clear themes emerged from the qualitative data. First, teachers, principals, and superintendents all said that their first priority was to advocate for all children. With that said, teachers, principals, and superintendents all stated that if there were a child in their class with two moms/dads, they would be sensitive to that child's needs and consider reading such literature. Otherwise, the literature would not be used. It appears that teachers are assuming that they would always be aware of a gay/lesbian parent/family member and only when made aware of such families would they consider reading inclusive literature. It further suggests that these teachers don't believe that including gay/lesbian families in their multicultural curriculum is beneficial to all children. When a few teachers were asked how this exclusion was different from waiting until there is a member of a cultural or ethnic group in their class to read a book depicting that culture, their responses were always the same— "I hadn't thought of it that way!" In a discussion on the works of Freire and Shor in *Writing Pedagogy: A Dialogue of Hope*, Anne-Loise Brookes and Ursula A. Kelly discuss whether or not those in power are capable of "dismantling the system": "The silent dominant have difficulty reading marginally, and I do not expect such men to discuss the problems of women or gay men or lesbians. What I do expect of them is that they examine their own positions of power as effects of and as affecting oppressed others. In answer to your question, 'How necessary is it for both women and men to problematize gender/sexual orientation?' I would respond, 'Not how necessary, but how?' " (Weiler & Mitchell, 1992, p. 279).

Richard A. Friend, in *Choices, Not Closets: Heterosexism and Homophobia in Schools,* wrote, "Often silencing (systematic exclusion) occurs by ignoring or denying the presence of lesbian, gay, and bisexual people, rendering them invisible" (1993, p. 212). This silencing or systematic exclusion was pervasive in my interviews, as evidenced by such comments as:

"I get a strong feeling that the school district runs in a quiet fashion . . . keeps everything under the radar. I think you need to pick your battles. I think going under the radar is not a bad thing, because you can do it (read such books) but when it becomes a big deal, teachers won't want to take the risk anymore." (school principal)

"We don't want to cross the line in terms of advocacy so that it puts us in a position that we are advocating. Prudence dictates support without appearing to be taking sides."
"We need to be careful. We certainly wouldn't let things go (if there was someone) who needed support but we don't ask the question. I have never seen this as an issue here, ever." (school superintendents)

"If it wasn't brought up we wouldn't have to talk about it."
"I haven't had any children with gay parents." (teachers)

Further evidence of systematic silencing came from a superintendent who said, "For all I know, that has occurred (the reading of gay/lesbian literature). Teachers deal with families. It should be on a case-by-case basis; don't take the books out unless a child is present with same-sex parents (elementary). The middle school librarian has some books on homosexuality or same-sex families. She makes those books available to students who *express an interest.*" Friend (1993) discusses this as a common situation whereby

If the school library does have any books on homosexuality, they are frequently kept behind the reference desk. This systematically excludes information by making it inaccessible to students. A catch-22 is created, whereby students may need the books in order to begin to feel more comfortable with asking for the books. This systematic exclusion of information, resource materials, empathetic support, and/or role models contributes to cementing the layers of silencing in schools. (p. 215)

As a result, Friend (1993) suggests that the teacher's challenge is "to work to understand the socio-emotional context in which students exist and provide resources for overcoming and dismantling the systems that lead to silencing and victimization while supporting resources that build equity" (p. 235).

A second theme that emerged and is a direct result of the first is that teachers were generally unaware of titles that depict gay/lesbian families or are inclusive of all family structures. This is contradictory, in the sense that most teachers said that their first priority was to advocate for all children and that they would be sensitive to children's needs. Yet, many were unable to recognize any titles that could be used to do so. When asked the question, "Do you know any literature depicting same-sex families?" most teachers said "no" or "I have seen some but don't know the titles." When asked if they were familiar with specific titles, most recognized *Heather Has Two Mommies,* and about one-third of the respondents were able to mention a few others (yet none of them actually owned these books). Only one principal was aware of other titles enough to discuss the stories (she actually owned some of the books mentioned).

Many teachers used their concern that the available books are of poor literary quality as the reason they did not have any in their possession. Many indicated that once the literature available becomes better, it will be "easier" to use. Teachers also wanted literature that did not make homosexuality the main issue, preferring literature in which homosexuality is "embedded" and therefore less likely to "push people's buttons." Since few teachers were able to identify any such books to begin with, one wonders how they could reasonably judge the content.

Teachers also expressed uncertainty that they would receive support and concern that they would be scrutinized by parents and then not supported by the administration if parents did complain. Tellingly, all of the teachers said that they were unaware of any existing policy that addressed the removal of support for teachers who connected the use of LGBT literature to a curriculum unit. They imagined becoming targets of parental complaints, and vulnerable to punishment from administration, even though no such policies existed.

Conclusion

What arises at every level of the education system is silence and invisibility with regard to LGBT issues. Homophobia is not expressed through consciously hurtful comments or acts, but rather through a series of assumptions that LGBT material does exist and could be covered should the need present itself. Homophobia also is evident in the unwillingness to follow up, to ensure access to LGBT books, to seek knowledge in how to use them in class. LGBT literature, if acquired, read, and discussed, could open exactly the types of critical dialogue needed to inform and empower teachers and administrators to utilize these materials with students. I envision open discussion forums, communication between board members and the community, superintendents, principals, teachers, librarians, and parents. In this way, practical information, such as awareness of titles, can be developed, accessibility to these texts can be opened, and strategies for connecting LGBT literature to curriculum can be established, thereby easing personal discomfort and enhancing learning. I am calling for open discussion to break the homophobia that thrives within a series of silences, so that school systems do not wait until one of its students faces a crisis, but genuinely educates for inclusivity so that all children can benefit.

References

Allington, R. L., & Cunningham, P. M. (1996). *Schools that work: Where all children read and write.* New York: HarperCollins.

American Library Association, Office of Intellectual Freedom. (2000). *OIF censorship database 1990-2000: Challenges by type.* Chicago, IL: Author.

Au, K. H. (1993). *Literacy instruction in multicultural settings.* Orlando, FL: Harcourt Brace College Publishers.

Baker, L., & Wigfield, A. (1999). Dimensions of children's motivation for reading and their relations to their reading activity and reading achievement. *Reading Research Quarterly, 34,* 452-477.

Brookes, A., & Kelly, U. A. (1992). Writing pedagogy: A dialogue of hope. In K. Weiler & C. Mitchell (Eds.), *What schools can do* (pp. 265-281). Albany, NY: State University of New York Press.

Casper,V., Cuffaro, H., Schultx, S., Silin, J., & Wickens, E. (1996). Toward a more thorough understanding of the world: Sexual orientation and early childhood education. *Harvard Educational Review, 66*(2), 227-293.

Christensen, L. (1992). Tales from and untracked class. *Rethinking Schools, 2*(1), 14-16.

COLAGE. (2001). *Children of gays and lesbians everywhere.* Retrieved November 2005, from www.colage.org/research/facts.html.

Day, F. A. (2000). *Lesbian and gay voices.* Westport, CT: Greenwood Publishers.

Friend, R. A. (1993). Choices, not closets: Heterosexism and homophobia in schools. In L. Weis & M. Fine (Eds.), *Beyond silenced voices* (pp. 209-235). Albany, NY: State University of New York Press.

Gollnick, D., & Chinn, P. (1990). *Multicultural education in a pluralistic society.* Columbus, OH: Merrill.

Harris, V. (Ed.). (1992). *Teaching multicultural literature in grades K-8.* Norwood, MA: Christopher-Gordon.

Irwin, J. (1996). *Empowering ourselves and transforming schools: Educators making a difference.* Albany, NY: SUNY Press.

Kozik-Rosabal, G. (2000). "Well, we haven't noticed anything bad going on," said the principal: Parents speak about their gay families and schools. *Education and Urban Society, 32*(3), 368-389.

Langer, J. (1995). *Envisioning literature: Literacy understanding and literature instruction.* New York: Teachers College Press.

McGill-Franzen, A., Lanford, C., & Adams, E. (1997). *Learning to be literate: A comparison of five urban early childhood programs.* Albany, NY: University of Albany, State University of New York, National Research Center on English Learning and Achievement.

Muse, D. (Ed.). (1997). *Multicultural resources for young readers.* New York: The New Press.

Nichols, S. L. (1999). Gay, lesbian, and bisexual youth: Understanding diversity and promoting tolerance in schools. *The Elementary School Journal, 99*(5), 505-519.

Newman, L. (1997). Heather and her critics. *The Horn Book Magazine, 73*(2), 149-153.

Newman, L. (2000). *Heather has two mommies* (2nd ed.). Los Angeles: Alyson Wonderland.

Nieto, S. (2002). *Language, culture, and teaching: Critical perspectives for a new century.* Mahwah, NJ: Lawrence Erlbaum.

Purves, A. C., & Beach, R. (1972). *Literature and the reader.* Urbana, IL: National Council of Teachers of English.

Schall, J., & Kauffman, G. (2003). Exploring literature with gay and lesbian characters in the elementary school. *Journal of Children's Literature, 29*(1), 36-44.

Schneider, J. J. (2001). No blood, guns, or gays allowed! The silencing of the elementary writer. *Language Arts, 78*(5), 415-425.

Shor, I. (1986). *Culture wars: School and society in the conservative restoration, 1969-1984.* Boston: Routledge & Kegan Paul.

Sims, R. (1982). *Shadow and substance.* Urbana, IL: National Council of Teachers of English.

Smith, F. (1985). *Reading without nonsense.* New York: Teachers College Press.

Walker-Dalhouse, D. (1992). Fostering multicultural awareness: Books for young children. *Reading Horizons, 33*, 47-54.

Weiler, K., & Mitchell, C. (Eds.). (1992). *What schools can do: Critical pedagogy and practice.* Albany, NY: State University of New York Press.

Wigfield, A., & Guthrie, J. T. (1995). *Dimensions of children's motivations for reading: An initial study (Research Rep. No. 34).* Athens, GA: National Reading Research Center.

Willhoite, M. (1990). *Daddy's roommate.* Boston: Alyson Wonderland.

RESOURCES FOR EMBRACING LESBIAN, GAY, BISEXUAL, AND TRANSGENDER (LGBT) FAMILIES IN OUR CLASSROOMS

Kay Emfinger

The following chapter details tools, resources, and materials to get beyond tokenism and to authentically embrace all families. This piece evolved from my own treacherous journey of navigating the school system as a lesbian parent, silenced in a sea of heteronormativity that ranged from having my partner's name removed from school records to a total absence of teacher knowledge of appropriate resources to "welcome" our family into the classroom community. My child's experience in a barren wasteland of curricula void of subject matter relevant to <u>her reality</u>, and the wounds of words unspoken and images unportrayed, spurred my research and fueled my desire as a parent, teacher, and teacher educator to proactively connect teachers with the vital resources they need. As you read, use the following questions as a guide and call to begin your own quest for knowledge. What is the responsibility of schools to embrace all families, regardless of their sexual orientation? Are you one of the many teachers who have limited knowledge of LGBT culture? How can you garner strategies to acknowledge and embrace the presence of same sex families? How will you help children connect with the subject matter and tasks and make it relevant to <u>their</u> reality? How might a welcoming classroom be a tool for combating hate? Who should bear the burden of making sure that classroom culture is reflective of all students?

This resource chapter is organized into four subsections: 1) background, 2) books, 3) multimedia, and 4) support and informational organizations for each of the audience categories, students, parents, and teachers. *Resources for Embracing Lesbian, Gay, Bisexual, and Transgender Families in Our Classrooms* provides the reader with information, insights, and strategies—ranging from commonplace to controversial.

Background

All people need to see themselves reflected in media . . . the books and magazines they read, the television/movies they watch, the Internet sites they visit. Quality media affirms emotions and mirrors life experiences. While media portraying LGBT families is sparse, it has grown tremendously in the last decade to include a range of venues from books to television networks. Media references are detailed in two major sections, books and multimedia. Books referenced vary in genre, quality, availability, and targeted age ranges. In an effort to provide an exhaustive listing, books have not been critiqued for quality. Online booksellers are excellent sources for critical reviews by both experts and lay readers. In order to inform the reader, descriptive key phrases in italics follow some references, particularly instances in which the title does not sufficiently indicate the content and/or audience.

A plethora of children's books are published each year. However, relatively few portray alternative families. Of the books that do make it to press, many focus on parental sexuality rather than families engaged in day-to-day activities. Rarely are LGBT characters portrayed as supporting characters in the normal flow of the text or illustrations (Siegel, 2003). In response to this hole in the market and the ever-increasing need expressed by gay Baby Boomers, several publishers and distributors have sprung up in the last several years. However, drawing an analogy to the 30-plus years it took to fill the void in African American children's literature, LGBT children's literature still has at least several decades to go before it becomes mainstream. Readers will note incomplete bibliographical information for several references, as many online desktop publishing companies do not include the geographical locations of their publications. This phenomenon possibly results from LGBT self-publishers' needs to ensure family security and privacy in a world that is generally oppressive and threatening to the LGBT population. Even in this information age, there are many barriers to quality children's literature. Books with LGBT characters are: 1) frequently banned books—thus inaccessible in libraries; 2) self published—thus leading to high cost and limited availability in mainstream bookstores; and 3) poor quality, due to lack of experienced writers and illustrators.

The multimedia sections encompass online resources, audio and video recordings, and television networks. Online resources make up the bulk of these sections. Until very recently, media moguls considered LGBT topics taboo, thus limiting information flow and media access. With the explosion of technology in the 1990s, the LGBT community effectively utilized the Internet to build alliances, provide information and support networks, and communicate in a safe arena, thus building solidarity.

Technology in the 21st century continues to revolutionize access to information about LGBT culture. Since the dawn of the century, three broadcasting companies have launched LGBT programming that is available via cable television, satellite, or the Internet ("GLAAD Media Awards," 2005). Major networks aired shows with LGBT characters, such as *Will & Grace*. Cable networks produced ongoing series portraying LGBT characters dealing with relevant issues, such as *Queer as Folk* and *The L Word* ("Out of the Closet," 2005). None of these offerings are "family programming" aimed at LGBT parents and their elementary-age children. New on the horizon are *The Gay Parenting Show*, a podcast (retrieved 11/26/2005 from http://gayparenting.the podcastnetwork. com/) and *South of Nowhere*, a teen drama launched on N, Nickelodeon's teen network ("Working on Television Portrayals of Gay Teens," 2005). These offerings bring us one step closer to filling the gap so that no family will be left behind.

Children, teachers, and parents need access to supportive environments and information via organizations and support groups. These resource sections include parenting groups, children's groups, chat boards, pen-pal opportunities, newsletters, family events, national support groups, camps, and information clearinghouses. Two major resource areas not included in this text are AIDS-related issues and children's sexual orientation/coming out process. These expansive topics deserve solo or targeted publications in order to communicate this critical information effectively.

This guide provides an impetus for pedagogical action, offering teachers the opportunity to explore these sources and seek additional venues with the larger educational community. Invite colleagues to ponder these points: What policies does your school have in place to confront homophobia? What supports are available for teachers who are working to design welcoming environments? Are there forums in your school for open conversation about strategically planning a welcoming, inclusive environment (e.g., changing school policies and forms to include same-sex families)? Can funds be allocated to purchase the collection of resources needed to effectively confront homophobia? What representations of LGBT culture exist in the school for students to feel validated? How can you be proactive in your classroom, school, and larger community?

Books for Children

Alden, J. (1992). *A boy's best friend*. Boston: Alyson Publications. *Non-traditional families*

Aldrich, A. (2003). *How my family came to be: Daddy, papa, and me*. New Family Press. *Told from a preschooler's point of view*

Burks, S. (2004). *While you were sleeping*. Little Man Publishing. *Non-traditional families, Adoptive families*

Combs, B. (2000). *ABC: A family alphabet book*. Illustrated by Desiree Keane & Brian Rappa. Ridley Park, PA: Two Lives Publishing. *Non-traditional families*

Combs, B. (2000). *123: A family counting book*. Illustrated by Danamarie Hosler. Ridley Park, PA: Two Lives Publishing. *Non-traditional families*

Considine, K. (2004). *Emma and Meesha my boy: A two-mom story*. Philadelphia: Xlibris.

De Haan, L., & Nijland, S. (2000). *King & king*. Berkeley, CA: Ten Speed Press. *Gay fairytale, gender roles*

De Haan, L., & Nijland, S. (2004). *King & king & family*. Berkeley, CA: Ten Speed Press. *Gay fairytale, gender roles*

dePaola, T. (1979). *Oliver Button is a sissy*. Orlando, FL: Harcourt Brace & Co. *Bullying, gender roles*

Dykstra, L. (2005). *Uncle Aiden*. Vancouver, BC: Baby Bloc Publishers.

Edmonds, B. L. (2000). *Mama eat ants, yuck*. Illustrated by Matthew Daniele. Eugene, OR: Hundredth Munchy Publications. *Non-traditional families*

Ferro, U. (2005). *Tanny's meow*. Illustrated by Ariella Huff. West Tilsbury, MA: Marti Books. *Non-traditional families*

Fierstein, H. (2002). *The sissy duckling*. Illustrated by Henry Cole. New York: Simon & Schuster Books for Young Readers. *Bullying, gender roles*

Freeman, M. (2002). *Trouble with babies*. New York: Holiday House.

Garden, N. (2004). *Case of the stolen scarab*. Ridley Park, PA: Two Lives Publishing. *LGBT supporting characters*

Garden, N. (2000). *Holly's secret*. New York: Farrar, Straus, and Giroux. *Non-traditional families*

Garden, N. (2004). *Molly's family*. New York: Farrar, Straus, & Giroux.

Gonzalez, R. (2005). *Antonio's card/La tarjeta de Antonio*. San Francisco: Children's Book Press. *Non-traditional family, Bilingual*

Gordon, S. (2000). *All families are different*. Amherst, NY: Prometheus Books.

Gregg, J. C. (2005). *Flying free*. North Charleston, SC: BookSurge Publishing. *Non-traditional families*

Guitman, A., & Hallensleben, G. (2003). *Daddy kisses board book*. San Francisco: Chronicle Books.

Guitman, A., & Hallensleben, G. (2004). *Mommy hugs board book*. San Francisco: Chronicle Books.

Guitman, A., & Hallensleben, G. (2005). *Mommy loves board book*. San Francisco: Chronicle Books.

Harding, B., & Harding, V. (2003). *Going to fair day*. Illustrated by Chris Bray-Cotton. Alexandria, NSW, Australia: Bulldog Books. (Available from Two Lives Publishing Company, http://www.twolives.com/ Phone: 610-532-2852).

Harding, B., & Harding, V. (2003). *My house*. Illustrated by Chris Bray-Cotton. Alexandria, NSW, Australia: Bulldog Books.

Harding, B., & Harding, V. (2005). *Koalas on parade*. Illustrated by Chris Bray-Cotton. Alexandria, NSW, Australia: Bulldog Books.

Harding, B., & Harding, V. (2005). *The rainbow cubby house*. Illustrated by Chris Bray-Cotton. Alexandria, NSW, Australia: Bulldog Books.

Henkes, K. (1989). *Jessica*. Illustrated by Kevin Henkes. New York: Greenwillow Books. *Female friendships*

Hoffman, E. (1999). *Best best colors*. Illustrated by Celeste Henriquez. St. Paul, MN: Redleaf Press. *Non-traditional families, gay pride, bilingual*

Howe, J. (1996). *Pinkey and Rex and the bully*. New York: Aladdin. *Bullying, gender roles*

Pendleton Jimenez, K. (2000). *Are you a boy or a girl?* Toronto, ON: Green Dragon Press.

Judes, M. (2001). *Max, the stubborn little wolf*. New York: HarperCollins. *Gender roles*

Kemp, J., & Walters, C. (2003). *Dad mine*. China: Little, Brown.

Krakow, K. (2002). *The Harvey Milk story*. Ridley Park, PA: Two Lives Publishing. *LGBT history/biography*

Lituchy, J., & Lituchy, S. (2004). *What makes a family*. Ridley Park, PA: Two Lives Publishing.

Marcus, E. (2000). *What if someone I know is gay?: Answers to questions about gay and lesbian people*. New York: Price Sterne Sloan.

Meyers, S. (2004). *Everywhere babies*. Singapore: Redwagon Books.

Moss, P. (2004). *Say something*. Gardiner, ME: Tilbury House Publishing. *Teasing/ bullying*

Newman, L. (2000). *Heather has two mommies* (2nd ed.). Illustrated by Dianna Souza. Boston: Alyson Publications.

Newman, L. (2002). *Felicia's favorite story*. Illustrated by Adriana Romo. Ridley Park, PA: Two Lives Publishing. *Non-traditional families*

Newman, L. (2004). *The boy who cried fabulous*. Berkeley, CA: Ten Speed Press. *Gender Roles, Bullying*

Numeroff, L. (1998). *What daddies do best*. New York: Simon & Schuster.

Okimoto, J. D., & Aoki, E. H. (2002). *White swan express*. New York: Clarion. *Adoption, LGBT supporting characters*

Parr, T. (2003). *The family book*. Boston: Little, Brown.

Richardson, J., & Parnell, P. (2005). *And tango makes three*. New York: Simon & Schuster. *Non-fictional account of same-gender parenting in the animal kingdom*

Rylant, C. (1998). *Van Gogh café*. New York: Scholastic. *Fictional chapter book with gay supporting characters*

Setterington, K. (2004). *Mom and mum are getting married*. Illustrated by Alice Priestley. Toronto, ON: Second Story Press.

Simon, N. (2003). *All families are special*. Illustrated by Teresa Flavin. Morton Grove, IL: Albert Whitman & Co.

Snow, J. (2004). *How it feels to have a gay or lesbian parent: A book by kids for kids of all ages*. Binghamton, NY: Harrington Park Press.

Stafford, A. (2005). *Aisha's moonlit walk*. Boston: Skinner House Books. *Non-traditional supporting characters, alternative religion*

Valentine, J. (2004). *The daddy machine* (2nd ed.). Illustrated by Lunette Schmidt. Boston: Alyson Publications. *Non-traditional families*

Valentine, J. (2004). *The duke who outlawed jelly beans and other stories* (2nd ed.). Boston: Alyson Publications. *Fairytale with non-traditional characters*

Valentine, J. (2004). *One dad, two dads, brown dad, blue dad* (2nd ed.). Illustrated by Melody Sarechky. Boston: Alyson Publications. *Non-traditional families*

Willhoite, M. (1990). *Daddy's roommate*. Boston: Alyson Publications. *Non-traditional families*

Wilson, B. (2002). *Clear spring*. New York: Feminist Press. *Chapter book with non-traditional supporting characters*

Zolotow, C. (1972). *William's doll*. Illustrated by William Pene Du Bois. Mexico: HarperCollins. *Gender roles*

Children's Multimedia

Children of Lesbians and Gays Everywhere (COLAGE). (n.d.). *Books for children with LGBT parents.* Retrieved January 16, 2007, from www.colage.org/resources/kids_books.htm

Gay, Lesbian, Straight Education Network (GLSEN). (n.d.). *Grades K-6 Booklink.* Retrieved January 16, 2007, from www.glsen.org/cgi-bin/iowa/all/booklink/K-6.html

Higgins, P. (Producer), & Bailey, G. (Director). (October 4, 2005). *Postcards from Buster: Buster's outdoor journeys.* Hollywood, CA: Paramount. (Available from many online booksellers in VHS and DVD formats). *Non-traditional family in supporting roles*

Hunt, D. (Producer), & Scagliotti, J. (Director). (December 6, 2005). *Oliver Button is a Star* (Video Tape). USA: Hunt and Scagliotti Productions. *Bullying, Embracing differences*

Nash, V. (2005). *Rainbow sprinkles: Songs for our children celebrating our diverse lives.* (CD available from Two Lives Publishing Company, www.twolives.com/ Phone: 610-532-2852).

Children's Organizations

Children of Lesbians and Gays Everywhere (COLAGE)
www.colage.org/index.htm
415-861-KIDS
3543 18th Street #1, San Francisco, CA 94110
This organization provides newsletters, pen pals (www.colage.org/programs/penpals/), camp listings (www.colage.org/resources/camps.htm), conferences, and media advocacy.

Books and Articles for Educators

Casper, V., & Schultz, S. (1999). *Gay parents/straight schools: Building communication and trust.* New York: Teachers College Press.

Copple, C. (2003). *A world of difference: Readings on teaching young children in a diverse society.* Washington, DC: National Association for the Education of Young Children.

Derman-Sparks, L., and the A.B.C. Task Force. (1989). *Anti-bias curriculum: Tools for empowering young children.* Washington, DC: National Association for the Education of Young Children.

Emfinger, L. K. (2004). A model for evaluating diversity in teacher education. *Focus on Teacher Education, 5,* 1-4, 7.

Family Pride Coalition. (1999). *Opening doors: Educational issues for LGBT parents.* Washington, DC: Family Pride Coalition.

Family Pride Coalition. (2003). *Opening more doors: Educational issues for LGBT parents.* Washington, DC: Family Pride Coalition.

Kissin, R. (Ed.). (2002). *Getting ready for Benjamin: Preparing teachers for sexual diversity in the classroom.* New York: Rowman & Littlefield.

Koerner, M., & Hulsebosch, P. (1996). Preparing teachers to work with children of gay and lesbian parents. *Journal of Teacher Education, 47*(5), 347-354.

Lamme, L. L., & Lamme, L. A. (2001/2002). Welcoming children from gay families into our schools. *Educational Leadership, 59,* 65-69.

Lesbian and Gay Parenting Association. (2000). *Preventing prejudice: LGBT lesson plan guide for elementary schools.* San Francisco: Women's Educational Media.

Letts, W., & Sears, J. T. (Eds.). (1999). *Queering elementary education: Advancing the dialogue about sexualities and schooling.* Lanham, MD: Rowman & Littlefield.

Lipkin, A. (1998). *Understanding homosexuality, changing schools*. Boulder, CO: Westview Press.

Out for Equity/Out4Good. (2000). *Safe schools manual*. Minneapolis, MN: Out for Equity/Out4Good of St. Paul and Minneapolis. (Available from www.glsen.org)

Pinar, W. (Ed.). (1998). *Queer theory in education*. Mahwah, NJ: Lawrence Erlbaum.

Ryan, D., & Martin, A. (2000). Lesbian, gay, bisexual, and transgender parents in the school systems. *School Psychology Review, 29*(2), 207-216.

Schiedewing, N., & Davidson, E. (1992). *Open minds to equality: A sourcebook of learning activities to affirm diversity and promote equality*. Boston: Allyn & Bacon.

Schwartz, W. (1999, September). Family diversity in urban schools. *ERIC Digest*, 148.

Shinew, D., Thomas-Jones, D, & Tan, G. (2005, April). *Lesbian moms in straight schools: Parents' perceptions of their children's experiences in schools*. Paper presented at the annual meeting of the American Educational Research Association, Montreal, Canada.

Stern-LaRosa, C., & Bettmann, E. (2000). *The Anti-defamation League's Hate hurts: How children learn and unlearn prejudice*. New York: Scholastic.

Multimedia for Educators

Chasnoff, D. (Director). (2000). *That's a family!* (Video). USA: Women's Educational Media. *Includes curriculum guide*

Children of Lesbians and Gays Everywhere (COLAGE). (Spring, 2003). *Tips for making classrooms safer for students with lesbian, gay, bisexual, and transgender parents*. Retrieved January 16, 2007, from www.colage.org/pubs/safe_classrooms.html

GALE-BC. (Producer). (Jan. 2004). *Challenging homophobia in schools: A K-12 resource*. (Video). British Columbia: Gay and Lesbian Educators of British Columbia. (Available from glsen.org).

Gay, Lesbian, Straight Education Network (GLSEN). (n.d.). *Educator resources*. Retrieved January 16, 2007, from www.glsen.org/cgi-bin/iowa/educator/educator/index.html

Gillespie, P. (Editor), & Kaeser, G. (Photographer). (1999). *Love makes a family: Portraits of lesbian, gay, bisexual, and transgender parents and their families*. (Photo exhibit). Amherst, MA: University of Massachusetts Press Family Diversity Project.

Human Rights Campaign Foundation (HRC). (n.d.). *Youth/schools*. Retrieved January 16, 2007, from www.hrc.org/Template.cfm?Section=Youth_Schools&Template=/TaggedPage/TaggedPageDisplay.cfm&TPLID=26&ContentID=10314. *Includes books/videos on school issues, school safety, summer camps, children & prejudice, evaluating schools, talking with children about LGBT family and sexuality issues*

Lesbian and Gay Parents Association. (Producer). (Feb.1995). *Both of my moms' names are Judy: Children of lesbians and gays speak out*. (Video). San Francisco: Lesbian and Gay Parents Association. (Available from glsen.org). *Training materials and supplemental guide available*

National Film Board of Canada. (Producer), & Padgett, J. (Director). (2000). *Sticks and stones*. (Video). Ottawa, ON: National Film Board. (Available from www.glsen.org). *Targets ages 5-12, focuses on families, gender stereotypes, and name-calling*

Partners Against Hate. (n.d.). *For educators*. Retrieved January 16, 2007, from www.partnersagainsthate.org/educators/index.html

Spadola, M. (Producer/Director). (2000). *Our house: A very real documentary about kids of gay and lesbian parents*. (Video). Brooklyn, NY: Icarus Films. *Available in DVD & VHS, 9-page study guide*

Wolpert, E. (Producer/Director). (2000). *Start seeing diversity: The basic guide to an anti-bias classroom*. (Video). Boston: Ellen Wolpert. (Available from glsen.org). *Developed to create responsive child care programs; includes discussion guide*

Women's Educational Media. (Producer). (2000). *It's elementary: Talking about gay issues in school.* (Video). San Francisco: Women's Educational Media. *Available in full-length and training versions, aimed at parents and educators, models how to approach this topic*

Organizations for Educators

Gay, Lesbian, and Straight Educators Network (GLSEN)
122 West 26th St., Suite 1100
New York, NY 10001
212-727-0135, www.glsen.org

Gay and Lesbian Educators of BC (GALE-BC)
P.O. Box 93678 Nelson Park PO
Vancouver, BC V6E 4L7
604-684-9872; www.galebc.org

Parents, Families, and Friends of Lesbians and Gays (PFLAG)
1101-14th St. NW, Suite 1030
Washington, DC 20005
202638-4200, www.pflag.org

Teaching Tolerance
400 Washington Ave.
Montgomery, AL 36104

Teens Educating and Confronting Homophobia (TEACH)
Planned Parenthood of Toronto
36B Prince Arthur Avenue
Toronto, ON, M5R 1A9
416-961-0113, ext. 230

Triangle Program of Oasis Alternative Secondary School
c/o Steve Solomon
Human Sexuality Program
416-397-3755

Books for LGBT Parents

Benkov, L. (1995). *Reinventing the family: Lesbian and gay parents.* Three Rivers, MI: Three Rivers Press. *Comprehensive examination of gay and lesbian parenting via case studies*

Clunis, D. M., & Green, G. D. (2003). *The lesbian parenting book: A guide to creating families and raising children* (2nd ed.). Seattle, WA: Seal Press. *"The Dr. Spock" for lesbian families—Detailed accounting of child development, valuable list of parenting resources*

Drucker, J. (1998). *Lesbian and gay families speak out: Understanding the joys and challenges of diverse family life.* New York: Perseus Publishing. *An in-depth look at gay and lesbian parenting in the United States*

Garner, A. (2005). *Families like mine: Children of gay parents tell it like it is.* New York: Harper Paperbacks. *Steeped in real stories and extensive research*

Gillespie, P. (Ed). (1999). *Love makes a family: Portraits of lesbian, gay, bisexual, and transgender parents and their families.* Photographs by Gigi Kaeser. Amherst, MA: University of Massachusetts Press. *LGBT family portraits and interviews, designed to accompany The Family Diversity Project Photo exhibit*

Goss, R., & Strongheart, A. A. (Eds.). (1997). *Our families, our values: Snapshots of queer kinship.* Binghamton, NY: Haworth Press. *Intellectually engaging collection of essays*

Green, J. (2000). *The velveteen father: An unexpected journey to parenthood.* New York: Ballantine Books. *Memoir of a gay journalist's journey into parenthood*

Johnson, S. M., & O'Connor, E. (2001). *For lesbian parents: Your guide to helping your family grow up happy, healthy, and proud.* New York: Guilford Press. *Lesbian version of "What to expect when you're expecting"*

Johnson, S. M., & O'Connor, E. (2002). *The gay baby boom: The psychology of gay parenthood.* New York: New York University Press. *Summary of findings from The Gay and Lesbian Family Study*

Lev, A. I. (2004). *The complete lesbian and gay parenting guide.* New York: Penguin. *Humorous accounts of joys and struggles of "gender variant" families*

Martin, A. (1993). *The lesbian and gay parenting handbook: Creating and raising our families.* New York: Perennial. *Practical parenting handbook covering a vast array of subjects*

McGarry, K. (2003). *Fatherhood for gay men: An emotional and practical guide to becoming a gay dad.* Binghamton, NY: Harrington Park Press. *Author's journey to parenthood, including questions and challenges of becoming a gay parent*

Moraga, C. (1997). *Waiting in the wings: Portrait of a queer motherhood.* Ann Arbor, MI: Firebrand Books. *A Chicana lesbian writer's journey into parenthood.*

Snow, J. E. (2004). *How it feels to have a gay or lesbian parent: A book by kids for kids of all ages.* Binghamton, NY: Harrington Park Press.

Stevenson, M. R., & Cogan, J. C. (Eds.). (2003). *Everyday activism: A handbook for lesbian, gay, and bisexual people and their allies.* New York: Routledge. *Action guide for promoting change in discriminatory policies affecting sexual minorities*

Strah, D. (2003). *Gay dads: A celebration of fatherhood.* New York: Penguin. *Twenty-five parenting vignettes*

Tasker, F. L., & Golombok. (1998). *Growing up in a lesbian family: Effects on child development.* New York: Guilford Press. *Longitudinal study*

Wright, J. M. (1998). *Lesbian step-families: Ethnography of love.* Binghamton, NY: Haworth Press. *Qualitative study defines, describes, and interprets lesbian step-parenting roles, Includes guidelines for counselors*

Multimedia for LGBT Parents

The Advocate. (n.d.). *The Advocate Home Page.* Retrieved January 16, 2007, from www.advocate.com *Home of Alyson Books, LGBT News site*

Burns, A., & Burns, C. (Producers/Directors). (March, 2004). *Mothers and babies: Lesbians creating families.* (DVD). Chicago: Birth Talk Productions. *Childbirth education video*

Families Like Mine. (n.d.). *Home Page.* Retrieved January 16, 2007, from www.familieslikemine.com *Advice page, newsletter, workshops*

Gay.Com. (n.d.). *Families.* Retrieved January 16, 2007, from www.gay.com/families/

Gay Parent Magazine. (n.d.). Retrieved January 16, 2007, from www.gayparentmag.com

The Gay Parenting Show. (n.d.). Retrieved January 16, 2007. From http://gayparenting.thepodcast-network.com/

Here! TV. (n.d.). *Raising family.* Retrieved January 16, 2007, from www.heretv.com *Gay and lesbian parenting talk show aired on Here! TV, a gay TV network*

In the Life. (n.d.). *Pride Edition.* Retrieved January 16, 2007, from www.inthelifetv.org *Gay and lesbian newsmagazine on public television*

Logo. (n.d.). www.logoonline.com/ *Gay and lesbian cable channel hosted by MTV*

Planet Out Parenting. (n.d.). *Families.* Retrieved January 16, 2007, from www.planetout.com/families/parenting/

Pride Parenting. (n.d.). *Home page.* Retrieved January 16, 2007, from www.prideparenting.com

Transfamily. (n.d.). *Home page.* Retrieved January 16, 2007, from www.transfamily.org/ *Transgender resources and chat board for kids*

Transparentcy. (n.d.). *Home page.* Retrieved January 16, 2007, from www.transparentcy.org *Transgender parenting information & advocacy*

Organizations for LGBT Parents

COLAGE (Children of Lesbians and Gays Everywhere)
415-861-5437, www.colage.org

Human Rights Campaign (HRC)
202-628-4160, www.hrc.org

Family Pride Coalition
202-331-5015, www.familypride.org
Fax: 202-331-0080
Parenting groups, newsletter, family events, national support groups, information clearinghouse, direct services, such as information and referrals, custody/visitation project

National Gay and Lesbian Task Force
212-604-9830, www.ngltf.org

Our Family Coalition
415-981-1960, www.ourfamily.org

References

The Gay Parenting Show. (n.d.). Retrieved November, 26, 2005, from http://gayparenting.the podcastnetwork.com/

GLAAD media awards to premier on MTV network's LOGO channel. (2005, July). *GLAAD Media Matters, 1.*

Out of the closet. (2005, October). *GLAAD Media Matters, 6.*

Siegel, S. (2003, Sept.-Oct.). Children's alternative media project: Filling the niche of children's books with gay characters. *Gay Parent Magazine, 4,* 12-15.

Working on television portrayals of gay teens. (November, 2005). *GLAAD Media Matters, 3.*

Andrew M.A. Allen, Ph.D. (OISE/U. Toronto). Andrew is a former elementary classroom teacher. He is an Assistant Professor in the Faculty of Education at the University of Windsor. He teaches Introduction to Issues in Education and Mathematics Methodology in the preservice program and Sociological Aspects of Education in the graduate program. His scholarly interests include the social and cultural structures and norms of the classroom and their effect on both teaching and learning. He has a driving interest also in teacher candidates' emerging teacher identity and factors contributing to and affecting the process of learning to teach.

Theresa Bouley is an Associate Professor in the Center for Early Childhood Education at Eastern Connecticut State University. She specializes in the areas of early childhood education, language and literacy acquisition, and literature-based reading and writing. Her research interests also include multicultural literature and literacy. She has a Ph.D. in Curriculum and Instruction from the University of Connecticut. You can reach her at Bouleyt@easternct.edu

Barbara Brush is a poet and an instructor of Rhetoric and Writing at San Diego State University.

Tonya Callaghan is a Ph.D. student in the Department of Curriculum, Teaching and Learning at the Ontario Institute for Studies in Education of the University of Toronto. The Social Sciences and Humanities Research Council of Canada has awarded Tonya a Canada Graduate Scholarship to build upon her University of Alberta Master's of Education thesis entitled, "The Catholic Closet: The Institutionalization of Homophobia in Canadian Catholic Schools." The holder of two degrees from the University of Calgary (B.A. English, B.Ed. Secondary English), Tonya Callaghan has over 10 years of teaching experience in national and international, rural and urban, Catholic and non-Catholic environments.

Dale R. Callender is a Counsellor, Delisle Youth Services. Dale's commitment to empowering youth and his work with high school youth in a North Toronto, Ontario, school has been highlighted and spoken about for years. He began his work at Delisle Youth Services and the "Delisle at Northern" school program in 1998. Previous to his work at Delisle, Dale spent nine years at the Aisling Discoveries Child and Family Centre, counselling in their residential group home and day treatment school programs. He brings his work in domestic violence, anger management development programs, youth crisis hostel work experience from Covenant House Toronto, and his experiences with multiple adolescent challenges and areas to his work. He has been involved in children and youth overnight and day camps for over 15 years. He has been the Director of Bolton Camp, Swallowdale Camp, and Outdoor Education/Camping at the YMCA Cedar Glen.

Katerina Cook is a princess of darkness, a wannabe goth, grade 4 student at a French language school, learning guitar and Polish in Toronto.

Carter Cook is a Canadian born in California in 1995. He moved to Toronto at age 3. He is a feminist, delivers lectures on bullying, and hopes to be an architect when he grows up.

Hilary Cook is a labour lawyer, photographer, femme, lesbian, and mother of Carter and Katerina. She serves on the board of EGALE Canada, an organization that advocates for the rights of LGBT people.

Cindy Cruz is the Provost's Academic Diversity Postdoctoral Fellow at Cornell University. A first-generation college graduate and seventh-generation Angeleno, Cindy continues her work in Third World feminist pedagogies, queer street culture, and mapping transgressive bodies.

Kay Emfinger is an Assistant Professor of Early Childhood at the University of Alabama at Birmingham. As a teacher educator, she strives to mentor future teachers to meet the diverse needs of children and families. Prior to her career in academe, Kay enjoyed 18 years of public school teaching. She is active in her community as an Advisor to BAGSLY, Birmingham Alliance of Gay, Straight, and Lesbian Youth. Kay lives in Birmingham, Alabama, with Shannon, her life partner of 22 years; their 10-year-old daughter, Elliot; and their dog, Lucy.

John J. Guiney Yallop is a parent, a partner, and a poet. He is also a Ph.D. Candidate in Educational Studies at The University of Western Ontario. In his research, John is using poetry to explore emotional landscapes. John lives with his partner and their daughter in Brampton, Ontario, Canada. Website: http://publish.edu.uwo.ca/john.guiney%20yallop/

Celia Haig-Brown is a Professor in the Faculty of Education at York University. She is the author and editor of four books, including *With Good Intentions: Aboriginal and Euro-Canadian Relations in Colonial Canada* (UBC Press 2006). She teaches courses in the foundations of education and research methodologies. Her own research focuses primarily on community-informed education in First Nations contexts. Sometimes she wears cowboy boots.

Didi Khayatt is a Professor in the Faculty of Education at York University, Toronto, Canada. She has published widely on issues of sexuality and equity in general.

Isabel Killoran is an Associate Professor in the Faculty of Education at York University, Toronto, Canada. She is also associated with the graduate programme in Critical Disability Studies. Isabel is a former elementary teacher. Her current focus is on preparing teachers to create and work effectively in inclusive settings.

Tim McCaskell is a long-time gay activist in Toronto. He worked with the Toronto Board of Education and Toronto District School board for 20 years, delivering and developing anti-racism and anti-homophobia programs for students. He is author of *Race To Equity: Disrupting Educational Inequality* (BTL Press Toronto 2005).

Lisa Ortiz is an autism specialist and teacher living in Portland, Oregon, with her amazing 6-year-old daughter, Malena; her loving partner of 4 1/2 years, Judi; and a menagerie of pets. She is happy to share that after leaving the district described in her story, she has enjoyed much success and happiness in the field of education in districts that know and follow the anti-discrimination laws of the beautiful state of Oregon.

Karleen Pendleton Jiménez is a writer and assistant professor in the School of Education at Trent University. She is the author of several short stories, published in a variety of anthologies, and the children's book *Are You a Boy or a Girl?* Her recent scholarly essays can be found in the collections *Learning, teaching & community, Chicana/Latina feminist pedagogies and epistemologies for everyday life* and *Cast Out: Queer Lives in Theater.*

janet romero-leiva is a queer feminist latina artist. exploring various means of creating discomfort y bellesa through language and image. creating a place and space for under/mis/un-represented bodies. searching for clean air and water, justicia y como amar sin condiciones.

Nichola Ward is a technical writer and frequent guest at Pussy Pen. Her "Little Sarah" character has graced many a stage. She has emceed at many events, including the OUTwrites OUTloud readings at the 519.

April Whatley Bedford is an Associate Professor and Chair of the Department of Curriculum and Instruction at the University of New Orleans. Her major professional interests are in children's literature, teacher development, and gender issues in education. April is actively involved in ACEI, the Children's Literature Assembly of National Council of Teachers of English, and the Children's Literature and Reading Special Interest Group of the International Reading Association. She is the 2007-2008 Chair of the Notable Books for a Global Society committee, an award given annually by IRA for the best children's and young adult literature promoting cultural understanding and acceptance of differences.

Kristopher Wells is a Killam Fellow and Social Sciences and Humanities Research Council of Canada (SSHRC) doctoral scholar in the Faculty of Education, University of Alberta. His research, teaching, and service work centres on creating safe, caring, and inclusive schools and communities for sexual minority students and teachers. He is a board member of the Society for Safe and Caring Schools and Communities and the Director of Youth Understanding Youth, a social/support group for sexual minority youth in Edmonton, Alberta. In 2005, his community service work was recognized with an Alberta Centennial Medallion as bestowed by the Alberta Legislature. Kristopher can be contacted via email at kris.wells@ualberta.ca.

Artwork

Brittany N. Guiney Yallop is 7 years old. She likes drawing, reading, and writing. She lives with her Daddy and Papa, and her pets, Whisker, Gamma, and Moon, in Brampton, Ontario, Canada.

"Sky" is a 10-year-old boy being raised by his two moms.

"Kory" is a 14-year-old boy being raised by his mom and his Barb.

"Louis" is a 14-year-old boy being raised by his mom and his stepmother.

"Liam" is a 7-year-old boy being raised by his two moms.